THE SPLENDOR OF AN AUTUMN MOON

The Splendor of an Autumn Moon

The Devotional Verse of Tsongkhapa

Translated and edited by

Gavin Kilty

Wisdom Publications • Boston

Wisdom Publications
199 Elm Street
Somerville MA 02144 USA
www.wisdompubs.org

Library of Congress Cataloging-in-Publication Data
Tsoṅ-kha-pa Blo-bzaṅ-grags-pa, 1357–1419.
The splendor of an autumn moon : the devotional verse of Tsongkhapa / translated and edited by Gavin Kilty.
p. cm.
ISBN 0-86171-192-0 (alk. paper)
1. Tsoṅ-kha-pa Blo-bzaṅ-grags-pa, 1357–1419—Translations into English. I. Kilty, Gavin. II. Title.
BQ7950.T753 E5 2001
294.3'4432—dc21 2001026206

ISBN 0-86171-192-0

06 05 04 03 02
6 5 4 3 2

Interior design by: Feron Design in 11-point Weiss
Cover design by: *tabula rasa* graphic design
Cover image: Tsongkhapa, 17th century, eastern Tibet, artist unknown.
From the collection of Shelley and Donald Rubin

Wisdom Publications' books are printed on acid-free paper and meet the guidelines for permanence and durability of the Committee on Production Guidelines for Book Longevity of the Council on Library Resources.

Printed in Canada.

Table of Contents

Introduction 1

Praise of the Buddha 9
The Unrivaled Lion of the Shakyas
སྐབས་གསུམ་པ་བཞུགས་སོ།།

Prayer to Sarasvati 21
དབྱངས་ཅན་མ་སྤྱན་དྲངས་བསྟོད་པ་བཞུགས་སོ།།

Praise of Manjushri 23
འཇམ་དབྱངས་བསྟོད་སྤྲིན་རྒྱ་མཚོ་བཞུགས་སོ།།

Praise to Amitayus 71
མགོན་པོ་ཚེ་དཔག་མེད་ལ་བསྟོད་པ་ཉི་གཞོན་འཆར་ཀ་བཞུགས་སོ།།

Praise to Amitabha 77
Gateway to the Highest Buddha Realm
མགོན་པོ་འོད་དཔག་མེད་ལ་བསྟོད་པ་ཞིང་མཆོག་སྒོ་འབྱེད་མ་བཞུགས་སོ།།

Prayer for Birth in Sukhavati, Realm of Bliss 83
བདེ་བ་ཅན་དུ་སྐྱེ་བའི་སྨོན་ལམ་བཞུགས་སོ།།

Praise of an Unnamed Sakya Lama 97
མཚན་མ་སྨོས་པའི་ས་སྐྱའི་བླ་མ་ཞིག་ལ་བསྟོད་པ།།

A Prayer to My Precious Dharma Master, Dragpa Jangchub 103
བདག་གི་བཀྲིན་ཅན་གྱི་རྩ་བའི་བླ་མར་གསོལ་འདེབས།།

A Harvest of Powerful Attainment 109
Prayer for Blessings of the Close Lineage
བྱིན་རླབས་ཉེ་བརྒྱུད་ཀྱི་བླ་རྣམས་ལ་གསོལ་འདེབས།།

In Praise of Maitreya, the Crown of Brahma 115
བྱམས་པའི་བསྟོད་ཆེན་བཞུགས་སོ།།

In Praise of Vajrapani, Keeper of the Secret Mantra 151
རྗེ་བཙུན་གསང་བདག་གི་བསྟོད་པ་བཞུགས་སོ།།

In Praise of the Extraordinary Deity Achala 163
ལྷག་པའི་ལྷ་མི་གཡོ་མགོན་པོ་ལ་བསྟོད་པ།།

In Praise of Vajra Sarasvati, Light of Wisdom 167
དབྱངས་ཅན་ཤེས་རབ་གསལ་བྱེད་མའི་བསྟོད་པ།།

In Praise of Goddess Namgyalma 179
རྣམ་པར་རྒྱལ་མའི་བསྟོད་པ་ས་གསུམ་རེ་སྐོང་མ།།

A Prayer for the Beginning, Middle, and End of Practice 193
ཐོག་མཐའ་མ་བཞུགས་སོ།།

The Essence of a Human Life 209
Words of Advice for the Lay Practitioner
དལ་རྟེན་ལ་སྙིང་པོ་ལེན་པར་བསྐུལ་བའི་ཚིགས་བཅད་བཞུགས་སོ།།

Dependent Arising 217
A Praise of the Buddha
རྟེན་འབྲེལ་བསྟོད་པ་བཞུགས་སོ།།

Verses of Benediction 247
On Publication of a New Edition of Perfection of Wisdom Sutras
ཤེར་ཕྱིན་གྱི་མདོ་པར་འདེབས་ཀྱི་སྨོན་ཚིགས།།

Praise of the Protector Dharmaraja 263
ཆོས་རྒྱལ་ནང་སྒྲུབ་ཀྱི་བསྟོད་པ་བཞུགས་སོ།།

Twenty-one Verse Rosary Prayer 269
ཕྲེང་བའི་གསོལ་འདེབས་ཚིགས་བཅད་ཉེར་གཅིག་མ།།

For As Long As 281
ཇི་སྲིད་ཐུབ་མཆོག།

Notes and Comments on the Poems 287
Glossary 299
About the Translator 305

Introduction

The purpose of this work is to show Tsongkhapa, the great Buddhist reformer, in his devotional aspect. Much has been written and translated of Tsongkhapa the scholar—the brilliant mind who unlocked the arcane mysteries of a Buddhism that had already been extant in Tibet for six hundred years previously and for a thousand years or so in India before that.

Tsongkhapa almost single-handedly rediscovered and clarified the message of the Buddha—a message that had become dissipated over the centuries. With an appetite for thorough research and an astonishing memory, he ploughed through the scriptures of ancient India and contemporary Tibet, searching to knit together the various strands of Buddha's thought. As a result, he produced some of the most authoritative literature on Buddhist philosophy and practice the world had ever known. He continues to be revered today and is thought of with immense gratitude by practitioners of all Tibetan Buddhist lineages.

Tsongkhapa was also a monk—and one who took his ordination very seriously. He ceaselessly strove to keep his vows pure and prayed to do so in all future lives. He researched the monastic code laid down by the Buddha and composed authoritative works on it as well. Buddhist practitioners throughout Tibet heaped great devotion upon him—and still he strove to live a simple contemplative life, spending much of his time in remote hermitages meditating and writing. Yet he never shirked from teaching when requested.

The story of the remarkable life of Tsongkhapa has been

well documented elsewhere, but this collection of works seeks to bring out a lesser-known side of this great scholar and meditator: the devotional poet. Tsongkhapa studied poetry, as did many of the great masters of his day and after, and in the colophon of many of his works he is referred to as the "Poet of the North." Historically, poetry in Tibetan literature was almost invariably religious and often indistinguishable from prayer or eulogy.

The poetry of Tsongkhapa and other renowned practitioners of ancient Tibet was addressed to objects of reverence found within the Buddhist pantheon. These included the Buddha himself, as well as the many deities of tantric practices, supernatural protectors, great bodhisattvas—the personifications of Buddha's qualities—as well as the teachings of the Buddha and, of course, the poet's own teachers and lamas.

Such reverence and heartfelt emotion finds its natural outlet in poetry. Emotion is a subject often considered unsuitable for expression by the dedicated Buddhist, and it is certainly true that some emotions are to be curtailed. Anger, for example, is rarely displayed in print, and in an exemplary practitioner, rarely in daily life. Excitement, too, is frowned upon for it disturbs a tranquil mind. However, the emotion evident in Tsongkhapa's poetry bespeaks deep faith and a love of the divine at its heart. In Tsongkhapa we hear awe and wonder in response to the discovery of a sublime path and of sublime beings with equally sublime qualities. We hear emotion arising from the realization that by good fortune, an astonishing spiritual opportunity has appeared. We hear relief that at last the way to a true happiness has opened up. We hear the delighted gratitude of encountering something so rare and so precious as the teachings of the Buddha. Such emotions do not stand still but swirl joyfully around the mind to pour out in poetry.

Also present in the poems of Tsongkhapa are emotions of sadness and compassion. Tsongkhapa often bewails his own lack of spiritual realization, lamenting that his mind is covered by dark unseeing ignorance. For so long, he says, he has been wandering lost in a thick fog of ignorance. He is genuinely distraught to have such an awesome realization about himself. But this is not impotent, defeatist sadness but rather an expression of the first two Noble Truths of Buddhism—suffering and its cause—coupled with knowledge of the last two Noble Truths—the path and suffering's cessation.

True compassion such as Tsongkhapa's is unable to rest while others suffer. It is notable that when Tsongkhapa and other great masters, notably the seventh Dalai Lama, bemoan moral laxity, material greed, and the flawed teachings of others, they do so with sadness and compassion for the suffering caused to others, and not with anger or a sense of righteousness.

And yet there is no fear of confident expression in the poems of Tsongkhapa and no room for false humility. Though Mahayana Buddhist works often use metaphors of triumph such as victory banners flying high, evil armies being conquered, the lion's roar that terrifies the foxes, a fame that spreads throughout the three worlds, and so on—these expressions spring from the joy of knowing that one walks the path of freedom and are not indications of arrogance or a will toward domination. When Tsongkhapa talks of defeating the "fox like false orators" in debate, his is the triumph of truth and purity over delusion.

Thus, the essence of the emotion embodied in Tsongkhapa's devotional works is faith and love. Tsongkhapa's emotion is a quiet emotion, not one shouted from the rooftops—maybe not one even expressed overtly in the presence of others—but in his poems it shines forth.

Tsongkhapa's poems are prayer, praise, or often a blend of both. Prayer without faith is empty mumbling, devoid of result. Prayer is for the future—a time in which paths can be lost, spiritual goals forgotten, friends can lead one astray, and the propensity and inclination for self-perpetuating pain is immense. Prayer with deep faith has power: it creates a propensity of mind directly affecting the petitioner's future actions and experience. But for prayer to be effective, it must be heartfelt. Through poetry the heartfelt prayer can be truly expressed.

It is, however, in the praises written by Tsongkhapa that his poetry comes into its own. The relationship between a practitioner and his source of refuge or between tantric meditator and deity is one of reverence. That reverence extends not only to the admirable qualities of mind but also to those of the voice and to physical characteristics, for these too are seen as manifestations of the enlightened mind. Therefore, it is not uncommon for Tsongkhapa to devote many verses to the perfection and beauty of a deity's body. He will lovingly describe features—rarely found even in the most romantic Western verse—such as the neck, shoulders, forehead, as well as more traditional seats of beauty such as the eyes and hair. For Tsongkhapa, every hair and every pore of the deity and the lama is a physical manifestation of a purity, wisdom, and compassion unknown on a more earthly plane.

Manjushri, the personification of Buddha's wisdom, has a voice possessing sixty-four endearing qualities. His voice is more beautiful than all the angels of heaven. It permeates everywhere and is manifest in a manner expressly pleasing to the listener. To hear and to marvel at such a voice is to recognize it as a manifestation of Manjushri's enlightened mind.

These qualities of body, speech, and mind are often

likened in the poems to extraordinary natural phenomena. The use of these reflects the exposure of ancient Tibetan life to natural phenomena but also demonstrates, I believe, that Tsongkhapa saw the divine all around him.

The meter of Tibetan poetry is syllabic, aiding its primary recitation mode of chanting. Syllables are usually in stressed couplets except the last of each line being a single. The accent is on the first syllable. There is no fixed number of syllables although nine is common. A typical line, then, would run DUM-da DUM-da DUM-da DUM-da DUM. There is no rhyming scheme, although Tsongkhapa sometimes wrote using various techniques, such as starting each line with succeeding letters of the alphabet or with same vowel, whole poems where only the inherent vowel sound *a* is used, repeating the final word or syllable of each line at the beginning of the next, and so on. Needless to say, these do not translate well.

These days Western academics are divided on what constitutes the nature of prayer, on the merits of faith and devotion, and even on the validity of prayer itself. Some see such devotional renderings as having no place in a modern society, but one wonders if they are missing something. This form of spiritual practice can be analyzed and researched, but until one is touched by its beauty, its power, and its self-evident worth, no amount of description will ever suffice.

I have tried, therefore, to translate these devotional works of Tsongkhapa in a manner that brings out their spiritual beauty and to reveal the deep love and faith of this most remarkable of men.

Gavin Kilty
May 2001

The Poems

སྐྱབས་གསུམ་པ་བཞུགས་སོ།

༄༅། །སྐྱབས་གསུམ་པ་དང་དབང་པོའི་དགྲ།།
དྲི་ཟ་གདེངས་ཅན་གྲུབ་པའི་གཙོ།།
ཀུན་གྱི་གཙུག་རྒྱན་ནོར་བུ་ཡིས།།
གང་གི་ཞབས་པད་མཛེས་བྱས་པ།།

གསེར་འོད་འཕྲུག་པའི་དཔལ་གྱིས་བརྗིད་པའི་སྐུ།།
དྲི་ཟའི་དབྱངས་ཀྱིས་བསྒྲུན་དུ་མེད་པའི་གསུང་།།
ཉི་མ་བྱེ་བའི་མདངས་ལས་གསལ་བའི་ཐུགས།།
མཐའ་ཡས་འགྲོ་བའི་འདྲེན་མཆོག་ཤཱཀྱའི་ཏོག།

དག་པའི་མཁའ་ལ་ཤར་བའི་གཟའ་སྐར་རྣམས།།
ཆུ་གཏེར་དབུས་ན་ཡོངས་སུ་གསལ་བ་བཞིན།།
དང་བའི་ཡིད་མཚོར་ཁྲོད་ཀྱི་ཡོན་ཏན་གྱི།།
གཟུགས་བརྙན་མ་འདྲེས་གསལ་བར་རབ་བཀོད་ནས།།

Praise of the Buddha

The Unrivaled Lion of the Shakyas

Indra, king of the gods,
his enemy the Asura leader,
Pramudita, celestial musician king,
naga kings and great rishis
beautify your lotus feet with the jewels of their crowns.

Glorious body bathing in splendor of its golden glow,
voice unrivaled even by melodies of celestial music,
mind brighter than ten million suns,
guide supreme for infinite living beings,
paragon of the Shakyas.

Moon and stars on a cloudless night
appear crystal-clear in the midst of a lake,
so in the clear waters of my untroubled mind
are your qualities reflected one by one.

ཟླ་ཟེར་ཕོག་པའི་ཆུ་སྐྱེས་གཞོན་ནུ་བཞིན།།
ལག་པའི་སོར་མོ་སྙིང་གའི་ངོས་སུ་ཟུམ།།
རྩེ་གཅིག་ཡིད་ཀྱིས་ཁྱོད་སྐུར་མངོན་ཕྱོགས་ཏེ།།
ཅུང་ཟད་བསྟོད་ལ་ཐུགས་རྗེ་ཅན་ཁྱོད་དགོངས།།

སྐར་མའི་ཚོགས་ཀྱིས་མཁའ་ལ་ཟླ་བ་བཞིན།།
རྒྱལ་སྲས་དཔའ་བོ་རྣམས་ཀྱིས་ཀུན་ནས་བསྐོར།།
བ་ལང་ཁྱུ་ཡི་ཐོག་མར་ཁྱུ་མཆོག་བཞིན།།
དགྲ་བཅོམ་འཁོར་གྱི་ཚོགས་ཀྱིས་མདུན་དུ་བདར།།
ནམ་མཁའི་ཁྱོན་ཀུན་འགེངས་པའི་འོད་ཟེར་གྱི།།
དྲ་བ་སྟོང་གིས་ཡོངས་སུ་དཀྲིགས་པའི་སྐུ།།
ནམ་མཁའི་ལམ་ནས་ཆོ་འཕྲུལ་དུ་མ་ཡིས།།
ངང་པའི་རྒྱལ་པོ་བཞིན་དུ་ལྡིང་ཞིང་གཤེགས།།

དེ་ཚེ་རིང་ནས་བསྐྲུན་པའི་བཟང་པོའི་ལས།།
ཡོངས་སུ་སད་པའི་ལྷ་མི་སྟོང་ཕྲག་བརྒྱ།།
ཁྱོད་ཞལ་མཐོང་བའི་མོད་ལ་མི་བསྐྱུན་ཡིད།།
ཉེས་བརྒྱའི་འཆིང་བ་ཀུན་ནས་ལྷོད་པར་གྱུར།།

Fingertips fold at my heart like a lotus touched by moonlight,
single-pointedly I hold you before me.
You of great compassion heed this modest praise.

Ringed by noble bodhisattvas
as the moon is circled by stars,
leading your arhat entourage
as the mighty bull leads the herd,
the skies were filled with a million garlands of golden light
as you soared through the sky
to arrive like the king of swans
in a magical display of corporal power.

At that time thousands of gods and men beheld your face,
awakened by seeds of wholesome deeds stored over ages,
their untamed minds at once loosened
from the chains of countless faults.

དཔའ་བོ་ཁྱོད་ཀྱིས་བྱང་ཆུབ་ཤིང་དྲུང་དུ།།
མཁྱེན་བརྩེའི་དཔུང་གིས་ཡིད་སྤྲུབས་བདག་པོའི་སྡེ།།
མ་ལུས་ཟིལ་གྱིས་མནོན་པར་མཛད་པ་ནི།།
དྲག་པོའི་རླུང་དང་ཉེ་བའི་སྤྲིན་ནག་བཞིན།།
མདའ་མཚོན་གོ་ཆ་མ་བཟུང་བར།།
རང་ཉིད་གཅིག་པུས་བྱེ་བའི་བདུད།།
མ་ལུས་ཕམ་མཛད་གཡུལ་གྱི་ལས།།
ཁྱོད་ལས་གཞན་པ་སུ་ཡིས་ཤེས།།

དེ་ལྟར་ཁྱོད་ཀྱིས་བྱམས་པའི་མེས།།
འདོད་ལྷའི་སྙིང་ནི་རབ་གདུངས་ཀྱང་།།
བརྩེ་བའི་གཏེར་ཁྱོད་ལུས་ཅན་ལ།།
རིས་སུ་ཆད་པར་གྱུར་པ་མེད།།
ཁྱོད་ནི་འགྲོ་བའི་དོན་གྱི་སླད།།
ཅུང་ཟད་ཙམ་ཡང་མི་ངལ་ཞིང་།།
འགྲོ་བ་རྣམས་ཀྱང་ཁྱོད་ཀྱི་ནི།།
ཡོན་ཏན་བརྗོད་ལ་ངལ་མ་གྱུར།།

Under your bodhi tree, great warrior,
like a violent wind in a dark storm,
you overwhelmed Mara's hosts
with an army of compassion and wisdom.
Without weapon, without armor,
you routed unaided a million demons.
Other than you, who could fight such battles?

With the fire of love
you scorched the hearts of lustful gods,
while remaining to all a jewel of compassion
without favor or displeasure,
unceasing, even momentarily, in your work for others,
who are unceasing likewise in praise of your qualities.

རྒྱ་མཚོའི་ཀློང་ལྟར་རབ་ཏུ་ཟབ་པའི་ཐུགས།།
ལྷ་ཡི་རྔ་བཞིན་ལེགས་པར་འདོམས་པའི་གསུང་།།
ལྷུན་པོའི་སྡོ་ལྟར་མངོན་པར་འཕགས་པའི་སྐུ།།
མཐོང་ཐོས་དྲན་པས་དོན་ལྡན་མཛད་པ་ཁྱོད།།
འཇིག་རྟེན་ཀུན་གྱི་སེམས་ཅན་ཐམས་ཅད་ཀྱིས།།
དུས་གཅིག་ཉིད་དུ་ཐེ་ཚོམ་དོན་ཞུས་ཀྱང་།།
དེ་དག་རེ་རེའི་མདུན་དུ་འདང་དེ་སྙེད་ཀྱི།།
སྐུ་དང་གསུང་གི་བཀོད་པ་དུས་གཅིག་ཏུ།།
མཛད་པ་མཛད་ཀྱང་རྟོག་པ་ཉེར་ཞི་བ།།
ཁྱོད་ཀྱི་སྐུ་གསུང་ཐུགས་ཀྱི་གསང་བ་ཡི།།
ཚུལ་འདི་རྒྱལ་སྲས་རང་རྒྱལ་ཉན་ཐོས་ཀྱིས།།
ཇི་ཙམ་བརྟགས་ཀྱང་བློ་ཡི་ཡུལ་མིན་ན།།
ཚངས་དང་དབང་པོ་སོགས་ཀྱིས་སྨོས་ཅི་འཚལ།།

མཁའ་ལྡིང་དབང་པོས་མཁའ་ལ་བགྲོད་བགྲོད་ནས།།
ནམ་ཞིག་རང་སྟོབས་བྲི་བས་ལྡོག་གྱུར་གྱི།།
ནམ་མཁའ་ཟད་པས་ལྡོག་པར་མི་འགྱུར་བཞིན།།
ཁྱོད་ཀྱི་ཡོན་ཏན་བརྗོད་པའང་དེ་ལྟར་ལགས།།

Mind as deep as an ocean,
words resounding like the celestial drum,
body taller even than Meru,
you are meaningful to see, hear, or bring to mind.
Were every living being of every world
to raise simultaneously individual doubts,
in front of each would you simultaneously display
as many creations of body and of word,
and yet you would not have stirred.
Such mysteries of body, speech, and mind
are not in the experience of bodhisattvas,
hearers, and solitary practitioners, however they try.
What need to mention Brahma, Indra, and others?

The mighty garuda hawk wings its way
onward, onward through the skies
but on tiring turns and heads for home.
The skies, however, lie unhindered by such limitation.
To talk of your qualities is likewise.

གཡོག་རྩལ་རབ་ཏུ་རྫོགས་པའི་མཁའ་ལྡིང་གིས།།
བགྲོད་པའི་ལམ་དུ་བྱིའུའི་རྩོལ་བ་ལྟར།།
སྟོབས་བཅུ་མདའ་བ་གང་དུ་གཡེགས་པ་ཡི།།
ལམ་མཆོག་དེར་ནི་འཇུག་པར་འདོད་པ་བདག །
གནས་ལུགས་དོན་ལ་ལྟ་བའི་བློ་མིག་ཉམས།།
ངེས་འབྱུང་བྱང་ཆུབ་སེམས་ཀྱི་འཁོར་བས་དབུལ།།
སྟོབས་ལྡན་ཉོན་མོངས་དགྲ་བོས་རྒྱུན་དུ་གཙེས།།
བདག་འཛིན་གཙོང་རོང་ཟབ་མོའི་སྐྱབས་སུ་ལྷུང་།།
འདི་འདྲའི་ཉམ་ཐག་གནས་སུ་གྱུར་ལགས་པ།།
བརྩེ་ཆེན་ཁྱོད་ཀྱིས་ཡལ་བར་འདོར་ལགས་ན།།
དམན་པ་རྣམས་ལ་ཆེས་ཆེར་བརྩེ་བའི་མགོན།།
ཁྱོད་ལས་གཞན་པ་གང་ལས་སྐྱབས་སུ་བཟུང་།།
སྙིགས་མ་ལྔ་ཡིས་ཧ་ཅང་སྡུགས་པ་ཡི།།
ཞིང་འདི་གཞན་གྱིས་སྤངས་དུས་མགོན་ཁྱོད་ཀྱིས།།
ཡོངས་སུ་བཟུང་སྟེ་རྒྱལ་བ་སྲས་བཅས་ཀྱིས།།
པད་དཀར་ལྟ་བུ་བསྔགས་པའི་དགོས་པའང་ཅི།།

Like a tiny bird yearning to follow the path
traveled by the mighty garuda
in whom the art of flight is perfected,
I long to travel that great highway
to the throne of the ten powers,
but my mind's eye is of sight too weak
to see the reality of phenomena.
I am impoverished, moreover,
by the lack of bodhi mind and true renunciation,
persecuted constantly by enemy-like delusions of mind,
cast headlong into the pit of grasping to self.
Were I abandoned by you in such a wretched state,
what other guardian who gazes on the pitiful
with such tremendous love could I turn to for refuge?
When this realm, sullied by the five remains,
was ignored by others but adopted by you,
what need was there for buddhas and bodhisattvas
to praise and liken you to the white lotus?

འོན་ཀྱང་ཁྱོད་ཀྱི་འཕྲིན་ལས་གདུལ་བྱ་ལ།།
མ་བརྟགས་བཏང་སྙོམས་ཙུང་ཟད་མི་མངའ་བས།།
སྐལ་ངན་བདག་གི་ཉེས་པ་ཕོ་ནར་ཟད།།
དེ་ཕྱིར་ཁྱོད་ལ་སྐྱོན་གྱི་སྐབས་མེད་པས།།

དེང་ནས་བྱང་ཆུབ་སྙིང་པོར་བདུད་སྡེ་ལས།།
ཇི་སྲིད་རྒྱལ་བར་མ་གྱུར་དེ་སྲིད་དུ།།
སྐྱེ་ཞིང་སྐྱེ་བར་ཁྱོད་ཀྱིས་རྗེས་བཟུང་ནས།།
གསུང་གི་བདུད་རྩིས་ངོམས་པ་མེད་པར་ཤོག །།

Within your deeds however,
no trace of neglect or indifference
toward any disciple is found.
Solely by my own faults, therefore,
am I rendered so unfortunate,
and no failing is attached to you.

Therefore, until under the bodhi tree
I emerge victorious over the hosts of Mara,
I pray to be cared for life after life by you
and never tire of your nectar-like words.

དབྱངས་ཅན་མ་སྤྱན་དྲངས་བསྟོད་པ་བཞུགས་སོ།།

ཆུ་འཛིན་དཀར་པོ་གློག་ཕྲེང་དྲ་བ་ཅན།།
མཁའ་ཡི་མཛེས་བྱེད་འདྲ་བའི་ཡིད་འཕྲོག་མ།།
དྲི་ཟའི་ན་ཆུང་དབུས་ན་འཛེ་སྒེག་མཁན།།
རིངས་ནས་བརྩེ་བའི་ལྷ་མོ་ད་ཚུར་སྤྱོན།།
པད་མའི་བཞིན་ལ་གཡོ་ལྡན་བུང་བའི་མིག །
མཐོན་མཐིང་རལ་པའི་རྩེ་ན་འོད་དཀར་ཅན།།
རོལ་སྒེག་གར་གྱིས་བསྒྱིངས་པའི་དབྱངས་ཅན་མ།།
ད་དུང་བདག་ལ་ངག་གི་དབང་ཕྱུག་སྩོལ།།
རོལ་རྩེད་གར་གྱིས་ཉམས་ལྡན་རི་དྭགས་མིག །
མིག་གིས་བལྟ་བས་མི་ངོམས་ཡིད་འཕྲོག་མ།།
མ་ལྟར་བརྩེ་བ་ཁྱོད་ཀྱིས་བདག་གི་ངག །
ངག་དབང་ལྷ་མོ་ཉིད་དང་མཚུངས་པར་མཛོད།།
སྟོན་ཟླ་རྒྱས་པའི་དཔལ་ལས་ལྷག་པར་མཛེས།།
ཚངས་དབྱངས་སྙན་པའི་གདངས་ཀྱང་ཟིལ་གྱིས་གནོན།།
ཟབ་ཡངས་རྒྱ་མཚོའི་འཛིང་ལྟར་དཔག་དཀའ་བ།།
དབྱངས་ཅན་ལྷ་མོའི་སྐུ་གསུང་ཐུགས་ལ་འདུད།།
ཨོཾ་སྭ་རྭ་སི་ཧྲི་ཧིཾ་ཧིཾ།།

Prayer to Sarasvati

Captivating presence, stealing my mind,
like a lightning-adorned cloud beautifying the sky,
there amid a celestial gathering of youthful musicians.
Compassionate goddess, come here now!

Those alluring honeybee eyes in that lotus face,
that long, dark blue hair, glowing with white light,
there before me in a pose of seductive dance.
Grant me, Sarasvati, your power of speech.

Those beautiful, playful antelope eyes,
I gaze insatiably upon you, seducer of my mind.
Goddess of speech with a mother's compassion,
make our speech as one.

More beautiful than the splendor of a full autumn moon,
a voice eclipsing the sweetest melody of Brahma,
a mind as hard to fathom as the deepest ocean,
I bow before the goddess Sarasvati.

Om sarasiddhi hring hring

འཇམ་དབྱངས་བསྟོད་སྤྲིན་རྒྱ་མཚོ་བཞུགས་སོ།།

རིང་ནས་གོམས་པའི་ཐུགས་རྗེའི་ཆབ་ཀྱིས་རང་བདེ་འདོད་པའི་ཡིད་ཀྱི་མེ་དཔུང་བཅིལ།། ཟབ་མོའི་རང་བཞིན་ཇི་བཞིན་གཟིགས་པས་ཀུན་ཏུ་རྟོག་པའི་སྤྲོས་པའི་དྲ་བ་བཅད།། ཉིད་ཀྱིས་གཟིགས་གང་འགྲོ་ལ་བསྐྲུན་ཕྱིར་གཞན་ཕན་ཁུར་ཆེན་སྐྱོ་མེད་ཐུགས་ཀྱིས་འཁྱེར།། ལྷག་པའི་ལྷ་དེར་ཡིད་གཏད་དང་བའི་ཀླུང་གིས་བསྐྱོད་པའི་བསྟོད་ཚིག་མེ་ཏོག་ལ།།

ཉིན་བྱེད་འཆར་ཀའི་མདངས་ཀྱིས་རབ་འཕྱུད་པའི།།
ལྷུན་སྟུག་གསེར་གྱི་རི་བོའི་ངོས་བཞིན་དུ།།
དམར་སེར་འོད་ཀྱི་ཕུང་པོ་ལྷམ་མེ་བ།།
འཇམ་དབྱངས་མཁྱེན་པའི་གཏེར་ཁྱོད་ཡུད་ཙམ་དགོངས།།

མ་ལུས་ཞིང་དུ་འབད་པས་བཙལ་ན་ཡང་།།
ཁྱོད་ལས་གཞན་པའི་སྐྱབས་བཟང་མ་མཆིས་པས།།
བདག་ཡིད་ཁྱོད་ཀྱི་རྗེས་སུ་ཕྱོགས་པ་ནི།།
ཉི་མས་གདུངས་པའི་གླང་ཆེན་པད་མཚོར་བཞིན།།
དེ་ཕྱིར་ཁྱོད་ཀྱི་ཡོན་ཏན་བརྗོད་ལ་བདག །
ཡིད་ལ་རེ་བ་སྐྱོང་བར་བྱེད་པ་ཡི།།

Praise of Manjushri

Praise of His Form

The rains of compassion, so long your acquaintance,
have quenched the fires burning for self-fulfillment alone.
A pure, unhindered knowledge of the profoundest of truths
has cut forever the ubiquitous net of fabrication.

To grant your knowledge to others
you willingly shoulder the burden of selfless service.
Deity extraordinary, on the wind of faith and devotion
I cast these flowers of praise your way.

A glowing magnitude of orange light,
like a golden mountain kissed by the sun,
Manjushri, treasure of wisdom, hear me awhile.

Though I might search in every realm
I would find no greater refuge.
I turn my mind to you, therefore,
as a heat-tormented elephant plunges into a lotus pool.

གཏོང་བས་མཛེས་པའི་སྦྱིན་བདག་མཐོང་བ་ན།།
འབྱོར་བས་དམན་པའི་སློང་མོ་བ་བཞིན་གྱུར།།

ཁྱོད་སྐུ་རི་དབང་ཧི་བཞིན་མཐོ་ཞིང་དྲང་།།
ཉུ་གྲོའི་ལྗོན་པ་ལྟར་རྒྱས་རྒྱ་ཞེང་གབ།།
བཙོ་མའི་གསེར་ལྟར་དག་ཅིང་གསལ་བ་ཡི།།
པགས་པའི་མདོག་ནི་ལེགས་ཤིང་སྲབ་ལ་འཇམ།།

རྒྱལ་མཚན་ཏོག་ལྟར་སྤྱི་གཙུག་གནས་སུ་ནི།།
རིང་འཇམ་གནག་ལ་སྣུམ་པའི་རལ་པ་ཡི།།
ཐོར་ཅོག་མཛེས་པར་བཅིང་པའི་ཟུར་བུ་ནི།།
ཟུར་ཕུད་ལྔ་ལྡན་ཅུང་ཟད་གཡོན་དུ་འཕྱང་།།

རིན་ཆེན་རྩེ་ཕྲན་རྣམས་ཀྱིས་མཛེས་བྱས་པའི།།
དབྱིབས་ལེགས་གདུགས་བཞིན་ཀུན་ནས་རྒྱས་པའི་དབུ།།
སྐྲ་མཚམས་མཐོ་བར་ལེགས་པར་ཕྱེད་པ་ཡི།།
དཔྲལ་བའི་དབུས་ནི་ཟླ་བ་རྒྱས་པ་བཞིན།།

Speaking of your qualities, I am a destitute beggar,
whose eyes have seen a beautiful patron to fulfill his dreams.

Your body is as tall and erect as Meru,
as symmetrical as the *nyagrodha* tree.
Your skin is as pure and clear as burnished gold,
soft and gentle to the touch.

Long, shining, black soft hair,
beautifully gathered up into five plaits,
falling a little to the left,
like the crest of a victory banner.

Fully formed head, adorned by jewels,
beautifully shaped like a parasol,
hairline high, clearly defined,
a brow broad like the fullest of moons.

ཀུན་ད་དུང་དང་པདྨའི་རྩ་བ་ལྟར།།
དཀར་གསལ་གཡས་སུ་འཁྱིལ་ལེགས་རི་མོ་ཅན།།
དག་པའི་དངུལ་གྱི་འབུར་དང་འདྲ་བ་ཡི།།
དྲི་མེད་མཛོད་སྤུ་སྨིན་མའི་དབུས་ན་མཛེས།།
ཁ་དོག་ནག་ཅིང་ཅུང་ཟད་གུག་པ་ཡི།།
འཇམ་སྣུམ་སྤུ་མཉམ་སྨིན་ཚུགས་རིང་པོ་ཅན།།
སྡུག་ཅིང་འཇམ་ལ་མ་འཛིངས་སྒྲིག་ལེགས་པ།།
ཁྱུ་མཆོག་བཞིན་དུ་རྫི་མ་ཡིད་དུ་འོང་།།

ཨུཏྤལ་མཐིང་ཁའི་འདབ་མ་ཇི་བཞིན་དུ།།
སྤྱན་དཀྱུས་རིང་པོ་ཅུང་ཟད་ཟུམ་པ་ཡི།།
དཀར་ནག་ཆ་རྣམས་མ་འདྲེས་མཛེས་པ་ནི།།
འདམ་སྐྱེས་འདབ་མ་ཀུན་ནས་དྭངས་པ་བཞིན།།

རིམ་པར་འཚམ་ཞིང་ཀུན་ཏུ་མཐོ་བའི་ཤངས།།
བིམ་པ་ལྟར་དམར་ཡིད་དུ་འོང་བའི་མཆུ།།
དཀར་ཞིང་ཚད་མཉམ་ཐགས་བཟང་བཞི་བཅུའི་ཚེམས།།
འགྲམ་པ་ཀླུམ་རྒྱས་རི་དྭགས་རྒྱལ་པོ་བཞིན།།

Your eyebrows, black and curving,
soft, beautiful, so elegantly long,
each hair the exact same length,
eyelashes thick, soft, each separate hair
beautifully formed like those of the leading bull.

A circle of perfect hair as white as the water lily,
conch-like curling to the right, as well formed as the lotus root,
beautiful between the eyebrows like a drop of pure silver.

Eyes long and curving like blue *utpala* petals,
whites beautifully defined like bright lotus petals.

Nose set high, uniformly shaped,
lips as red as the *bimba* fruit,
forty pure white teeth, well-set, of equal size,
cheeks fully rounded like those of a lion.

སྲབ་མཉེན་རོ་མཆོག་མྱོང་བའི་ལྷུགས་ཀྱིས་ནི།།
ཞལ་གྱི་དཀྱིལ་འཁོར་ཀུན་ཏུ་ཁེངས་པར་མཛད།།
སྙན་ཤལ་བཟང་པོ་རིང་དུ་འཕྱུར་བའི་རྩེར།།
རིན་ཆེན་དུ་མས་སྤྲས་པའི་རྣ་ཆ་གཡོ།།

གཟི་འོད་འཁྲུག་པའི་རིན་ཆེན་ཕྲེང་བའི་རྒྱན།།
གང་དུ་འཕྱུར་བའི་དྲི་མེད་མགྲིན་པ་ནི།།
མཛེས་པའི་གསེར་གྱི་བུམ་པའི་མགྲིན་པ་བཞིན།།
རྒྱུ་ཡི་དྲ་བ་མི་མངོན་ལྷུམ་ཞིང་རྒྱས།།
ཕྱུག་ཞབས་བོལ་དང་ཕྲག་གོང་ལྟག་པའི་ཕྱོགས།།
ཡོངས་སུ་གང་བས་མི་མཉམ་མེད་པའི་སྐུ།།
གདོང་ལྷ་པ་བཞིན་ཀུན་ནས་རྒྱས་པའི་སྟོད།།
ལྷུན་པོའི་ངོས་ལྟར་རབ་ཏུ་ཡངས་པའི་བྲང་།།

དཔུང་པའི་མགོ་ནི་ལེགས་པར་ལྷུམ་པའི་ཕྱུག །
གླང་པོའི་རྒྱལ་པོའི་སྣ་ལྟར་རིང་ཞིང་མཛེས།།
ཉི་ཤུའི་སོར་མོ་མཛེས་པའི་དྲ་བ་ཡིས།།
ལེགས་པར་སྤྲེལ་བ་ངང་པའི་རྒྱལ་པོ་བཞིན།།

Smooth, slender tongue enclosed
by the mandala of your face,
enjoying only the best of tastes.

Ears endowed with long well-formed lobes,
adorned by ornaments jeweled and precious.

Perfectly formed neck
graced by dazzling jeweled garlands,
fully fleshed, no vein protruding,
as beautiful as that of a golden vase.

Calves, forearms, shoulder blades, upper back
all fully fleshed and uniform in their symmetry,
a torso like that of a lion, a chest as broad as Meru.

Delightfully curved shoulders, their beautiful arms
long and low as the royal elephant's trunk.

མདོག་སྨུམ་དམར་བའི་མདངས་ཆགས་སེན་མོ་ཡི།།
ཕྲེང་བས་རབ་དུ་དངར་བའི་སོར་མོ་ནི།།
དཔག་བསམ་ཡལ་འདབ་གཞོན་ནུའི་ལྷུག་ཕྲན་ལྟར།།
རིང་ཞིང་རྒྱུས་ལ་འཛམ་ཞིང་གཞོན་ཤ་ཆགས།།

གསལ་ཞིང་རྫོགས་ལ་སོ་སོར་མ་འདྲེས་པའི།།
རྩིབས་སྟོང་ལྡན་པའི་གསེར་གྱི་འཁོར་ལོ་མཆོག །
ཕྱག་དང་ཞབས་ཀྱི་མཐིལ་ན་བཀྲ་བ་ནི།།
རྒྱུ་ལས་རྒྱུ་ཡི་འབྱུར་ནི་གསལ་བ་བཞིན།།

དཔུང་རྒྱན་གདུ་བུས་མཛེས་པར་བྱུས་པ་ཡི།།
གཡས་པའི་ཕྱག་ན་དངོས་འཛིན་འཁྲི་ཤིང་གི །
ལྗོན་པ་དྲུངས་ནས་གཅོད་པའི་རལ་གྲི་ནི།།
འབར་བའི་འོད་ཀྱི་དྲ་བ་འཁྲོད་པ་བསྣམས།།
ཞི་སྒྲོ་གཉིས་སུ་མེད་པ་རྟེན་འབྲེལ་ལམ།།
མ་ལུས་གསལ་པར་སྟོན་པའི་གླེགས་བམ་མཆོག །
ཨུཏྤལ་སྔོན་པོའི་ལྟེ་བར་གནས་པ་ཡི།།
སྡོང་བུ་གཡོན་པའི་ཕྱག་གིས་ཐུགས་ཀར་འཛིན།།

Fingers and toes beautifully webbed
like those of the royal swan.

Fingers, long, full, soft, and young,
tipped by a row of glistening red nails
like slender shoots upon the celestial wish-fulfilling tree.

Golden wheels, each of a thousand spokes,
grace the soles of your feet, the palms of your hands,
so clear, so perfect, each spoke well defined,
works of art in relief like the matrix of a seal.

Your right arm, adorned with bracelets and armbands,
brandishing a blazing sword to cut to the root
the treelike creeper of clinging ignorance.

In your left hand a blue *utpala* stem at your heart,
petals cradling the supreme scripture that teaches with clarity
paths of dependent arising, sole gateway to freedom.

རབ་འབྱམས་ཚོན་གྱིས་ཁ་བསྒྱུར་སྤྲབ་ལ་འཛམ།།
སྣ་ཚོགས་དར་གྱི་སྨད་གཡོགས་གཡོ་བའི་སྟེང་།།
སིལ་སིལ་སྒྲ་སྒྲོག་གསེར་གྱི་འོག་པག་གིས།།
ཡིད་འོང་སྐེད་སྐབས་ཀུན་ནས་མཛེས་པར་བསྡམས།།

རྟ་མཆོག་བཞིན་དུ་གསང་གནས་སྦུབས་སུ་ནུབ།།
འཛམ་ཞིང་ཕྲ་བ་བ་སྤུའི་ཚོགས་རྣམས་ནི།།
ཟླ་མེད་རེ་རེར་བྱུང་ནས་གཡས་ཕྱོགས་སུ།།
རིམ་གྱིས་འཁྱིལ་ནས་སྐུ་ལ་གྱེན་དུ་ཕྱོགས།།

བགས་ཀྱིས་ཕྲ་ཞིང་ཟླུམ་པའི་བྱིན་པ་ལེགས།།
ཞབས་ཀྱི་མཁྲིག་པ་ལོང་བུའི་འབུར་གྱིས་དབེན།།
རུས་སྦལ་ལྟོ་བཞིན་ཞབས་མཐིལ་ཀུན་ནས་མཉམ།།
ཞབས་ཀྱི་བཞི་ཆ་ཕྱིར་འཕགས་རྟིང་པ་ཡངས།།
འདབ་དྲུག་པད་དཀར་དམར་སེར་ལྗེ་བའི་སྟེང་།།
དཀྱིལ་འཁོར་ཡོངས་རྫོགས་རྒྱུ་སྐར་བདག་པོའི་གདན།།
གང་དེར་སྒྲ་ལྡན་གདུ་བུས་མཁྲིག་མའི་ཕྱོགས།།
མཛེས་པའི་ཞབས་གཉིས་རྡོ་རྗེའི་སྐྱིལ་སྐྲུང་མཛད།།

From your waist, streamers flow fine and silken,
dyed in a million colors, tied about with a golden sash,
from each the tinkling sounds of a string of bells,

As with the king of horses your sexual organ hidden,
your bodily hair, soft and fine, each perfect strand
coiling to the right, reaching upward.

Fine calves, rounded, tapering beautifully into slenderness,
no protrusion upon your ankle joint,
soles flattened smooth like the underside of a turtle shell,
heel quarters heightened, their backs broad.

Within a six-petal lotus at its orange heart,
upon a moon-disc throne, a perfect circle,
your feet, adorned by tinkling bracelets,
rest in lotus pose.

བསོད་ནམས་ཚོགས་རབ་རབ་འབྱམས་རྒྱ་ལས་
འཕྲུངས་པའི་སྐུ་མཆོག་མཆོག་ཏུ་མཛེས་པ་ཁྱོད་ཀྱི་སྐུ།།
ནམ་མཁའི་མཐས་གཏུགས་གཏུགས་པ་མེད་པའི་
ཞིང་མཆོག་ཀུན་ཏུ་དུ་མའི་འགྲོ་ལ་མིག་འཕྲུལ་བཞིན།།
ལ་ལར་བལྟམས་ཤིང་ཞིང་གཞན་དུ་ཡང་བྱང་
ཆུབ་ཚུལ་སྟོན་སྟོན་པ་ཁྱོད་ཀྱི་སྐུ་ཡི་ནི།།
བཀོད་པ་མཆོག་འདི་འདི་དང་གཞན་དུ་མ་ལུས་
འགྲོ་ཀུན་ཀུན་མཁྱེན་གྱུར་ཀྱང་བརྗོད་མི་ནུས།།

ལི་ཁྲིའི་རྒྱ་མཚོར་རྟ་བདུན་འོད་སྟོང་ལྡང་པ་བཞིན།།
ལྟ་བས་མི་ངོམས་འོད་དཔུང་ཕྱོགས་བཅུར་འཕྲོ་བའི་སྐུ།།
གང་དེ་ཙུང་ཟད་བསྟོད་པའི་བསོད་ནམས་དེ་ཡིས་བདག །
འཇམ་དབྱངས་སྐུ་མཛེས་མིག་གི་ལམ་དུ་འབྲལ་མེད་ཤོག །

ནམ་ཞིག་ཁྱོད་སྐུ་མཐོང་བར་གྱུར་མ་ཐག །
སྲིད་པར་རིང་དུ་འཁྱམས་པས་དུབ་པ་བདག །
ལོག་པའི་ལམ་དུ་སོང་བའི་མ་རྒུངས་ཡིད།།
བྱང་ཆུབ་སེམས་ཀྱི་དབང་དུ་འགྱུར་བར་ཤོག །

Most beautiful of beautiful forms,
born supreme from a million causes of virtue supreme,
appearing among dwellers of infinite realms through infinite
space like tricks played upon their eyes.
In some you are born, while in others simultaneously
you show the ways of the enlightened.
Were every being of every realm to reach omniscience,
they could not explain the artistry of such manifested form.

By the merit I amass from this meager praise
may the captivating presence of Manjushri,
shining like the sun on a vermilion sea,
spellbindingly beautiful in a magnitude of light
radiating out to the ten directions,
be never lost from my sight.

And when my eyes light upon you,
I pray that my rapacious mind,
blundering along its ignorant ways,
wearied by long wandering through samsara,
be at once reined in under the domain
of the great mind of enlightenment.

གཞན་ཡང་གཟུངས་དང་མངོན་ཤེས་རྣམ་ཐར་སྒོ།།
སྨུ་མཐའ་ཡས་པའི་ཏིང་འཛིན་ཚོགས་ཐོབ་ནས།།
ཞིང་ཁམས་བྱེ་བར་རྒྱལ་རྣམས་བལྟ་བའི་ཕྱིར།།
དཔག་མེད་ལུས་ཀྱི་བཀོད་པ་སྟོན་པར་ཤོག །

དེར་ནི་མང་དུ་ཐོས་པའི་མཐར་སོན་ཏེ།།
མཐའ་ཡས་འགྲོ་བ་ཆོས་ཀྱིས་ཚིམ་བྱས་ནས།།
རིང་པོར་མི་ཐོགས་རྒྱལ་བ་ཀུན་གྱི་གཙོ།།
ངག་གི་དབང་པོའི་སྐུ་མཆོག་ཐོབ་པར་ཤོག །

When I acquire the four great powers of retention,
the sixfold clairvoyance, freedom's three gateways,
and a host of meditative concentrations on limitlessness,
may I then appear in forms beyond number
to gaze upon conquering buddhas in countless realms.

Having journeyed to learning's end
and satisfied countless beings with Dharma,
may I become without delay that supreme embodiment
of the power of speech, highest of all buddhas.

འོད་སྟོང་ཟེར་གྱི་ཕྲེ་བའི་གུར་ཀུམ་གཟུགས།།
དྭངས་པའི་མེ་ལོང་དཀྱིལ་ན་སྣང་བ་བཞིན།།
འཁྲིད་ལེགས་དབང་པོའི་གཞུ་བཞིན་རབ་བཀྲ་བ།།
འཇམ་པའི་དབྱངས་ཀྱིས་ངག་གི་དབང་ཕྱུག་སྐྱོལ།།

ཕྱོགས་བཅུའི་ཞིང་ཀུན་ཀུན་ནས་ཁེངས་པའི་སྒྲ་སྐད་
སྐད་ཀྱི་དབྱེ་བ་མཐའ་ཡས་པ།།
སེམས་ཅན་ཀུན་ཡིད་ཡིད་དང་མཐུན་པར་འཆོམ་
བྱེད་བྱེད་པོའི་གདངས་ཀྱང་ཟིལ་གནོན་པ།།

ཁྱོད་ཀྱི་གསུང་དབྱངས་དབྱངས་ཀྱི་ང་རོའི་དཀྱིལ་
འཁོར་འཁོར་བ་སྲིད་དུ་རྒྱུན་ཆགས་པའི།།
སྙན་པའི་གསུང་གང་གང་གི་རྣ་བའི་ལམ་དུ་ལྷུང་
ན་ན་རྒ་འཆི་བ་འཕྲོག་པར་བྱེད།།

Praise of His Speech

Like the fresh petals of the saffron flower
opened by the rays of the sun
reflected within a spotless mirror,
your pose is of a rainbow beauty.
Grant me, Manjushri, the powers of speech.

Your voice fills every corner of every realm,
a voice of manifestations beyond number,
a melody pleasing, a melody satisfying,
a melody eclipsing the melody of Brahma.

Your voice a vocal mandala of sound,
your words beautiful, unbroken in samsara,
banishing in those whose ears they fall upon,
death, old age, and sickness.

གསུང་མཉེན་འཇམ་ཞིང་ཡིད་འོང་ཡིད་དུ་འཐད།།
དག་ཅིང་དྲི་མེད་འོད་གསལ་སྙན་ལ་འཇེབས།།
མཉན་པར་འོས་ཞིང་མི་ཚུགས་སྙན་ཞིང་དུལ།།
མི་རྩུབ་མི་བརླང་རབ་འདུལ་རྣ་བར་སྙན།།

ལུས་སེམས་སྙིང་ནི་འཚིམ་བྱེད་དགའ་བདེ་བསྐྱེད།།
གདུང་མེད་ཀུན་ཏུ་ཤེས་བྱེད་རྣམ་རིག་བྱ།།
རྣམ་གསལ་དགའ་བྱེད་མངོན་པར་དགའ་བྱེད་ཅིང་།།
ཀུན་ཤེས་བྱེད་ཅིང་རྣམ་པར་རིག་པར་བྱེད།།

A voice whose words agreeable to all,
softly spoken, pleasing to the mind,
delivered in eloquence, pure and uncorrupted,
easily understood, soothing, worthy of hearing.

Gratifying, pacifying, unsurpassed by others,
never severe nor punishing, a panacea for all,
captivating to the listener, bringer of bodily bliss,
of mental joy and of peace to the soul.

Words bringing the joy of insight,
the happiness of uncorrupted perception,
words free from the grief that false promises bring,
full of knowledge, the bearer of wisdom.

Never vague nor mealy-mouthed,
bringing the joy of anticipation and foreseen fulfillment,
teaching the conceivable and inconceivable,
free from contradiction, fitting words
in tune with the disposition of listeners.

རིགས་ཤིང་འབྲེལ་ལ་ཟློས་པའི་སྐྱོན་དང་བྲལ།།
སེང་གེ་གླང་ཆེན་འབྲུག་དང་ལག་འགྲོའི་དབང་།།
དྲི་ཟ་ཀ་ལ་པིང་ཀ་ཚངས་པ་དང་།།
ཤང་ཤང་ཏེའུ་དབང་པོའི་དབྱངས་ལྷུར་སྙན།།

ཛ་སྒྲ་མ་ཁེངས་མི་དམའ་ཀུན་རྗེས་ཞུགས།།
ཚིག་ཟུར་ཕྱིན་ཅིང་མ་ཚང་མེད་པ་དང་།།
མ་ཞུམ་མི་ཞན་རབ་དགའ་ཁྲབ་ཅིང་ཆུབ།།
རྒྱུན་ཆགས་འབྲེལ་ཞིང་སྒྲ་ཀུན་རྫོགས་པར་བྱེད།།

དབང་པོ་ཀུན་འཚིམ་མ་སྨད་མི་འགྱུར་ལ།།
མ་བརྟགས་འཁོར་གྱི་དཀྱིལ་འཁོར་ཀུན་ཏུ་གྲགས།།
དུག་གསུམ་སེལ་བྱེད་བདུད་དཔུང་ཚར་གཅོད་ཅིང་།།
རྣམ་པ་ཀུན་གྱི་མཆོག་དང་ལྡན་པར་འབྱུང་།།

Free from the fault of repetition,
words comparing to the roar of a lion,
as unhindered as the trumpeting elephant,
as deep as the bellowing dragon,
as noble as the words of the naga king,
as soft and sweet as gandarva music,
as enticing as the song of the *kalapinga* bird,
as resonating as the sound of Brahma,
as auspicious as hearing the voice
of the half-human griffin.

It is the voice of authority,
the sound of the drum of victory,
empty of pride yet never downtrodden,
full of prophecy, never vague nor half taught.

Forever fulfilling, never afraid,
unconcerned for the rewards of fame,
a joyful voice, all-encompassing, masterful,
unending, and fulsome.

དེ་ལྟར་བཞི་ཡིས་ལྷག་པའི་དུག་བཅུའི་དབྱངས།།
གསུང་ཅིག་ཉིད་ལའང་མ་ཚང་མེད་པར་ནི།།
ཇི་སྲིད་ནམ་མཁའི་མཐས་ཁྱབ་དེ་སྲིད་པའི།།
སྐལ་ལྡན་རྣ་བའི་ལམ་དུ་བདེ་བ་སྟེར།།

དེ་ཚོ་ཉེ་བར་གནས་ལ་ཧ་ཅང་ཆེ་བར་མི་སྣང་རིང་
ན་གནས་ལ་ཆུང་མིན་པར།།
སྣ་ཚོགས་ཚོན་དང་ཕྲད་པའི་ཤེལ་བཞིན་གྲངས་
མེད་གདུལ་བྱའི་རང་རང་སྐད་དང་མཐུན་པར་ནི།།
སྤྱི་གཙུག་མཛོད་སྤུ་མགྲིན་པ་ལ་སོགས་ཁྱོད་སྐུའི་ཆ་
ཤས་ཀུན་ནས་འབྱུང་བར་རབ་སྟོན་ཀྱང་།།
དེ་དག་ཀུན་ལ་རྟོག་པ་ཉེར་ཞི་འདི་ནི་ནམ་མཁས་
ཚངས་དབྱངས་སྒྲོག་ན་མཚོན་པར་ནུས།།

Accomplished in every sound, every language,
uplifting, not open to ridicule or contempt,
instantaneously there, yet unhurried,
pervading samsara's every corner,
dispelling the poisons of greed, hate, and ignorance,
victorious over Mara's hosts, simply the best.

These qualities, in number sixty-four,
not found lacking in even your tiniest sliver of speech,
will continue to be music of joy to the ears of the fortunate
for as long as space pervades.

When near, not too loud, when far, never too faint;
like crystal in contact with many a color.
A voice in accord with the tongues of limitless listeners,
it arises from your crown, the circle of hair on your brow
your throat, and indeed from any part of your precious body,
and yet all thought and intention to speak have been stilled,
as all-pervading space is free from thought
yet filled with the voice of Brahma.

སློག་དམར་མཛེས་པའི་སྣ་རྒས་བཅིངས་པ་ཡི།།
ཆར་སྤྲིན་ནང་གི་འབྲུག་སྒྲ་ཟབ་མོ་བཞིན།།
འཇམ་དབྱངས་གསུང་བསྙོད་བསོད་ནམས་འདི་ཡིས་བདག །
ཁྱོད་གསུང་རྣ་བའི་ལམ་དུ་འབྲལ་མེད་ཤོག །

གསུང་རྒྱུན་རྣ་བའི་བུ་གར་ཞུགས་མ་ཐག །
སྐལ་ལྡན་རྗེས་འཛིན་ཡོག་སྒྲ་ཆར་གཅོད་ཅིང་།།
སྟེབ་ལེགས་ཚིག་གིས་བློ་གསལ་ཡིད་འཕྲོག་པའི།།
འཆད་རྩོད་རྩོམ་པའི་གནས་རྣམས་མཐར་སོན་ཤོག །

ཐ་དད་འགྲོ་བའི་སྐད་ལ་ཐོགས་མེད་པའི།།
ངེས་ཚིག་སོ་སོ་ཡང་དག་རིག་པ་མཆོག །
བདེ་བླག་ཐོབ་ནས་འགྲོ་བ་ཐམས་ཅད་ཀྱི།།
ཐེ་ཚོམ་གཅོད་པའི་མཆོག་ཏུ་བདག་གྱུར་ཅིག །

ཁྱོད་ཀྱིས་ཇི་ལྟར་རྗེས་སུ་གདམས་པ་ཡི།།
གསུང་གི་མཚམས་ལས་ནམ་ཡང་མི་འདའ་བར།།
གུས་པས་རྩེ་གཅིག་ཉམས་སུ་བླངས་པ་ཡིས།།
གསུང་གི་དབང་ཕྱུག་སྨྲར་དུ་འགྱུབ་པར་ཤོག །

By the wealth of merit gathered from this praise
of the speech of Manjushri whose voice compares
to the deep dragon roar within the rain cloud
girdled by beautiful lightning flashes,
may your words forever rain into my ears.

No sooner than your voice settles upon my ears,
may I gather the fortunate about me,
defeat those who peddle distorted views
and with poetry of voice and word may I journey
to perfection in the arts of teaching, logic, and composition
that captivate the souls of the wise.

May I gain without hardship
specialist knowledge mastering words and sounds
to penetrate with ease the language of differing beings,
and may I be unrivaled in such skills
to dispel the doubts of every living being.

By never straying beyond the bounds set by your teachings,
and practicing wholeheartedly and devotedly,
I pray that I may swiftly attain to the glories of your speech.

བྱ་རུའི་མདངས་དང་འདྲེས་པའི་གསེར་ཟངས་མདོག །
མདོག་ལེགས་ཤེས་བྱ་མ་ལུས་ལྷང་ངེར་མཁྱེན།།
མཁྱེན་རབ་དབང་ཕྱུག་འཇམ་དབྱངས་འགྲོ་བའི་སྐྱབས།།
སྐྱབས་མཆོག་ཁྱོད་ཀྱིས་རབ་འབྱམས་ཤེས་རབ་སྐྱོལ།།

དངོས་འཛིན་ཆང་གིས་རབ་ཏུ་སྨྱོས་པས་བླང་དོར་
དཔྱོད་པའི་བློ་གྲོས་ཉམས།།
ཉོན་མོངས་གདུག་པའི་སྦྲུ་ཡི་ལག་པས་དགེ་བའི་
ལྗོན་པ་ཀུན་ཏུ་འཇོམས།།
སྲིད་པའི་ཞགས་པས་ཡིད་ནི་དྲངས་པས་
རྙེད་བཀུར་གླང་མོའི་ཕྱིར་འབྲང་བ།།
བག་མེད་ནགས་ཁྲོད་ཀུན་ཏུ་རྒྱུ་བའི་གདུལ་
དཀའི་ཡིད་ཀྱི་གླང་པོ་ཆེ།།

Praise of His Mind

Of a color, the blend of coral hue
and the burnish of the finest gold,
the beautiful color of one whose knowledge
alights freely on every phenomenon known.
A cornucopia of knowledge, Manjushri,
protector of all, protector supreme,
grant me this ocean of knowledge.

This elephant of the mind,
intoxicated by the wines of holding phenomena as real,
weakening discernment of right and wrong,
its trunk of vicious delusion tearing up the trees of virtue,
led on and on by the leads of desire
in pursuit of the she-elephant of fame and fortune,
crashes wildly through the deep forests of unawareness.

དྲན་ཤེས་བག་ཡོད་ཐག་པས་དམ་བཅིངས་ནས།།
ཡང་དག་རིགས་པའི་ལྕགས་ཀྱུ་རྣོན་པོ་ཡིས།།
འཕགས་མཆོག་བྲེ་བས་བགྲོད་ཅིང་བསྔགས་པ་ཡི།།
རྟེན་འབྲེལ་དམ་པའི་ལམ་བཟང་སྲོལ་དུ་བཙུད།།

རྩོལ་དེ་སྐྱོ་མེད་བརྩོན་པའི་ཤུགས་དྲག་གིས།།
དཔག་མེད་བསྐལ་པར་ཡང་དང་ཡང་གོམས་པས།།
སྒྱུ་མ་ལྟ་བུའི་ཏིང་འཛིན་རྡོ་རྗེ་ཡིས།།
མཐར་འཛིན་རི་བོ་མིང་གི་ལྷག་མར་མཛད།།

སླར་ཡང་མཐའ་ཡས་རྒྱལ་བའི་དབང་པོ་རྣམས།།
རབ་མཆོག་མཆོད་སྤྲིན་རྒྱ་མཚོས་མཉེས་བྱས་པས།།
དྲི་མེད་མགུར་ནས་ཚངས་དབྱངས་ང་རོ་ཡིས།།
དགོངས་པ་གཅིག་གིས་གསུངས་པའི་གདམས་པ་མཆོག །

Such a hard-to-tame elephant of the mind you reined in
with the ropes of memory, mindfulness, and awareness,
and with the sharp hook of flawless reasoning
set it upon the true and good path of dependent arising,
well traveled, well-praised by countless noble beings.

For immeasurable eons again and again
you practiced with tireless and powerful endeavor until,
with the vajra of the meditative concentration
upon the illusion-like nature of all phenomena,
you crumbled the great mountain of extremes
till only its name remained.

Again, by delighting countless buddhas
with boundless horizons of offerings supreme,
you brought forth their pure Brahman-like voices,
their minds in accord, their teachings supreme,
to eradicate forever the manifold sickness that is samsara.

སྲིད་པའི་ནད་བརྒྱ་དྲུངས་འབྱིན་བདུད་བརྩིའི་ཟས།།
རྒྱུན་དུ་བསྟེན་པས་བགྲོད་པར་ཆེས་དཀའ་བའི།།
རྒྱལ་སྲས་སྤྱོད་པ་རླབས་ཆེའི་ཕ་རོལ་ཏུ།།
བགྲོད་པའི་བློ་གྲོས་ལུས་སྟོབས་རྒྱས་པ་ན།།
མཐའ་དག་འཛིན་པས་ནམ་ཡང་མི་རྫི་ཞིང་།།
མ་ལུས་འཁྲུལ་སྣང་འཛོམས་ལ་ཐོགས་མེད་པའི།།
ཏིང་འཛིན་ཀུན་གྱི་གཙོ་བོར་གྱུར་པ་གང་།།
རྡོ་རྗེ་ལྟ་བུར་གྲགས་པའི་ཏིང་ངེ་འཛིན།།

ཁྱོད་ཀྱིས་མངོན་དུ་མཛད་པ་དེ་ཡིས་མཐུས།།
སྒྱུ་མ་ལྟ་བུའི་ཡུལ་གྱི་སྣང་བ་དང་།།
རྨི་ལམ་ལྟ་བུའི་གསལ་ཞིང་རིག་པའི་བློ།།
སྦྱོང་སྣང་མ་ལུས་ཆོས་ཀྱི་དབྱིངས་སུ་ཞུགས།།
དེ་ཕྱིར་རྩ་བ་ཉམས་པའི་ལྗོན་ཤིང་བཞིན།།
མ་ལུས་འཛིན་པའི་ས་བོན་དྲུངས་ཕྱུང་བས།།
སྐྱོབ་པ་ཁྱོད་ལ་ནམ་མཁའ་ཇི་སྲིད་དུ།།
ཆོས་ཀྱི་སྐུ་ལས་གཡོ་བ་ག་ལ་ཞིག །

Sipping such nectar constantly
you nourished a body of wisdom to sustain you
on the hard road to perfection of bodhisattva practice,
where never again would you be cowed
by the delusion holding all phenomena as real,
and where the road to destruction of misperceived appearance
was seen clearly and without hindrance
by the supreme vajra-like meditative concentration.

By its power, this illusion-like appearance of phenomena
and this transparent and knowing dream-like mind,
which together embrace all experience, all appearance
melted into the space-like realm of dharmadhatu,
and like a tree with roots shriveled,
all seeds of clinging were forever laid to waste.
Therefore, my protector, for as long as space lasts,
how could you ever leave your dharmakaya?

དེ་ལྟར་མགོན་ཁྱོད་ཆོས་ཀྱི་དབྱིངས་ལས་ཙུང་
ཟད་གཡོ་བ་མེད་བཞིན་དུ།།
དུ་མའི་ཤེས་བྱ་གསལ་བར་སྣང་བ་མེ་ལོང་
ནང་དུ་གཟུགས་བརྙན་ནམ།།
ནམ་མཁའི་ལམ་ན་འཇའ་ཚོན་བཞིན་དུ་
སོ་སོར་མ་འདྲེས་རྫོགས་པར་མཁྱེན།།
མཁྱེན་བཟང་ཁྱོད་ཀྱི་མཁྱེན་པ་དེ་ཡང་སྐད་
ཅིག་ཉིད་ལ་དེ་ལྟར་ལགས།།

སྨྲིན་ལས་འཁྲོར་ལྡན་གནས་ཡིན་དབུལ་པོ་མིན།།
སེར་སྣས་དབུལ་པོའི་གནས་ཡིན་འཁྲོར་ལྡན་མིན།།
དེ་སོགས་རྟེན་འབྲེལ་མི་སླུའི་གནས་ཀུན་མཁྱེན།།
དེ་ཕྱིར་ཁྱོད་ནི་སྨྲ་བའི་གཙོ་བོ་ལགས།།

ཐོགས་མེད་སྲིད་པར་སོང་བ་ཐམས་ཅད་ཀྱི།།
དགེ་དང་མི་དགེའི་ལས་རྒྱུ་འབྲས་བུར་བཅས།།
གང་དེ་ཁྱོད་ཀྱི་མངོན་དུ་མ་གྱུར་མེད།།
དེ་སྐད་ཁྱོད་གསུང་འབྲུལ་མེད་མ་མཆིས་ལགས།།

Never stirring, therefore, from your dharmadhatu realm,
every phenomenon arises before you, my guide,
like images in a mirror, like the colors of a rainbow,
each individually and completely known at every instant.

From giving comes wealth has basis,
from giving comes poverty has not.
From miserliness comes poverty has basis,
from miserliness comes wealth has not.
Such consequences born from infallible dependent arising
are known by you and renders you
supreme, therefore, among teachers.

No deed, good or bad, nor corresponding result
found throughout samsara since time immemorial,
remains unseen and unknown by you.
Your words, therefore, contain nothing
falling foul of the law of dependence.

ཆགས་ལ་གནས་ཤིང་སྡུད་ལ་མོས་པ་དང་།།
དེ་ལས་ལྡོག་སོགས་མོས་པ་སྣ་ཚོགས་ཚུལ།།
མངོན་གསུམ་གཟིགས་ཕྱིར་ཁྱོད་ཀྱི་མཛད་པ་ཀུན།།
འགྲོ་ལ་དོན་དུ་མི་འགྱུར་ཡོད་མ་ལགས།།

བཅོ་བརྒྱད་ཁམས་ཀྱི་རབ་དབྱེ་མཐའ་དག་ལ།།
ཁྱོད་ཀྱི་ཀློག་ཏུ་གྱུར་པ་གང་ཡང་མེད།།
དེ་ཕྱིར་ཁྱོད་ནི་གདུལ་བྱའི་གནས་རྣམས་ཀྱི།།
གདུལ་བའི་དུས་ལས་ཅུང་ཟད་འདའ་མ་ལགས།།

སྲིད་པར་རྒྱུ་བ་རྣམས་ཀྱི་དད་སོགས་ཀྱི།།
དབང་པོ་རྣོ་རྟུལ་དབང་པོ་མེད་པ་ལ།།
མཁྱེན་པ་ཐོགས་མེད་འཇུག་པ་དེ་སླད་ཁྱོད།།
ཆོས་སྟོན་ཚུལ་ལ་ཤིན་ཏུ་མཁས་པ་ལགས།།

མངོན་པར་མཐོ་ཞིང་ངེས་པར་ལེགས་པ་དང་།།
ངན་སོང་གནས་རྣམས་ཀུན་ཏུ་བགྲོད་པའི་ལམ།།
ཀུན་ལ་མཁྱེན་པ་སྒྲིབ་པ་མེད་པའི་ཕྱིར།།
ཁྱོད་ནི་འགྲོ་བའི་བཤེས་གཉེན་བཟང་པོ་ལགས།།

Some beings dwell in manifest desire
yet are disposed toward anger,
others dwell in open anger
but are disposed to desire.
Such dispositions are all manifest to you.
There are no deeds of yours, therefore,
that are not of benefit to others.

The eighteen realms of phenomena in all their divisions
lie manifest and unhidden before you.
You do not miss, even by a fraction, therefore,
the times of those ripe for training.

Of those tumbling through samsara
some are developed, some are weak.
You see unfettered their differing strengths of faith,
of wisdom, memory, perseverance, and concentration.
You are, therefore, wiser than wise in teaching.

The paths leading to wholesome rebirths, nirvana,
and to every suffering realm
are known by you, manifest to you.
You are, therefore, the good spiritual guide.

བསམ་གཏན་གཟུགས་མེད་སེང་གེ་རྣམ་པར་བསྒྲིངས།།
ཐོད་རྒྱལ་ལ་སོགས་ཏིང་འཛིན་མཐའ་དག་གིས།།
འཇུག་ལྡང་ཀུན་བྱང་རྩལ་ལ་མ་རྫོངས་པས།།
སྙོམས་འཇུག་རྣམས་ཀྱི་ཕ་རོལ་སོན་པ་ལགས།།

ཐོག་མེད་འཁོར་བར་ཡོངས་སུ་འདྲིས་བགྲིས་པའི།།
རང་གཞན་ཚེ་རབས་དན་རྟགས་དང་བཅས་པར།།
སྐད་ཅིག་ཙམ་གྱིས་ཁོང་དུ་ཆུད་པས་ན།།
ཁྱོད་ནི་སྔོན་གྱི་མཐའ་ལ་མཁས་པ་ལགས།།

འདི་ཙམ་དུས་ན་འདི་ནས་ཤི་འཕོ་ཞིང་།།
ལེགས་སྤྱོད་ཉེས་སྤྱོད་ལས་རྣམས་ཇི་ལྟ་བར།།
གང་དུ་སྐྱེ་བའི་གནས་ཀུན་རབ་མཁྱེན་པས།།
ཁྱོད་ནི་ཕྱི་མའི་མཐའ་ལ་མཁས་པ་ལགས།།

གང་ཞིག་ཟག་པ་ཟད་པའི་མྱང་འདས་དང་།།
གང་གིས་ཟད་བྱེད་འཕགས་ལམ་བརྒྱད་ཀྱི་ལམ།།
དེ་དག་ཀུན་ལ་སྒྲིབ་མེད་མངོན་སུམ་སྤྱན།།
དེ་ཕྱིར་ཁྱོད་ནི་སྐྱབས་ཀྱི་དམ་པ་ལགས།།

Knowing the stages of every meditative concentration,
specifically the fearless lion pose
and those of the form and formless realms,
alongside techniques of entering and leaving such equipoise,
you have traveled to the mastery of meditative equilibrium.

You are wise in knowledge of the past,
thoroughly acquainted with beginningless samsara;
your own past lives, those of others,
their causes, details, and signs
are instantaneously manifest to you.

You are wise in knowledge of the future;
that such a being at such a time will leave such a body
and by such deeds, good or bad, be reborn in such a place
is fully known to you.

Knowing that the end of delusion is the end of suffering,
that the ending of delusion is by the eightfold noble path,
is knowledge manifest before your eyes.
You are, therefore, the greatest of great protectors.

དེ་ལྟར་གནས་དང་གནས་མིན་ལས་ཀྱི་
རྣམ་སྨིན་མོས་པ་འཇིག་རྟེན་ཁམས།།
དབང་པོའི་རིམ་པ་ཀུན་འགྲོའི་ལམ་དང་
ཉོན་མོངས་རྣམ་བྱང་སྔོན་གྱི་གནས།།
འཆི་འཕོ་སྐྱེ་དང་ཟག་པ་ཟད་པ་མཁྱེན་པ་
ཐོགས་པ་མེད་འཇུག་པ།།
གང་ལ་མངའ་བ་ཁྱོད་ཀྱི་ཡུལ་དུ་མ་གྱུར་
ཤེས་བྱའི་གནས་དེ་གང་།།

སྲིད་པར་འཁྲུམས་པ་རྣམས་ཀྱི་ཐོག་མེད་ནས།།
བདག་བདེའི་ཕྱིར་དུ་གཞན་ལ་གནོད་པའི་ལམ།།
དྲག་པོའི་རྩོལ་བས་ཀུན་ཏུ་བསྟེན་ན་ཡང་།།
ངལ་བ་འབྲས་བུ་མེད་པས་གོལ་བ་ལྟར།།

Therefore, facts and fiction concerning actions and results,
every deed and their every ripening,
dispositions of every being,
divisions of the realms of phenomena,
differing abilities of living beings,
every path, good or bad,
the ways and stages of eliminating delusion,
knowledge of the past and future,
the constitution of the end of delusion;
these ten your mind penetrates with ease.
Where is there anything unknown by you?

Those wandering on lost in samsara
have since time immemorial pursued
with elephantine effort a path strewn
with the pain and hurt caused to others
all for the sake of their own happiness,
and yet, since the longed-for fruits
of such hardship are nowhere to be seen,
it is an erroneous path.

གཞན་ལ་ཅུང་ཟད་ཙམ་ཡང་མི་འཚེ་བར།།
རང་ཉིད་ཕྱིར་དུ་ཉིན་མཚན་བར་མེད་པར།།
བརྒྱ་ཕྲག་བརྩོན་པས་ཐར་པ་བསྒྲུབ་དེ་ཡང་།།
ཡང་དག་ལམ་ལ་རྒྱབ་ཀྱིས་ཕྱོགས་པར་གཟིགས།།

དེ་ཕྱིར་རྒྱལ་བ་ཀུན་གྱི་ལམ་གཅིག་པུ།།
ལུས་ཅན་མཐའ་དག་རྗེས་སུ་འཛིན་པའི་མ།།
རྒྱལ་སྲས་དཔའ་བོ་གཡུལ་དུ་འཇུག་པའི་སྒོ།།
སྙིང་རྗེའི་ལམ་བཟང་རིང་ནས་གོམས་པར་མཛད།།

སྡུག་བསྔལ་རྨི་ལམ་དུ་ཡང་མི་འདོད་ཅིང་།།
ཕུལ་བྱུང་བདེ་ལ་ཚོག་ཤེས་མེད་པར་ནི།།
འགྲོ་བའི་འདི་ཀུན་ཁྱད་པར་ཡོད་མིན་ན།།
གཞན་བདེ་ཡལ་བར་འདོར་རྣམས་ཆེས་འཁྲུལ་བར།།

Similarly, the path upon which
even the tiniest harm to others is forsworn,
where night and day without respite
for the sake of one's happiness alone
the goal of freedom from samsara is pursued
with dedicated and wholehearted effort,
is seen, nevertheless, by you
as a path leading away from the one true path.

And so, for time beyond time
you have lived the great path of compassion,
the practice that alone journeys to enlightenment,
the true mother that cares for every living being,
the armor worn by the courageous bodhisattva.

Insofar as we all run from suffering
even experienced within a dream,
and yet always fall short of satisfaction
even within the heights of sublime happiness,
living beings cannot be differentiated.
It is therefore great self-delusion
to have no thought for the happiness of others.

བརྩེ་ལྡན་ཁྱོད་ཀྱིས་གཟིགས་ནས་བདག་དང་གཞན༎
མཉམ་པ་ཉིད་དུ་མཐོང་ནས་བྱང་ཆུབ་སེམས༎
ཐོག་མ་ཉིད་དུ་གོམས་པར་མཛད་པ་ཡིས༎
སེམས་ཅན་ཐམས་ཅད་ཁྱོད་ཀྱིས་བདག་གིར་གཟུང་༎

བདག་བདེར་སྲེད་པ་ཡང་དག་ལམ་གྱི་གེགས༎
གཞན་ཉིད་གཅེས་འཛིན་ཡོན་ཏན་ཀུན་གྱི་གཏེར༎
དེ་ཕྱིར་ཁྱོད་ཀྱིས་བདག་གཞན་བརྗེ་བའི་ཚུལ༎
ཡང་ཡང་གོམས་པས་འགྲོ་ཀུན་བདག་ཏུ་མཛད༎

དེ་ལྟར་སྙིང་རྗེའི་མ་ཡིས་ལན་མང་དུ༎
ལུས་སྦྱོབས་རྫོགས་པར་བསྐྱངས་པའི་བཙོམ་ལྡན་ཁྱོད༎
ཕུན་ཚོགས་ཡོན་ཏན་རྣམས་ཀྱི་མཐར་ཕྱིན་ཡང་༎
ཞི་བའི་བདེ་བས་འཁྲོག་པར་ག་ལ་འགྱུར༎

You, therefore, out of immense compassion,
at the outset of your quest for the bodhi mind,
held the view of self and others as undifferentiated
and cherished every living being as your own.

To be attached to one's own happiness
is a barrier to the true and perfect path.
To cherish others is the source
of every admirable quality known.
By practicing again and again, therefore,
the exchange of self for others,
you held all others as self.

Mighty conqueror, your Mahayana body
was nourished again and again to final fulfillment
on your journey to perfection of glorious qualities
by that great mother of compassion.
How could you have ever been lured away
by the tranquillity of nirvana?

འདབ་བཟང་དབང་པོ་ལྷ་ཡི་ལམ་ཞུགས་པ།།
དེར་གནས་མ་ཡིན་འཛིན་པར་མི་ལྷུང་ལྟར།།
སྲིད་ཞིར་མི་གནས་ཁྱོད་ཐུགས་བསྐྱོད་པས་བདག །
འཇམ་དབྱངས་མཁྱེན་བརྩེ་ཡིད་ལ་འབྲལ་མེད་ཤོག །

མཐར་འཛིན་གོ་སྐབས་འཕྲོག་པའི་ལྟ་བ་དང་།།
འགྲོ་ཀུན་བུ་སྡུག་ལྟར་མཐོང་སྙིང་རྗེ་གཉིས།།
ཡིད་ལ་བདེ་བླག་ཉིད་དུ་འགྲུབ་གྱུར་ནས།།
ལུས་ཅན་ཐེག་པ་མཆོག་ལ་འཁྲིད་པར་ཤོག །

ཆོས་ཀུན་ཚིག་དོན་མི་བརྗེད་དྲན་པའི་གཟུངས།།
དྲི་བ་ཀུན་གྱི་ལན་ལྡོན་སྤོབས་པ་མཆོག །
མྱུར་དུ་བསྐྱེད་ནས་ཆོས་ཀྱི་ཕོངས་རྣམས་ལ།།
ལེགས་བཤད་དགའ་སྟོན་འགྱེད་པར་བདག་འགྱུར་ཅིག །

The mighty garuda takes to the skies
but does not dwell there nor will ever fall to earth.
By praising the mind of one who similarly
dwells not in nirvana nor falls to samsara,
may I be never parted from
the wisdom and compassion of Manjushri.

May I without hardship nourish the wisdom,
snuffing out the growth of extreme views,
alongside the compassion that looks upon
every living being as a dearest child,
and may I lead them all to the great Mahayana.

May I develop soon the *dharani* powers of memory
holding all words, all meanings of every teaching,
alongside the supreme wisdom-led confidence
to answer every question put by others,
and may I give to those bereft of Dharma
a veritable feast of the best of teachings.

སྣ་ཚོགས་གདུལ་བྱའི་བསམ་པ་ཇི་བཞིན་དུ།།
མི་རྟོག་བཞིན་དུ་རེ་བ་སྐོང་བ་ཡི།།
འཇམ་དབྱངས་ཐུགས་ཀྱི་དཔལ་གྱིས་མྱུར་དུ་བདག །
སྡོན་ལྷས་ནམ་མཁའ་ཇི་བཞིན་མཛེས་གྱུར་ཅིག །

ཕྱོགས་བཅུའི་ཞིང་ན་མཐའ་ཡས་རྒྱལ་བས་
རྒྱུན་ཆད་མེད་པར་རབ་བསྔགས་པ།།
གང་གི་སྣན་པས་འཇིག་རྟེན་གསུམ་བཀང་
འཇམ་པའི་དབྱངས་ཞེས་རབ་ཏུ་གྲགས།།
གང་དེའི་ཡོན་ཏན་ཅུང་ཟད་གུས་པས་བརྗོད་པའི་
བསྟོད་སྤྲིན་རྒྱ་མཚོ་འདི།།
གང་ཞིག་འཛིན་ཅིང་ཀློག་པ་དེ་ཡི་ཡིད་ལ་
འཇམ་དབྱངས་མྱུར་འཇུག་ཤོག ། །

May the wonder that is the mind of Manjushri
fulfilling the myriad hopes of differing disciples
with equally myriad displays of spontaneity
soon beautify my mind as the full autumn moon
shines and beautifies the crystal-clear night.

In every realm above, below, and at the eight compass points
innumerable buddhas cover him constantly with praise.

Manjushri! His name resounds, the three worlds echo with his fame. Whoever takes to heart and recites this vast cloud-like praise that touches but a fraction of his qualities, yet is delivered with devotion, may the blessings of Manjushri soon enter their minds.

མགོན་པོ་ཚེ་དཔག་མེད་ལ་བསྟོད་པ་ཉི་གཞོན་འཆར་ཀ་བཞུགས་སོ།།

ཉིན་གཞོན་འཆར་ཀའི་མདངས་ལྡན་ལི་ཁྲི་ལྟར།།
ཡིད་འོང་དམར་སེར་དྲ་བས་ཁེབས་པ་ཡི།།
འདབ་སྟོང་གེ་སར་རྩེ་ན་ཟླ་གདན་ལ།།
ཧྲཱི་ལས་བྱུང་བའི་མགོན་པོ་ཚེ་དཔག་མེད།།

པདྨ་རཱ་གའི་ལྷུན་པོ་དབང་པོའི་གཞུས།།
ཀུན་ནས་ཀླུབས་པ་ཇི་བཞིན་ཁྱོད་ཀྱི་སྐུ།།
སྣ་ཚོགས་གོས་དང་ནོར་བུའི་རྒྱན་མང་གིས།།
ཀུན་ནས་མཛེས་པར་བྱས་ལ་ཕྱག་འཚལ་ལོ།།

འཁྲི་ཤིང་གཞོན་ནུའི་ཡལ་འདབ་ལྟར་མཉེན་པའི།།
ཕྱག་གཉིས་དབུས་ན་འཆི་མེད་བདུད་རྩི་ཡིས།།
ལེགས་པར་གང་བའི་ལྷུང་བཟེད་རབ་བསྣམས་ནས།།
ཚེ་ཡི་དངོས་གྲུབ་སྩོལ་ལ་ཕྱག་འཚལ་ལོ།།

Praise to Amitayus

Like *sindhura* powder kissed by the light of the rising sun,
the beautiful orange glow of the corolla carpet spread
upon a thousand-petal lotus capped by a full-moon circle
cradles the syllable *Hrih* from which arises
the guide and protector Amitayus.

I prostrate to you,
a mountain of red lotuses
garlanded by Indra's rainbow,
resplendent in silks, jewels, and ornaments.

In your gentle hands,
soft as the fresh young leaves of the celestial tree,
a bowl brimming with immortality's nectar.
I prostrate to you who grants power over life and death.

བྱང་བ་ལྷུར་ནག་རལ་པའི་ཐོར་ཅོག་ནི།།
སྤྱི་བོར་མཛེས་པའི་ལན་བུ་རིང་དུ་འཕྱང་།།
འཛམ་གཉེན་སྣ་ཚོགས་དར་གྱི་སྨད་གཡོག་ཅན།།
མཚན་དཔེའི་གཟི་བརྗིད་འབར་ལ་ཕྱག་འཚལ་ལོ།།

ཤུགས་དྲག་དད་པས་བསྐྱོད་པའི་ཐལ་སྦྱར་ཞིང་།།
ཡིད་འཕྲོག་ཤིན་ཏུ་སྙན་པའི་ང་རོ་ཡིས།།
ཁྱོད་ཀྱི་ཡོན་ཏན་ལེགས་པར་བརྗོད་པ་ལ།།
ལེགས་ཚོགས་ཐམས་ཅད་སྩོལ་ལ་ཕྱག་འཚལ་ལོ།།

ཡེ་ཤེས་མཚོན་གྱིས་མི་ཤེས་དྲ་བ་བཅད།།
སེམས་ཅན་ཀུན་ལ་སྙིང་རྗེ་རྒྱུན་ཆད་མེད།།
འགྲོ་ཀུན་དྲན་པའི་འཁུར་གྱིས་མི་ངལ་བ།།
གཏན་གྱི་སྐྱབས་གནས་ཁྱོད་ལ་ཕྱག་འཚལ་ལོ།།

མཚན་ཙམ་བཟུང་བས་དུས་མིན་འཆི་བ་འཇོམས།།
ཡིད་ལ་དྲན་པས་སྲིད་པའི་འཇིགས་ལས་སྐྱོབ།།
སྐྱབས་སུ་བསྟེན་ན་གཏན་གྱི་བདེ་སྟེར་བ།།
ཁྱོད་ལ་རྣམ་པ་ཀུན་ཏུ་ཕྱག་འཚལ་ལོ།།

Hair as dark as the black bee,
beautifully tied on your head, long plaits falling to either side,
soft flowing silks gracing your lower body.
I prostrate to you, your body blazing with marks and signs
of a great being possessed of inner qualities.

Moved by great faith I bring my palms together
and with mind captivated and in voice melodious
speak in praise of your qualities.
I prostrate to you, bestower of all happiness and joy.

A sharp blade of wisdom cutting away the entanglement of
ignorance,
a stream of unending compassion for every sentient being,
never tiring from the burden of freeing living beings,
to you, a true refuge, I prostrate.

Just to recall your name is to destroy an untimely death,
to hold you in mind is to be guarded from samsara's fears,
to rely upon you for refuge is joy forever.
In every way possible, I prostrate to you.

སྐྱོན་བྲལ་ཁྱོད་ལ་གུས་པས་བསྟེན་པ་བདག །
གནས་སྐབས་མི་འདོད་ཉེར་འཚེ་ཞི་བ་དང་།།
མཐར་ཐུག་བདེ་བ་ཅན་དུ་པ་སྨྱོ་ལས།།
ཇུས་ཏེ་སྐྱེས་ནས་ཁྱོད་མཉེས་བསྐྱེད་པར་ཤོག །

By my devotion to one as perfected as you,
may I at all times avoid unwished-for hindrance,
finally to be lotus-born in the realm of Sukhavati,
there to please you with the offering of practice.

མགོན་པོ་འོད་དཔག་མེད་ལ་བསྟོད་པ་

ཞིང་མཆོག་སྒོ་འབྱེད་མ་བཞུགས་སོ།།

ན་མ། ཤྲཱི་གུ་རུ་མཉྫུ་གྷོ་ཥཱ་ཡ།

བདེ་གཤེགས་ཀུན་གྱིས་བསྔགས་པའི་བདེ་བ་ཅན།།
རྣམ་དག་ཞིང་གི་དབང་ཕྱུག་བཅོམ་ལྡན་འདས།།
ལྷ་མིའི་སྟོན་པ་མགོན་པོ་ཚེ་དཔག་མེད།།
རྒྱལ་བའི་དབང་པོས་འགྲོ་ལ་འཆི་མེད་སྩོལ།།

སྣ་ཚོགས་སྟོང་གི་དབྱེ་བ་མཐའ་ཡས་པའི།།
དྭངས་བའི་རྒྱ་ལ་སྤྲིན་བྲལ་ཟླ་གཟུགས་བཞིན།།
སྐལ་ལྡན་གྲངས་མེད་འགྲོ་ལ་ཅིག་ཅར་དུ།།
རྣམ་པ་དུ་མར་སྟོན་པ་ཁྱོད་ཀྱི་སྐུ།།

མཐའ་ཡས་གདུལ་བྱའི་སོམ་ཉིའི་དྲྭ་བ་རྣམས།།
སྐད་ཅིག་ཉིད་ལ་སོ་སོར་གཅོད་མཛད་ཅིང་།།
ཡང་དག་དོན་ལ་བློ་གྲོས་མིག་འབྱེད་པའི།།
རྒྱུན་མི་འཆད་པར་སྒྲོག་པ་ཁྱོད་ཀྱི་གསུང་།།

Praise to Amitabha
Gateway to the Highest Buddha Realm

Homage to Guru Manjughosha!

Glorious conqueror, lord of Sukhavati,
pure realm exalted by every buddha,
Protector Amitayus, teacher of men and gods,
grant with the power of the victorious Buddha
the nectar of immortality to every living being.

Like the moon on a cloudless night reflected
in the clear waters of a million different receptacles,
great teacher, you appear simultaneously in differing
manifestations
to untold numbers of fortunate beings.
Such is your form.

In an instant you dispel entangled webs of doubt
from the minds of countless disciples,
and in unceasing discourse and exposition
you open wisdom eyes to the truth.
Such is your speech.

ཤེས་བྱ་ཀུན་ལ་རབ་འབྱམས་མཁྱེན་པ་འཕྲོ།།
རྒྱུད་ལྡའི་འགྲོ་ལ་ཐུགས་རྗེའི་གཞན་དབང་གྱུར།།
མཁྱེན་བརྩེ་ནུས་པས་སྲིད་ཞིའི་འཇིགས་ལས་སྐྱོབ།།
འབད་རྩོལ་མཚན་མས་མི་གཡོ་ཁྲོད་ཀྱི་ཐུགས།།

ཉིན་བྱེད་ཟེར་གྱིས་ལྷ་ཡི་ལམ་ལ་བཞིན།།
དཔག་ཡས་ཞིང་ཀུན་མཐའ་མེད་འོད་དཔུང་གིས།།
ཡོངས་སུ་འགེངས་པའི་གཟི་བརྗིད་ཕུང་པོའི་སྐུས།།
སྐལ་ལྡན་བདག་གི་མིག་གི་དགའ་སྟོན་སྒྲུབས།།

སྙན་པའི་འབྲུག་སྒྲ་རྨ་བྱའི་སྙིང་ལ་བཞིན།།
ཐོས་པ་ཙམ་གྱི་བདེ་བའི་མཆོག་སྟེར་བའི།།
ཡན་ལག་ལྡ་དང་ལྡན་པའི་ཚངས་དབྱངས་ཀྱིས།།
རྣ་བའི་ལམ་དུ་བདུད་རྩིའི་ཟེགས་མ་འཐོར།།

ནམ་མཁའི་དབྱིངས་སུ་སྤྲིན་ཕུང་ཞི་བ་བཞིན།།
སྟོང་པའི་ངང་དུ་རིག་པ་ཞུགས་གྱུར་པས།།
སྤྲོས་ཀུན་ཉེར་ཞི་ཞི་བའི་ཐུགས་མཆོག་གིས།།
ཀུན་རྟོག་ཡིད་ཀྱི་དམིགས་གཏད་ཐམས་ཅད་ཞི།།

Perfect wisdom reaching out to every phenomenon,
swayed by compassion for beings of the five realms,
protecting them with love, wisdom, and power
from fears of samsara and nirvana
and yet unstirred by any sign of effort.
Such is your mind.

Like the sun streaming across the open sky,
millions upon millions of realms are filled
with the limitless light of your dazzling form,
a joyous treat for my fortunate eyes.

As dragon-like thunder is music to the peacock's ears,
so to hear your voice is to engender great bliss,
as its Brahma-like melody adorned by five qualities
falls upon my ears like nectar.

Like clouds disappearing into the sky,
cognition absorbs into emptiness' sphere
and your highest of minds stilled of all fabrication
stills all concept-driven projections of my mind.

རྒྱལ་བ་ཀུན་གྱིས་དཔག་མེད་བསྐལ་པ་རུ།།
བརྗོད་ཀྱང་ཕ་མཐའ་རྙེད་པར་མི་སླ་བའི།།
ཁྱོད་ཀྱི་ཡོན་ཏན་ཕུང་པོ་ཅི་འདྲ་བ།།
དེ་འདྲ་བདག་གིས་བརྗོད་པའི་ཡུལ་ལས་འདས།།

དེ་ཕྱིར་མི་ཟད་ཡོན་ཏན་གཏེར་གྱུར་ཅིང་།།
ཉེས་པའི་ས་བོན་མཐའ་དག་གཏན་སྤངས་པ།།
ཁྱོད་དང་མཚུངས་པའི་སྟོན་པ་གཞན་ཡོད་མིན།།
དེ་སླད་ཁྱོད་ཉིད་གཅིག་པུ་འགྲོ་བའི་སྐྱབས།།

སྐྱོབ་པ་ཁྱོད་ཀྱིས་སྨོན་ལམ་བྱེ་བ་བརྒྱུས།། ལེགས་པར་བསྒྲུབ་པའི་ཞིང་
མཆོག་དམ་པ་གང་།། སྡུག་བསྔལ་རྣམས་ཀྱི་མིང་ཡང་མི་འབྱུང་བས།།
བདེ་བ་ཅན་ཞེས་ཡོངས་སུ་གྲགས་པ་དེར།། ཚེ་འདིའི་སྣང་བ་ནུབ་པར་
གྱུར་ཙམ་ན།། འདབ་སྟོང་པད་མའི་སྦུབས་སུ་སྐྱེས་མ་ཐག །
ཆུ་སྐྱེས་དབུས་ནས་ཐོགས་པ་མེད་བྱུང་སྟེ།། ཁྱོད་སྐུ་མཐོང་ནས་གསུང་
གིས་ཚིམ་པར་ཤོག །
མགོན་པོ་ཁྱོད་ལས་ཐེག་མཆོག་གཏམ་ཐོས་ནས།། སྲིད་པའི་འདམ་དུ་
བྱིང་རྣམས་བསྒྲལ་ཕྱིར་དུ།། སྤྱན་རས་གཟིགས་དང་མཐུ་ཆེན་ཐོབ་
གཉིས་ཀྱིས།། ཇི་ལྟར་སྤྱོད་པ་དེ་ལྟར་བདག་གྱུར་ཅིག །

Your qualities, their limits hard to find,
even if buddhas spoke of them for eons beyond measure,
are well beyond my powers of description.

You remain, therefore, an unending treasure of qualities,
every root of every fault forever destroyed,
no other teacher compares with you,
sole refuge for all living things.

I pray my protector, when this life fades,
to be reborn in that highest of realms,
formed from your billion prayers,
famed and renowned as Sukhavati, realm of bliss,
where even names of sufferings remain unheard,
there to take birth within the celestial lotus flower,
arising unhindered among its thousand petals,
to behold your form, to be sated by your words,
and having heard from you, protector, the sounds of the
  Mahayana,
may I do as Avalokiteshvara and Vajrapani have done,
and free those sunk in swamps of existence.

བདེ་བ་ཅན་དུ་སྐྱེ་བའི་སྨོན་ལམ་བཞུགས་སོ།།

ཕུལ་བྱུང་མཛད་པས་འགྲོ་ལ་མི་ཟད་དཔལ་སྟེར་ཞིང་།།
ལན་གཅིག་དྲན་པས་འཆི་བདག་འཇིགས་པ་རིང་དུ་དོར།།
རྟག་ཏུ་བརྩེ་བས་འགྲོ་ལ་བུ་བཞིན་དགོངས་གྱུར་པ།།
ལྷ་མིའི་སྟོན་པ་ཚེ་དཔག་མེད་ལ་ཕྱག་འཚལ་ལོ།།

ཐུབ་པའི་དབང་པོས་ལན་གྲངས་དུ་མ་རུ།།
ལེགས་པར་ཡོངས་སུ་བསྔགས་པའི་ཞིང་གི་མཆོག །
བདེ་བ་ཅན་དུ་སྐྱེ་བའི་སྨོན་ལམ་འགའ།།
བརྩེ་བའི་དབང་གིས་ཇི་ལྟར་ནུས་བཞིན་བརྗོད།།

བླང་དོར་གནས་རྣམས་མ་རིག་འཐུག་པོས་བསྒྲིབས།།
ཁོང་ཁྲོའི་མཚོན་གྱིས་མཐོ་རིས་སྲོག་འཕྲོག་ཅིང་།།
འདོད་སྲེད་ཞགས་པས་འཁོར་བའི་བཙོན་རར་བཅིངས།།
ལས་ཀྱི་ཆུ་བོས་སྲིད་པའི་རྒྱ་མཚོར་ཁྱེར།།
ན་རྒའི་སྡུག་བསྔལ་ཐ་ཆླབས་མང་པོས་གཡེངས།།
མི་བཟད་འཆི་བདག་ཆུ་སྲིན་ཁར་ཆུད་པས།།

Prayer for Birth in Sukhavati, Realm of Bliss

With deeds exalted, you grant splendor unending;
once remembered, you hurl far all fear of the lord of death;
with constant love, you look on others as sons and daughters.
Amitayus, teacher of gods and men, I bow before you.

I will write, swayed by compassion, as best I can
a prayer for birth in Sukhavati, land of bliss,
praised again and again by the mighty Buddha
as the highest of realms.

All knowledge of right and wrong covered
  by layers of ignorance,
all future life in higher realms murdered
  by the weapons of anger,
lying trussed by the ropes of desire in the prison of samsara,
I am carried helplessly to the oceans of existence
  by rivers of karma,
tossed by endless waves of aging, sickness, and other suffering,

མི་འདོད་སྡུག་བསྔལ་ཁུར་གྱིས་ནོན་གྱུར་པ།།
མགོན་མེད་བདག་གི་ཉམ་ཐག་ང་རོ་ཡིས།།

ཡིད་ལ་སྨོན་པ་འགྲུབ་པའི་དཔང་པོ་རུ།།
ཕོངས་པའི་གཉེན་གཅིག་འདྲེན་པ་འོད་དཔག་མེད།།
སྤྱན་རས་གཟིགས་དབང་རྒྱལ་སྲས་མཐུ་ཆེན་ཐོབ།།
འཁོར་དང་བཅས་ལ་གུས་པས་གསོལ་འདེབས་ན།།
དཔག་མེད་བསྐལ་པར་བདག་ཅག་རྣམས་ཀྱི་ཕྱིར།།
ཐུགས་མཆོག་བསྐྱེད་པའི་དམ་བཅའ་མ་བསྙེལ་བར།།
འདབ་བཟང་གཙོ་བོ་ལྷ་ཡི་ལམ་ལ་བཞིན།།
རྫུ་འཕྲུལ་སྟོབས་ཀྱིས་བརྩེ་བས་འདིར་གཤེགས་ཤིག །

thrown to the jaws of that savage monster the lord of death,
to languish under the weight of unwanted suffering.

Without protector and with anguished cries I ask with devotion,
as witnesses to the yearnings of my mind,
Amitabha, guide and sole friend to the deprived,
powerful Avalokiteshvara Bodhisattva, Vajrapani and
  entourage,
to not forget the vows of the supreme bodhi mind
made over countless eons for our sakes
and like the mighty garuda hawk swooping through the skies,
to come, with the power of miracles, in great compassion
  before me.

⁂

བདག་དང་གཞན་གྱི་དུས་གསུམ་དང་འབྲེལ་བའི་ཚོགས་གཉིས་ཀྱི་རྒྱ་མཚོ་རྣམས་ཕྱོགས་གཅིག་ཏུ་བསྡོམས་པའི་མཐུ་ལ་བརྟེན་ནས། བདག་འཆི་བའི་དུས་ཉེ་བར་གནས་པ་ན་འདྲེན་པ་འོད་དཔག་ཏུ་མེད་པ་སྲས་ཀྱི་ཐུ་བོ་གཉིས་ལ་སོགས་པའི་འཁོར་གྱིས་བསྐོར་བ་མངོན་སུམ་དུ་མཐོང་ཞིང་། དེའི་ཚེ་རྒྱལ་བ་འཁོར་དང་བཅས་པ་ལ་དམིགས་པའི་རབ་ཏུ་དད་པ་དྲག་པོ་སྐྱེས་ཏེ།། གནད་གཅོད་ཀྱི་སྡུག་བསྔལ་མེད་པ་དང་། དད་པ་ཡུལ་དང་བཅས་པ་མི་བརྗེད་པའི་དྲན་པས། ཤི་འཕོས་མ་ཐག་ཏུ་རྒྱལ་བའི་སྲས་པོ་བརྒྱད་རྫུ་འཕྲུལ་གྱིས་ལྷགས་ཏེ་བདེ་བ་ཅན་དུ་འགྲོ་བའི་ལམ་ཇི་ལྟ་བ་བཞིན་དུ་བསྟན་པ་ལ་བརྟེན་ནས་བདེ་བ་ཅན་གྱི་ཞིང་དུ་རིན་པོ་ཆེའི་པད་མ་ལས་ཐེག་པ་ཆེན་པོའི་རིགས་ཅན་དབང་པོ་རྣོན་པོ་ཤ་སྟག་ཏུ་སྐྱེ་བར་གྱུར་ཅིག །སྐྱེས་མ་ཐག་ཏུ་གཟུངས་དང་། ཏིང་ངེ་འཛིན་དང་། དམིགས་པ་མེད་པའི་བྱང་ཆུབ་ཀྱི་སེམས་དང་། ཟད་མི་ཤེས་པའི་སྤོབས་པ་ལ་སོགས་པ་ཡོན་ཏན་གྱི་ཚོགས་དཔག་ཏུ་མེད་པ་ཐོབ་པ་དང་། སྟོན་པ་བླ་ན་མེད་པ་འོད་དཔག་ཏུ་མེད་པ་ལ་སོགས་པས་ཕྱོགས་བཅུའི་རྒྱལ་བས་སྲས་དང་བཅས་པ་ཐམས་ཅད་མཉེས་པར་བྱས་ནས་ཐེག་པ་ཆེན་པོའི་བཀའ་ལུང་ཡང་དག་པར་ཉོད་པར་གྱུར་ཅིག དེ་རྣམས་ཀྱི་དོན་ཇི་ལྟ་བ་བཞིན་དུ་ཁོང་དུ་ཆུད་ནས་སྐད་ཅིག་རེ་རེ་ལ་འང་སངས་རྒྱས་ཀྱི་ཞིང་རབ་འབྱམས་སུ་རྫུ་འཕྲུལ་གྱིས་ཐོགས་མེད་དུ་བགྲོད་ནས་བྱང་ཆུབ་སེམས་དཔའི་སྤྱོད་པ་རླབས་པོ་ཆེ་ཐམས་ཅད་ཡོངས་སུ་རྫོགས་པར་བྱེད་པར་གྱུར་ཅིག །དག་པའི་ཞིང་དུ་སྐྱེས་ནས་ཀྱང་བརྩེ་བ་ཤུགས་དྲག་པོས་ཀུན་ནས་བསླང་སྟེ་ཐོགས་པ་མེད་པའི་རྫུ་འཕྲུལ་གྱིས་གཙོ་བོར་མ་དག་པའི་ཞིང་དུ་ཕྱིན་ནས་སེམས་ཅན་ཐམས་ཅད་ཀྱི་རང་རང་གི་སྐལ་བ་ཇི་ལྟ་བ་བཞིན་དུ་ཆོས་བསྟན་པ་ལ་བརྟེན་ནས་རྒྱལ་བས་བསྔགས་པའི་ལམ་རྣམ་པར་དག་པ་ལ་འགོད་ནུས་པར་གྱུར་ཅིག །སྤྱོད་པ་རྨད་དུ་བྱུང་བ་དེ་དག་མྱུར་དུ་རྫོགས་པར་བྱས་པའི་བློ་ནས་མཐའ་ཡས་པའི་འགྲོ་བའི་དོན་དུ་རྒྱལ་བའི་གོ་འཕང་བདེ་བླག་ཏུ་ཐོབ་པར་གྱུར་ཅིག །ནམ་ཞིག་ཚེ་ཡི་འདུ་བྱེད་གཏོང་བ་ན།།

By the power of the immense twin accumulation of spiritual merit stored by others and myself in past, present, and future, I pray that when death draws near I see before me my guide Amitabha, his two main disciples, his entourage, and others. At that time may I have strong faith in this great conqueror and his entourage and be free from the pains of dying. By recalling and holding in my mind objects of faith, I pray that as soon as my consciousness has left this body, the eight bodhisattvas arrive by miraculous power to show the way to Sukhavati, there to be born within a jeweled lotus, of intelligent mind and of Mahayana family.

Once born in Sukhavati may I gain immediately the powerful dharani memory, meditative concentration, the objectless bodhi mind, inexhaustible confidence, and countless other qualities. By pleasing the highest of teachers, Amitabha and all buddhas and bodhisattvas of the ten directions, may I take with propriety the Mahayana teachings.

When I have absorbed and understood the true meanings of these teachings, may I be able to travel in an instant and without hindrance to limitless Buddha realms by miraculous power, there to perfect every powerful practice of the bodhisattva.

Though born in pure Sukhavati, I pray that I be able to journey, with unhindering miraculous power motivated by fierce compassion, to impure realms, there to teach every living being the Dharma according to disposition and so bring them to that immaculate path hailed by the Buddha.

By quickly perfecting these exalted practices may I, for the benefit of countless living beings, easily attain the enlightened state of a buddha.

འཁོར་ཚོགས་རྒྱ་མཚོས་བསྐོར་བའི་འོད་དཔག་མེད།།
མིག་གི་ལམ་དུ་གསལ་བར་མཐོང་གྱུར་ནས།།
དད་དང་སྙིང་རྗེས་བདག་རྒྱུད་གང་བར་ཤོག །
བར་དོའི་སྣང་བ་ཤར་བ་གྱུར་མ་ཐག །
རྒྱལ་སྲས་བརྒྱད་ཀྱིས་མ་ནོར་ལམ་བསྟན་ཏེ།།
བདེ་བ་ཅན་དུ་སྐྱེས་ནས་སྤྲུལ་པ་ཡིས།།
མ་དག་ཞིང་གི་འགྲོ་བ་འདྲེན་གྱུར་ཅིག །

དེ་ལྟ་བུའི་གོ་འཕང་མཆོག་མ་ཐོབ་པའི་སྐྱེ་བ་ཐམས་ཅད་དུའང་རྒྱལ་བའི་བསྟན་པ་ལུང་དང་རྟོགས་པ་ལ་ཐོས་པ་དང་བསམ་པ་དང་སྒོམ་པ་རྣམ་པར་དག་པ་སྒྲུབ་པའི་རྟེན་ཤ་སྟག་ཐོབ་པར་གྱུར་ཅིག །རྟེན་དེ་ཡང་མཐོ་རིས་ཀྱི་ཡོན་ཏན་བདུན་གྱི་རྒྱུན་དང་མི་འབྲལ་བར་གྱུར་ཅིག །དེ་ལྟ་བུའི་གནས་སྐབས་ཐམས་ཅད་དུའང་སྔོན་གྱི་གནས་ཇི་ལྟ་བ་བཞིན་དུ་དྲན་པའི་ཚེ་རབས་དྲན་པ་ཐོབ་པར་གྱུར་ཅིག །སྐྱེ་བ་ཐམས་ཅད་དུ་སྲིད་པ་མཐའ་དག་ལ་སྙིང་པོ་མེད་པར་མཐོང་ཞིང་ཐར་པའི་ཡོན་ཏན་གྱིས་ཡིད་འཕྲོག་པའི་བསམ་པས་ཀུན་ནས་བསླང་སྟེ། བཅོམ་ལྡན་འདས་ཀྱིས་ལེགས་པར་གསུངས་པའི་ཆོས་འདུལ་བ་ལ་རབ་ཏུ་བྱུང་བ་བྱེད་པར་གྱུར་ཅིག །རབ་ཏུ་བྱུང་བའི་ཚེ་ན་ཡང་ཉེས་ལྟུང་ཕྲ་མོས་ཀྱང་མ་གོས་པར་ཚུལ་ཁྲིམས་ཀྱི་ཕུང་པོ་མཐར་ཕྱིན་པར་མཛད་པའི་སྒོ་ནས་བྱང་ཆུབ་ཆེན་པོ་བརྙེས་པ་དགེ་སློང་མི་འཁྲུགས་པ་ལྟ་བུར་གྱུར་ཅིག །

When the amalgamations of this life are spent,
may I plainly behold in my path of vision
Amitabha encircled by vast entourage,
and may my mind be filled with faith and compassion.
Once the bardo visions have appeared,
may I be shown the path by the eight bodhisattvas
and, born in Sukhavati, may I by manifestation
become a spiritual guide for impure realms.

❋

Should I not attain such exalted states, may I in every life incarnate solely in a form capable of engaging in authentic study, contemplation, and meditation upon scripture and practice of the Buddhadharma.

May that form be endowed always with the seven desirable features of higher realms.

In every such existence may I gain the memory that recalls perfectly all my past lives.

In every life may I see all existence as being without essence, be driven by a mind captivated by the virtues of nirvana, and be ordained into the monastic discipline so excellently taught by the Buddha.

Once ordained may I live as the monk Akshobhya who, unsullied by the slightest fault, perfected morality and gained great enlightenment.

གཞན་ཡང་སྐྱེ་བ་ཐམས་ཅད་དུ་ཀུན་ནས་ཉོན་མོངས་པ་དང་རྣམ་པར་བྱང་བའི་ཚུལ་ཇི་ལྟ་བ་བཞིན་དུ་ཁོང་དུ་ཆུད་ནས་མཐར་ཕྱིན་པའི་ཡན་ལག་ཆོས་རྣམས་ཀྱི་ཚིག་དང་དོན་མ་ལུས་པ་མི་བརྗེད་པར་འཛིན་པའི་གཟུངས་ཕུན་སུམ་ཚོགས་པ་ཐོབ་པར་གྱུར་ཅིག །རང་ཉིད་ཀྱིས་བཟུང་བ་བཞིན་དུ་གཞན་ལ་སྟོན་པ་ལ་ཐོགས་པ་མེད་པའི་སྤོབས་པ་རྣམ་པར་དག་པ་ཐོབ་པར་གྱུར་ཅིག །གཞན་ཡང་སྐྱེ་བ་ཐམས་ཅད་དུ་དཔའ་བར་འགྲོ་བ་ལ་སོགས་པའི་ཏིང་ངེ་འཛིན་གྱི་སྒོ་རྣམས་དང་། ཤའི་མིག་ལ་སོགས་པའི་སྤྱན་རྣམས་དང་། རྫུ་འཕྲུལ་གྱི་ཡུལ་ཤེས་པ་ལ་སོགས་པའི་མངོན་པར་ཤེས་པ་རྣམས་ཐོབ་པ་དང་མི་འབྲལ་བར་གྱུར་ཅིག །གཞན་ཡང་སྐྱེ་བ་ཐམས་ཅད་དུ་བླང་དོར་གྱི་གནས་རྣམས་རང་སྟོབས་ཀྱིས་འབྱེད་ནུས་པའི་ཤེས་རབ་རླབས་ཆེ་བ་ཐོབ་པར་གྱུར་ཅིག །ཀུན་ནས་ཉོན་མོངས་པ་དང་རྣམ་པར་བྱང་བའི་ཆ་ཤས་ཕྲ་ཞིང་ཕྲ་བ་རྣམས་ཇི་ལྟ་བ་བཞིན་དུ་མ་འདྲེས་པར་འབྱེད་ནུས་པའི་ཤེས་རབ་གསལ་བ་ཐོབ་པར་གྱུར་ཅིག །མ་རྟོགས་པ་དང་ལོག་པར་རྟོག་པ་དང་ཐེ་ཚོམ་གྱི་བསམ་པ་སྐྱེས་མ་ཐག་ཏུ་མ་ལུས་པར་འགོག་ནུས་པའི་ཤེས་རབ་མྱུར་བ་ཐོབ་པར་གྱུར་ཅིག །གཞན་གྱིས་ཚད་གཟུང་མི་ནུས་པར་གསུང་རབ་ཀྱི་ཚིག་དོན་ལ་གཏུགས་པ་མེད་པར་འཇུག་པའི་ཤེས་རབ་ཟབ་པ་ཐོབ་པར་གྱུར་ཅིག །མདོར་ན་འཆལ་བའི་ཤེས་རབ་ཀྱི་སྐྱོན་ཐམས་ཅད་དང་བྲལ་བའི་ཤེས་རབ་ཀྱིས་གསུང་རབ་ཀྱི་ཚིག་དོན་འབྱེད་པ་ལ་ཐབས་མཁས་པའི་ཤེས་རབ་ཀྱི་སྒོ་ནས་བྱང་ཆུབ་སེམས་དཔའི་སྤྱོད་པ་ཐམས་ཅད་ཀྱི་མཐར་སོན་པ་རྗེ་བཙུན་འཇམ་པའི་དབྱངས་ལྟ་བུར་གྱུར་ཅིག །དེ་ལྟར་ཤེས་རབ་ཆེ་བ་གསལ་བ་མྱུར་བ་ཟབ་པ་བདེ་བླག་ཏུ་རྙེད་ནས་སྐལ་ལྡན་རྗེས་སུ་འཛིན་པ་དང་ལོག་སྨྲ་ཚར་གཅོད་པ་དང་། མཁས་པ་མགུ་བ་སྐྱེད་པའི་ཡན་ལག་རྒྱལ་བའི་གསུང་རབ་མཐའ་དག་ལ་དམིགས་པའི་འཆད་པ་དང་རྩོད་པ་དང་རྩོམ་པ་ལ་མཁས་པའི་ཕ་རོལ་ཏུ་ཕྱིན་པ་ཐོབ་པར་གྱུར་ཅིག

Furthermore, in every life having fully comprehended the ways of deluded states of mind and the paths of purification and freedom, may I develop the powerful and accomplished dharani memory to maintain total recall over every word and meaning of every branch and division of the teachings. And in the same way that I retain these dharmas, may I gain a pure and unhindered confidence to teach them likewise to others.

Furthermore, in every life may I master and never be apart from the ways of meditative concentrations such as the warrior-like *shurangama samadhi*. May I acquire supernatural sight such as that unhindered by matter, as well as clairvoyance such as that which knows the ways of miraculous powers.

Furthermore, in every life may I develop that great wisdom that, self-reliantly and unaided, is able to separate right from wrong.

May I develop the clear wisdom that unerringly separates to the subtlest degree deluded states of mind from paths of purification and freedom.

May I develop the swift wisdom that holds the power to counter, as soon as they appear, all doubts, fallacious views, and incomprehension.

May I develop the deep wisdom that penetrates unopposed the meanings of scripture unfathomable to others.

In short, with wisdom stripped of all deluded insight may I rise to the wisdom skillful in unlocking the meanings of scripture in order to travel, as the noble Manjushri has done, to the perfection of every bodhisattva practice.

Having gained without difficulty great, clear, swift, and deep wisdom may I, in order to gather the fortunate, crush false orators, and to please the wise, perfect the arts of teaching, debating, and composition that focus upon the entire teachings of the Buddha.

གཞན་ཡང་སྐྱེ་བ་ཐམས་ཅད་དུ་རང་གི་དོན་གཙོ་བོར་འཛིན་པའི་ཡིད་ལ་བྱེད་པ་དང་། བྱང་ཆུབ་སེམས་དཔའི་སྤྱོད་པ་རླབས་པོ་ཆེ་ལ་སྒྱིད་ལུག་ཅིང་ཞུམ་པའི་བསམ་པ་ཐམས་ཅད་བཀག་ནས་གཞན་གྱི་དོན་ལྷུར་ལེན་ཅིང་སྙིང་སྟོབས་མཆོག་གི་ཕ་རོལ་ཏུ་སོན་པ་ལ་ཐབས་མཁས་པའི་བྱང་ཆུབ་ཀྱི་སེམས་ཀྱི་སྒོ་ནས་བྱང་ཆུབ་སེམས་དཔའི་སྤྱོད་པ་ཐམས་ཅད་ཀྱི་ཐར་སོན་པ་རྗེ་བཙུན་སྤྱན་རས་གཟིགས་དབང་ཕྱུག་ལྟ་བུར་གྱུར་ཅིག །གཞན་ཡང་སྐྱེ་བ་ཐམས་ཅད་དུ་རང་དང་གཞན་གྱི་དོན་ལ་འཇུག་པ་ན་བདུད་དང་མུ་སྟེགས་དང་ཕས་ཀྱི་རྒོལ་བ་ཐམས་ཅད་འཇོམས་པར་བྱེད་པ་ལ་ཐབས་མཁས་པའི་ནུས་པའི་སྒོ་ནས་བྱང་ཆུབ་སེམས་དཔའི་སྤྱོད་པ་ཐམས་ཅད་ཀྱི་མཐར་སོན་པ་རྗེ་བཙུན་གསང་བའི་བདག་པོ་ལྟ་བུར་གྱུར་ཅིག །སྐྱེ་བ་ཐམས་ཅད་དུ་ལེ་ལོ་སྤངས་པའི་བརྩོན་འགྲུས་ཀྱི་བྱང་ཆུབ་ཀྱི་སྤྱོད་པ་ཡོངས་སུ་རྫོགས་པར་བྱེད་པ་ལ་དང་པོ་ཐུགས་བསྐྱེད་པ་ནས་སྐད་ཅིག་ཀྱང་གཡེལ་བ་མེད་པར་རླབས་པོ་ཆེའི་བརྩོན་འགྲུས་ཀྱི་སྒོ་ནས་བྱང་ཆུབ་ཆེན་པོ་བརྙེས་པ་མཉམ་མེད་ཤཱཀྱའི་རྒྱལ་པོ་ལྟ་བུར་གྱུར་ཅིག །སྐྱེ་བ་ཐམས་ཅད་དུ་བྱང་ཆུབ་སྒྲུབ་པའི་བར་ཆད་ལུས་དང་སེམས་ཀྱི་ནད་ཐམས་ཅད་འཇོམས་པར་བྱེད་པ་ལ་མཚན་ནས་སྨོས་པ་ཙམ་གྱིས་ལུས་ངག་དང་ཡིད་གསུམ་གྱི་ཟུག་རྔུ་ཐམས་ཅད་ཞི་བར་བྱེད་ནུས་པ་བདེ་བར་གཤེགས་པ་སྨན་པའི་རྒྱལ་པོ་ལྟ་བུར་གྱུར་ཅིག། །

གཞན་ཡང་སྐྱེ་བ་ཐམས་ཅད་དུ་ཇི་ལྟར་འདོད་པ་བཞིན་ཚེ་མཐར་ཕྱིན་པ་ལ་མཚན་ནས་སྨོས་པ་ཙམ་གྱིས་དུས་མ་ཡིན་པའི་འཆི་བ་ཐམས་ཅད་འཇོམས་པར་བྱེད་ནུས་པ་རྒྱལ་བ་ཚེ་དཔག་ཏུ་མེད་པ་ལྟ་བུར་གྱུར་ཅིག །ཚེའི་བར་ཆད་འབྱུང་དུ་ཉེ་བ་ན་སྐྱོབ་པ་ཚེ་དཔག་ཏུ་མེད་པས་འཕྲིན་ལས་བཞི་གང་གིས་འདུལ་བ་དང་རྗེས་སུ་མཐུན་པའི་སྐུའི་སྣང་བ་རབ་ཏུ་བསྟན་པ་མཐོང་ཞིང་། མཐོང་མ་ཐག་ཏུ་ཚེའི་བར་དུ་གཅོད་པ་མ་ལུས་པ་ཉེ་བར་ཞི་བར་གྱུར་ཅིག །

Furthermore, in every life, having put an end to a way of thinking primarily concerned with self, to all laziness and weakness regarding the powerful practices of the bodhisattva, may I possess a bodhi mind wise in the accomplishment of supreme courage and the willingness to dedicate myself to others, and may I travel, as the noble Avalokiteshvara has done, to the consummation of every bodhisattva practice.

Furthermore, in every life, whenever I apply myself to the welfare of self and others, may I possess a skillful ability to demolish the hordes of Mara, defeat those of extreme views, thwart all enemies, and may I travel, as the noble Vajrapani has done, to the consummation of every bodhisattva practice.

To perfect the bodhisattva practice that dispels all laziness, may I in every life first create the bodhi mind, and by powerful endeavor undistracted for even an instant, may I reach great enlightenment as the unparalleled Shakyamuni has done.

To eradicate obstacles to practices of enlightenment such as illness to body or mind, may I in every life pacify, as the King of Physicians, the Medicine Buddha, has done, all pain of body, speech, and mind, merely by mentioning his name.

Furthermore, in every life may I have the power to live out my span of life as I would wish and, merely by mentioning his name, may I destroy all untimely death as the conqueror Amitayus has done.

Whenever life-threatening obstacles approach, may I behold in all clarity Amitayus in appropriate manifestation, who curbs the threat by way of the four kinds of Buddha activity, and with such a vision, may every hindrance to life be at once removed.

གང་གིས་འདུལ་བ་དང་འཚམ་པར་སྐུའི་སྣང་བ་བསྟན་པ་དེ་ཡང་མགོན་པོ་ཆེ་དཔག་ཏུ་མེད་པ་ཡིན་པར་ངོ་ཤེས་ནས་བཅོས་མ་མ་ཡིན་པའི་དད་པ་བརྟན་པོ་སྐྱེས་ཤིང་། དེའི་མཐུ་ལ་བརྟེན་ནས་སྐྱེ་བ་ཐམས་ཅད་དུ་རྒྱལ་བ་ཆེ་དཔག་མེད་ཀྱིས་དགེ་བའི་བཤེས་གཉེན་དངོས་སུ་མཛད་པ་དང་མི་འབྲལ་བར་གྱུར་ཅིག །གཞན་ཡང་སྐྱེ་བ་ཐམས་ཅད་དུ་འཇིག་རྟེན་དང་འཇིག་རྟེན་ལས་འདས་པའི་ཡོན་ཏན་ཐམས་ཅད་ཀྱི་རྩ་བ་ཐེག་པ་ཆེན་པོའི་དགེ་བའི་བཤེས་གཉེན་མཚན་ཉིད་དང་ལྡན་པས་མཉེས་བཞིན་དུ་རྗེས་སུ་འཛིན་པར་གྱུར་ཅིག །རྗེས་སུ་བཟུང་བའི་ཆེ་ན་ཡང་དགེ་བའི་བཤེས་གཉེན་ལ་མི་ཕྱེད་པའི་དད་པ་བརྟན་པོ་ཐོབ་སྟེ་སྒོ་ཐམས་ཅད་ནས་མཉེས་པ་ཁོ་ན་བྱེད་པར་གྱུར་ཅིག །མི་མཉེས་པ་སྐད་ཅིག་ཙམ་ཡང་མི་སྐྱེབ་པར་གྱུར་ཅིག །དགེ་བའི་བཤེས་གཉེན་གྱིས་གདམས་པ་དང་། རྗེས་སུ་བསྟན་པ་ཐམས་ཅད་མ་ཚང་བ་མེད་པ་འདོམས་པར་གྱུར་ཅིག །དེ་རྣམས་ཀྱི་དོན་ཐམས་ཅད་ཇི་ལྟ་བ་བཞིན་དུ་ཁོང་དུ་ཆུད་ནས་སྒྲུབ་པས་མཐར་ཕྱིན་པར་བྱེད་ནུས་པར་གྱུར་ཅིག །མི་དགེ་བའི་བཤེས་གཉེན་དང་སྡིག་པའི་གྲོགས་པོའི་དབང་དུ་སྐད་ཅིག་ཙམ་ཡང་མི་འགྲོ་བར་གྱུར་ཅིག །སྐྱེ་བ་ཐམས་ཅད་དུ་ལས་འབྲས་ལ་ཡིད་ཆེས་པའི་དད་པ་དང་། ངེས་འབྱུང་དང་། བྱང་ཆུབ་ཀྱི་སེམས་དང་། ལྟ་བ་རྣམ་པར་དག་པ་མཐའ་དག་པ་ཁོང་དུ་ཆུད་ནས་རྩོལ་བ་མེད་པའི་སྤྱོད་པ་རྒྱུན་མི་ཆད་དུ་འཇུག་པར་གྱུར་ཅིག །སྐྱེ་བ་ཐམས་ཅད་དུ་ལུས་དང་ངག་དང་ཡིད་ཀྱི་སྒོ་ནས་དགེ་བའི་རྩ་བ་ཇི་སྙེད་ཅིག་བྱས་པ་ཐམས་ཅད་གཞན་དོན་དང་བྱང་ཆུབ་རྣམ་པར་དག་པ་ཁོ་ནའི་རྒྱུར་གྱུར་ཅིག །

Recognizing such an appropriate manifestation to be none other than Amitayus, may I develop firm, uncontrived faith by whose power I will forever be in the presence of Amitayus as my spiritual teacher.

Furthermore, in life after life may I, pleasing him in return, be forever fostered by an accomplished Mahayana spiritual master, the source of every virtue of this world and beyond.

In his care, may I acquire in him a firm unshakable faith, pleasing him by every means possible, doing nothing, even for an instant, to disappoint him.

May my spiritual master impart to me every instruction and every teaching in its entirety. Having understood them faultlessly, may I practice them and be able to bring them to perfection.

May I never, even for a moment, fall under the sway of malevolent teachers and misleading friends.

Having developed, in every life, belief in cause and effect, renunciation, the bodhi mind, and the pure view, may I embark upon them continually with effortless experience.

In every life may every virtuous act gathered by way of body, speech, and mind be causes solely for the welfare of others and for the purest and highest enlightenment.

མཚན་མ་སློས་པའི་ས་སྐྱའི་བླ་མ་ཞིག་ལ་བསྟོད་པ།།

ཨོཾ་བདེ་ལེགས་སུ་གྱུར་ཅིག །

རིག་གནས་རྒྱ་མཚོའི་ཕ་རོལ་སོན་གྱུར་པས།།
གསུང་རབ་ནོར་བུའི་གླིང་ལ་མངའ་སྒྱུར་ཞིང་།།
སྙན་གྲགས་ཀུན་གྱི་རྣ་བའི་རྒྱན་གྱུར་པས།།
ངོ་མཚར་བསྔགས་པའི་གནས་གྱུར་ས་སྐྱ་པ།།

མཁྱེན་པས་ཤེས་བྱ་ཀུན་གྱི་དེ་ཉིད་གཟིགས།།
བརྩེ་བས་ལེགས་བཤད་དགའ་སྟོན་འགྲོ་ལ་སྩོལ།།
མཛད་པས་རྒྱལ་བ་མཉེས་པ་འབའ་ཞིག་སྒྲུབ།།
མཚན་ནས་བརྗོད་པར་དཀའ་བ་ཁྱོད་ལ་འདུད།།

ཁྱོད་ནི་བློ་གྲོས་དྲི་མ་མེད།། སྨྲ་མཐའ་བྲལ་བའི་ཤེས་བྱ་ལ།།
ལྷ་ཡི་ལམ་ལ་འོད་སྟོང་བཞིན།། འཇུག་པར་མཐོང་ཚེ་བདག་གི་ཡིད།།
ཡ་མཚན་གྱུར་ནས་དེ་ཡི་དཔེར།།
འཇམ་དཔལ་དབྱངས་ཀྱི་མཁྱེན་པ་བཙལ།།
དེ་ནས་དེ་གཉིས་དབྱེར་མེད་པར།། མཐོང་བས་བདག་གི་དཔེ་མ་རྙེད།།

Praise of an Unnamed Sakya Lama

May happiness prevail!

Sakya Lama, by crossing great oceans of knowledge
you became Lord of the jeweled isle of scripture,
your name and fame are ornaments to the ear,
worthy, therefore, of extraordinary praise.

Wisdom perceiving the reality of existence,
a love that gives to others a festival of the finest teachings,
activities solely dedicated to delighting the buddhas,
I bow to you, your name so hard to utter.

When I see your purest of pure intelligence
penetrating phenomena without boundary,
like a million sunbeams traversing the sky,
my mind is held in awe, and for comparison
I look to the mind of Manjushri only to find
you inseparable, and all comparison disappears.

རབ་འབྱམས་རྒྱལ་བའི་ཡེ་ཤེས་འཇམ་པའི་དབྱངས་།།
རབ་དཀར་གངས་རིའི་ལྗོངས་སུ་འགྲོ་རྣམས་ཀྱི།།
རབ་མཛེས་གཙུག་གི་རྒྱན་དུ་བྱོན་གྱུར་ནས།།
རབ་རིབ་མ་ལུས་སེལ་བའི་ས་སྐྱ་པ།།

མ་ལྷར་བརྩེ་བའི་ཐུགས་རྗེས་ལུས་ཅན་ཀུན།།
སྲིད་ལས་སྒྲོལ་བའི་ཐབས་ལ་ཤིན་ཏུ་དགའ།།
མཁྱེན་བརྩེའི་དཔུང་གིས་བདུད་སྡེའི་དཔུང་བཅོམ་ནས།།
བསྟན་པའི་རྒྱལ་མཚན་འཛིན་པ་ཁྱོད་ལ་འདུད།།

ཁྱོད་ཀྱིས་ཐུབ་བསྟན་ནོར་བུ་ཡི།།
དྲི་མ་རིགས་པའི་ཆུ་ཡིས་བཀྲུས།།
ཡིད་ཆེས་ལུང་གིས་བྱི་དོར་བྱས།།
སྒྲུབ་པའི་རྒྱལ་མཚན་རྩེ་རུ་མཆོད།།

ཉིན་མཚན་དུས་ནི་ཐམས་ཅད་དུ།།
བསྟན་པ་འབའ་ཞིག་དགོངས་པ་ཁྱོད།།
སྙིགས་དུས་འགྲོ་བ་སྐྱབས་མེད་ལ།།
རྒྱལ་བ་བས་ཀྱང་ཐུགས་རྗེ་ཆེ།།

Manjushri, wisdom of buddhas beyond number,
came to this land of the white snow mountain
as the beautiful crown jewel of its inhabitants
where you dispel all darkness, Sakya Lama.

A great mind of motherly love taking utter delight
in practices to lift every living being from samsara,
an armory of wisdom and compassion routing Mara's legions,
I prostrate to you, standard bearer of Buddha's teachings.

The jewel that is the teaching of Buddha,
you clean with waters of reasoning,
polish with trustworthy scripture,
and offer it upon the banner of practice.

Every minute of every day and night,
your mind exists only for Dharma.
For we helpless beings in degenerate times,
greater than the Buddha's is your love.

ཐ་སྙད་གཙུག་ལག་ནང་གི་སྤྱི་སྤྱོད་ཀྱི།།
བདེ་གཤེགས་དགོངས་པ་ཐམས་ཅད་ལེགས་རྟོགས་ནས།།
མ་རྟོགས་པ་དང་ཕྱོགས་རེས་ཆིམས་པ་དང་།།
ཇི་བཞིན་མིན་པར་རྟོག་པའི་འགྲོ་བ་ལ།།
ལྷག་པར་བརྩེ་བ་སྐྱེས་ནས་ཡིན་ལུགས་དོན།།
རྣར་སྙན་ཡིད་འབབ་གོ་བར་སླ་བ་ཡི།།
སྐྱོན་སྤངས་གསུང་གིས་ཡང་ཡང་འདོམས་མཛད་པ།།
ཁྱོད་ལ་བསམ་པ་དག་པས་བདག་ཕྱག་འཚལ།།

ས་སྟེང་འགྲན་ཟླ་བྲལ་བ་ཆོས་ཀྱི་རྗེ།།
ཤེས་བྱ་ཀུན་ལ་ཐོགས་མེད་འཇམ་པའི་དབྱངས།།
གནས་ལྔ་མངོན་དུ་གྱུར་པའི་པཎྜིཏ།།
གངས་ཅན་འགྲོ་བའི་སྐྱབས་གཅིག་ས་སྐྱ་པ།།
ཉེན་མཚན་ཀུན་ཏུ་གྲགས་པས་གསོལ་བ་འདེབས།།
སྐྱེ་ནས་སྐྱེ་བར་མཚན་དཔེའི་གཟི་འབར་བ།།
ཁྱོད་སྐུ་མཐོང་ཞིང་ཐེག་མཆོག་སྒྲོག་པ་ཡི།།
ཁྱོད་གསུང་རྒྱུན་ཆད་མེད་པར་ཐོས་པར་ཤོག

With insight into Buddha's every thought
collected in the great works of knowledge,
you hold special love for those of no understanding,
those who misunderstand, those content to partially
  understand,
showing them clearly, beautifully, simply,
the ways things are with unerring speech.
From the purest of minds, I prostrate to you.

Unrivaled on this earth, Lord of Dharma,
all existence manifest, noble Manjushri,
the five sciences at your fingertips, Pandita,
sole refuge for beings of this snowy land, Sakya Lama,
day and night with devotion I pray to you,
life after life may I behold your form,
ablaze with glorious enlightened features,
to listen unceasingly to your words
declaring the Mahayana.

བདག་གི་བཀྲིན་ཅན་གྱི་རྩ་བའི་བླ་མར་གསོལ་འདེབས།།

ན་མཿ། ཤྲཱི་མཉྫུ་གྷོ་ཥཱ་ཡ།

དཔག་ཡས་བསྐལ་པར་ཤིན་ཏུ་བྱ་དཀའ་བའི།།
ཐབས་ཆེན་ཚོགས་གཉིས་རྒྱ་ཆེན་བསྒྲུབ་པའི་མཐུས།།
སྐྱེ་དགུའི་སྤྱི་གཙུག་རྒྱན་དུ་བྱོན་གྱུར་པའི།།
ཆོས་རྗེ་རིན་པོ་ཆེ་ལ་གསོལ་བ་འདེབས།།

སྙན་པའི་གྲགས་པས་རྒྱ་མཚོའི་མཐའ་རུ་སོན།།
དུལ་བའི་སྤྱོད་པས་བྱང་ཆུབ་འབའ་ཞིག་སྒྲུབ།།
དཔལ་འབྱོར་བཟང་པོས་འགྲོ་བའི་རེ་བ་སྐོང་།།
ཆོས་རྗེ་རིན་པོ་ཆེ་ལ་གསོལ་བ་འདེབས།།

ངེས་འབྱུང་ཐུགས་ཀྱིས་སྲིད་ལ་རྒྱབ་ཀྱིས་ཕྱོགས།།
བསླབ་ལ་གུས་པས་ཀུན་སྤྱོད་ཡོངས་སུ་དག །
ཉེས་ལྟུང་ཕྲ་མོ་ཙམ་ཡང་རིང་དུ་དོར།།
ཆོས་རྗེ་རིན་པོ་ཆེ་ལ་གསོལ་བ་འདེབས།།

A Prayer to My Precious Dharma Master, Dragpa Jangchub

Homage to Manjughosha!

I pray to my Dharma master
who created, over eons beyond number,
the powerful and difficult to amass
twin accumulation of virtue and insight,
to become a crown jewel for living beings.

I pray to my Dharma master,
fame reaching far shores of oceans,
a disciplined life lived solely for enlightenment,
wealth fulfilling the hopes of others.

I pray to my Dharma master,
mind renounced, back turned upon samsara,
devoted to the moral law, every action pure,
the tiniest fault cast far away.

བདག་བདེ་གཞན་ལ་གཏོང་ལ་མ་ཞུམ་པའི།།
བདག་གཞན་བརྗེ་བའི་ཐུགས་རྗེ་ཆེན་པོ་ཡིས།།
བདག་ཉིད་གཅེས་འཛིན་རིང་དུ་སྤྱངས་པ་ཡི།།
ཆོས་རྗེ་རིན་པོ་ཆེ་ལ་གསོལ་བ་འདེབས།།

རྣམ་དག་དབང་ལས་བྱུང་བ་ཟབ་མོའི་ལམ།།
རྣམ་མཁྱེན་སྒྱུར་དུ་བགྲོད་པའི་རིམ་པ་གཉིས།།
རྣམ་པ་ཀུན་ཏུ་སྒྲུབ་ལ་མི་གཡེལ་བའི།།
ཆོས་རྗེ་རིན་པོ་ཆེ་ལ་གསོལ་བ་འདེབས།།

བྱམས་པའི་ཐུགས་ཀྱིས་གདུལ་བྱ་བུ་བཞིན་སྐྱོང་།།
མཁྱེན་པའི་སྤྱན་གྱིས་ཤེས་བྱའི་གནས་རྣམས་གཟིགས།།
བརྩོན་འགྲུས་མཆོག་གིས་ལེ་ལོའི་གོ་སྐབས་བཅོམ།།
ཆོས་རྗེ་རིན་པོ་ཆེ་ལ་གསོལ་བ་འདེབས།།

མཐོང་བའི་མོད་ལ་དད་པའི་མཆི་མ་འཁྲུག །
རིང་དུ་བསྟེན་ན་ལྷག་པར་དད་པ་འཕེལ།།
ཇི་ཙམ་བརྟགས་ཀྱང་སྐྱོན་གྱིས་མ་གོས་པའི།།
ཆོས་རྗེ་རིན་པོ་ཆེ་ལ་གསོལ་བ་འདེབས།།

I pray to my Dharma master,
huge compassion exchanging self for others,
undaunted in giving self-happiness to others,
all self-concern thrust far aside.

I pray to my Dharma master,
utterly undistracted from the practice of
the two stages of the swift journey to enlightenment
along the profound route arising from pure initiation.

I pray to my Dharma master,
fatherly love sheltering his son-like students,
all-seeing eyes discerning the reality of existence,
supreme endeavor barring the way to laziness.

I pray to my Dharma master,
unsullied by fault howsoever examined,
tears of faith upon seeing him,
surges of faith in devotion from afar.

དྲེགས་ལྡན་རྣམས་ཀྱིས་ཞབས་ལ་བཏུད་གྱུར་ཀྱང་།།
དྲེགས་པའི་རློམ་པ་རྡུལ་ཙམ་མ་མཆིས་ཤིང་།།
དྲེགས་པ་ཅན་ལ་ལྷག་པར་ཐུགས་བརྩེ་བའི།།
ཆོས་རྗེ་རིན་པོ་ཆེ་ལ་གསོལ་བ་འདེབས།།

འགྲོ་བའི་སྐྱབས་ཁྱོད་མི་ཕམ་མདུན་སའམ།།
མགོན་པོ་འོད་དཔག་མེད་པའི་ཞིང་མཆོག་སོགས།།
དག་པའི་ཞིང་ཁམས་གང་དུ་གཤེགས་པ་དེར།།
བདག་ཅག་རྣམས་ཀྱང་འཁོར་དུ་སྐྱེ་བར་ཤོག །

I pray to my Dharma master,
bowed to by the high and mighty
yet untouched by the pomposity of pride,
showing those with pride greater love still.

Be it in the presence of Maitreya
or in the great realm of Amitabha,
to whichever pure land you travel,
Protector, may we be born into your presence.

བྱིན་རླབས་ཉེ་བརྒྱུད་ཀྱི་བླ་རྣམས་ལ་གསོལ་འདེབས།།

ན་མ། ཤྲཱི་གུ་རུ་མཉྫུ་གྷོ་ཥཱ་ཡ།

མཁྱེན་པས་སྲིད་པའི་འཆིང་བ་མཐར་མཛད་ཅིང་།།
ཐུགས་རྗེས་ཞི་ལ་དགའ་བ་རིང་དུ་དོར།།
སྲིད་ཞིའི་མཐའ་ལ་མི་གནས་སྲིད་ཞིའི་མགོན།།
རྒྱལ་བ་རྡོ་རྗེ་འཆང་ལ་གསོལ་བ་འདེབས།།

རབ་འབྱམས་ཞིང་གི་རྟུལ་སྙེད་ལས་འདས་པའི།།
གྲངས་མེད་རྒྱལ་བ་རྣམས་ཀྱི་མཁྱེན་པའི་གཏེར།།
མཐའ་ཡས་གཅིག་ཏུ་བསྡུས་པའི་ཡེ་ཤེས་སྐུ།།
མགོན་པོ་འཇམ་པའི་དབྱངས་ལ་གསོལ་བ་འདེབས།།

རླབས་ཆེན་སྨོན་ལམ་རིང་ནས་བཏབ་པའི་མཐུས།།
རྗེ་བཙུན་འཇམ་དབྱངས་ཉིད་ཀྱིས་མངོན་སུམ་དུ།།
ཐེ་ཚོམ་དྲ་བ་མཐའ་དག་བསལ་གྱུར་པ།།
དཔའ་བོ་རྡོ་རྗེའི་ཞབས་ལ་གསོལ་བ་འདེབས།།

A Harvest of Powerful Attainment

Prayer for Blessings of the Close Lineage

Homage to my guru, the youthful Manjushri!

I pray to the mighty Vajra-holder,
wisdom breaking samsara's chains,
compassion discarding nirvana's joys.
Dwelling in neither, you are protector of both.

I pray to protector Manjushri,
single manifested form of wisdom
of the treasure of knowledge of innumerable buddhas
in number more than the atoms of countless realms.

I pray at the feet of Pawo Dorje,
whose tangled webs of doubt were blown away
by noble Manjushri in actual presence,
made manifest by the force of sustained and powerful prayer.

འཇིག་རྟེན་འཇིག་རྟེན་འདས་པའི་དགེ་ལེགས་ཀྱི།།
ཡོན་ཏན་ཀུན་གྱི་རྩ་བ་དྲིན་ཅན་རྗེ།།
ཡིད་ལ་དྲན་པ་ཙམ་གྱིས་དུས་ཀུན་ཏུ།།
མོས་གུས་རྩོལ་མེད་སྐྱེ་བར་བྱིན་གྱིས་རློབས།།

འདོད་ཆུང་ཆོག་ཤེས་ཞི་ཞིང་དུལ་བར་གནས།།
སྙིང་ནས་ཐར་པ་དོན་གཉེར་གསོང་པོར་སྨྲ།།
བག་ཡོད་ལ་སྦྱོར་གྲོགས་མཆོག་སྟེན་བྱེད་ཅིང་།།
དག་སྣང་ཕྱོགས་མེད་སྐྱེ་བར་བྱིན་གྱིས་རློབས།།

འཆི་བར་ངེས་ཤིང་ནམ་འཆི་ཆ་མེད་པ།།
ཚིག་ཙམ་མིན་པ་དྲན་ནས་ལོང་མེད་དང་།།
སྙིང་བཀར་ཆོས་ལ་གཏིང་ནས་ཞེན་ལོག་སྟེ།།
དགོས་མེད་རྒྱུད་ལ་སྐྱེ་བར་བྱིན་གྱིས་རློབས།།

ལུས་ཅན་མཐའ་དག་དྲིན་ཅན་མར་ཤེས་པས།།
ཉམ་ཐག་རྣམས་ཀྱི་སྡུག་བསྔལ་དྲན་གྱུར་ནས།།
རང་བདེ་འབའ་ཞིག་སྒྲུབ་ལས་ཡིད་ལོག་སྟེ།།
སྙིང་རྗེ་རྩོལ་མེད་སྐྱེ་བར་བྱིན་གྱིས་རློབས།།

By merely calling him to mind,
bless me that I develop for all time,
effortless devotion toward my master most kind,
source of all virtue, worldly and beyond.

Bless me that I be of few desires, at peace, a mind controlled,
of sincere quest for freedom, honest in speech,
practiced in awareness, reliant upon the best of friends,
and of pure view that falls not to bias.

Bless me that I develop in all naturalness
a sense of urgency with regard to time,
an utter disregard for fame and fortune
that arises from honestly contemplating upon
death's inevitability and its unannounced arrival.

Seeing all living beings to be my mothers most kind,
bless me that I, recalling the sufferings of the weak,
turn from practice born of self-interest
toward an effortless love and compassion.

མཐར་འཛིན་ནད་ཀུན་སེལ་བའི་སྨན་གཅིག་པུ།།
ཟབ་མོ་རྟེན་འབྲེལ་མཐའ་དང་བྲལ་བའི་དོན།།
འཕགས་མཆོག་ཀླུ་སྒྲུབ་ཡབ་སྲས་དགོངས་པ་དག །
ཇི་བཞིན་ཁོང་དུ་ཆུད་པར་བྱིན་གྱིས་རློབས།།

དགེ་འདིས་མཚོན་ནས་དུས་གསུམ་དང་འབྲེལ་བའི།།
བདག་གཞན་དགེ་བའི་རྩ་བ་ཇི་སྙེད་པ།།
དེ་དག་ཐམས་ཅད་སྐྱེ་ཞིང་སྐྱེ་བ་རུ།།
བྱང་ཆུབ་མཆོག་གི་རྗེས་སུ་མི་མཐུན་པའི།།
ཞེས་ཀྱི་ཁེ་འདོད་པ་དང་གྲགས་པ་དང་།།
འཁོར་དང་ལོངས་སྤྱོད་རྙེད་དང་བཀུར་སྟིའི་རྒྱུར།།
སྐད་ཅིག་ཙམ་ཡང་ནམ་ཡང་མི་སྨིན་པར།།
བླ་མེད་བྱང་ཆུབ་ཁོ་ནའི་རྒྱུར་གྱུར་ཅིག །

རྨད་བྱུང་སྲས་བཅས་རྒྱལ་བའི་བྱིན་རླབས་དང་།།
རྟེན་འབྲེལ་སླུ་བ་མེད་པའི་བདེན་པ་དང་།།
བདག་གི་ལྷག་བསམ་དག་པའི་མཐུ་སྟོབས་ཀྱིས།།
རྣམ་དག་སྨོན་པའི་གནས་འདི་འགྲུབ་པར་ཤོག

Bless me that I comprehend in a manner akin
to noble Nagarjuna and his spiritual successors
the meaning of dependent arising, profound and limit-free,
sole cure for diseases of holding to extremes.

I pray that every virtue of others and myself,
symbolized by the virtue of this prayer,
will never ripen—life after life—even for an instant,
as worldly profit, fame, attendants, wealth, adoration,
all of which are in discord with highest enlightenment,
but become instead causes for peerless buddhahood.

By the blessings of the awe-inspiring buddhas and
  bodhisattvas,
by the truth of unfailing dependent arising,
by the force of my wholehearted sincerity,
may this prayer be realized.

བྱམས་པའི་བསྟོད་ཆེན་བཞུགས་སོ།།

མཉེས་གཤིན་བྱམས་པས་རྟག་ཏུ་བརླན་ཡང་ནག་པོའི་རྩ་ལག་སྲེག །
ཤིན་ཏུ་བཅད་དཀའི་འཆིང་བ་བཅད་ཀྱང་སྙིང་རྗེས་དམ་དུ་བཅིངས།།
ཞི་བའི་བཏང་སྙོམས་རྒྱུན་དུ་ལྡན་ཡང་བདག་པས་གཞན་ལ་གཅེས།།
འཇམ་དབྱངས་ཞབས་ལ་གུས་པས་བཏུད་ནས་མི་ཕམ་མགོན་ལ་བསྟོད།།

གདོང་བཞི་མེས་པོའི་ཞལ་ནས་རབ་ཏུ་བསྔགས།།
སྤྱན་སྟོང་ལྡན་པས་དང་བས་རྒྱུན་དུ་ལྟ།།
དགའ་མའི་བདག་པོས་དྲེགས་པ་བཏང་ནས་འདུད།།
རྒྱལ་ཚབ་ཞབས་ལ་གུས་པས་ཕྱག་བགྱིའོ།།

In Praise of Maitreya, the Crown of Brahma

Although your mind is forever moist
with the gentle waters of love,
you burn and scorch, nevertheless,
celestial Mara and his friends of darkness.

Although you have long broken
the hardened chains of samsara,
you remain a prisoner, nonetheless,
of your own compassion.

Although you rest at ease in peaceful equipoise,
you cherish, nevertheless, others more than self.
Manjushri, I bow devotedly to your feet
and offer this praise to Maitreya.

Highly praised by the four-faced Brahma,
gazed upon continuously by thousand-eyed Indra,
bowed to by Kama, all celestial arrogance deflated,
Buddha's regent, I fall in reverence to your feet.

དང་བའི་མཚོ་ལ་འདབ་བརྒྱ་པ་
སྐྱེ་དེ་ཉིད་ལ་ཡང་ཉིན་བྱེད་འོད།།
དག་པའི་མཁའ་ལ་རྒྱུ་སྐར་མགོན་ཏེ་དེས་
ཀྱང་ཀུན་དའི་ཚལ་ལ་བཞིན།།
མཚན་དཔེའི་ཕྲེང་བས་གང་སྐུ་མཐོང་མ་
ཐག་ཏུ་འགྲོ་བའི་ཡིད་འཕྲོག་པ།།
བྱམས་མགོན་ཞབས་པད་སྐྱེ་ཞིང་སྐྱེ་བར་
བདག་གི་གཙུག་ན་མཛེས་གྱུར་ཅིག །

བདུད་འཇོམས་འཁོར་དུ་འཇིགས་པ་ཀུན་དང་བྲལ།།
མཚུངས་མེད་དཔའ་བོ་སྲིད་གསུམ་སྟོན་པ་མཆོག །
ཉམ་ངར་ལྷུང་བའི་འགྲོ་ལ་རྟག་ཏུ་གཟིགས།།
རྣམ་འདྲེན་ཁྱོད་ཀྱི་ཞབས་ལ་ཕྱག་འཚལ་ལོ།།

མཐའ་ཡས་ཤེས་བྱར་ཐོགས་པ་མེད་འཇུག་པའི།།
མཁྱེན་པའི་སྟོབས་ཀྱིས་མ་རུང་བདུད་ཀྱི་སྡེ།།
གནམ་ལྕགས་བབ་པའི་མེ་ཏོག་གཞོན་ནུ་བཞིན།།
པམ་མཛད་སྟོབས་བཅུའི་དཔལ་གྱིས་བརྗིད་པ་ཁྱོད།།

As the multipetaled lotus in a crystal-clear lake
is bathed in beauty by rays of the sun,
as the moon in a cloudless, evening sky
beautifies the lily grove,
so your body is beautified by marks of perfection,
stealing the minds of those who gaze upon it.
Maitreya, my guide, may your lotus feet,
life after life, beautify the crown of my head.

Destroyer of Mara, unafraid of reproach among others,
unrivaled conqueror, teacher supreme in all worlds,
looking always to those languishing in suffering's morass,
my guide, I bow to your feet.

With the power of wisdom penetrating countless phenomena
shattering Mara's unholy forces
like fresh flowers falling as a storm of hail,
you, resplendent with the wealth of ten powers.

ཕས་རྒོལ་གླང་པོ་དྲེགས་པའི་གླད་འགེམས་ཞིང་།།
ལེགས་བཤད་སྒྲ་ཆེན་འཁོར་དབུས་བསྒྲགས་པ་ཡིས།།
སྨྲ་བ་ངན་པའི་ཕ་སྐྱེས་མཐར་མཛད་པའི།།
མི་འཇིགས་བཞི་ལྡན་མི་ཡི་སེང་གེ་ཁྱོད།།

ཁེངས་པས་མཐོ་བའི་འཇིག་རྟེན་མེས་པོ་དང་།།
ཉག་ཕྲན་བདག་པོ་དགེ་སྦྱོང་བྲམ་ཟེ་སོགས།།
གང་གིས་སྨྲ་བར་མ་ནུས་འཁོར་ལོ་མཆོག །
བསྐོར་བས་འགྲོ་ལ་བྱམས་པའི་མགོན་པོ་ཁྱོད།།

སྐུ་དང་གསུང་ལ་འཁྲུལ་པའི་མིང་ཡང་མེད།།
དྲན་པ་མ་ཉམས་རྟག་ཏུ་མཉམ་པར་བཞག །
ཐ་དད་འཛིན་པ་མ་བརྟགས་བཏང་སྙོམས་ཀྱིས།།
དབེན་ཕྱིར་ཁྱོད་ཀྱི་སྤྱོད་པ་ཡོངས་སུ་དག །

Tearing into the arrogant brains of elephantine opponents,
a roar of perfect teachings in the midst of others,
soon scattering the foxes of false and faulty views,
you, of the fourfold fearlessness, a lion among men.

Brahma, grandfather of the world, elevated by conceit,
Kama of the Five Arrows, celestial deceiver,
puffed up practitioners, Brahmins and hosts of others
unable to compete or emulate
as you whirled the great wheel of Dharma,
you, my guide—so much love for others.

Your actions and speech alien to even the name of fault,
you are of unfailing memory,
your mind in constant meditative equipoise,
freed from the unthinking equanimity
of holding samsara and nirvana to be ultimately different.
A conduct of body, speech, and mind, therefore,
pure to perfection.

འདུན་པ་དང་ནི་བརྩོན་འགྲུས་དྲན་པ་དང་།།
ཏིང་འཛིན་ཤེས་རབ་རྣམ་པར་གྲོལ་བ་ལ།།
ཉམས་པའི་གོ་སྐབས་མ་ལུས་རིང་དུ་མཛད།།
དེ་ཕྱིར་ཁྱོད་ཀྱི་རྟོགས་པ་བླ་ན་མེད།།

དུས་གསུམ་ཐམས་ཅད་ཆགས་ཐོགས་མེད་པར་མཁྱེན།།
སྐུ་གསུང་ཐུགས་ཀྱི་འཕྲིན་ལས་རྣམ་པར་དག །
སྲིད་པའི་ཕྱི་མཐའ་ཇི་སྲིད་འགྲོ་བའི་དོན།།
མཛད་པའི་ཁུར་གྱིས་དགྱེས་བཞིན་འཇུག་པ་ཁྱོད།།

རྒྱ་ཆེའི་ཡོན་ཏན་ཕུང་པོ་རབ་རྫོགས་པས།།
ཕྲ་མོའི་སྐྱོན་ཡང་འཇུག་པའི་སྐབས་བཅོམ་པ།།
ཁྱོད་ཀྱི་བརྩེ་བའི་ཡུལ་དུ་གྱུར་པ་བདག །
སླེ་ལྟོགས་སློ་ནས་སླྲ་ལ་ཡུད་ཙམ་དགོངས།།

སྡུག་བསྔལ་རྒྱ་མཚོ་ཆེ་ལས་སྒྲོལ་བའི་གྲུ །
དལ་འབྱོར་ཚང་བའི་རྟེན་འདི་ཡིན་ན་ཡང་།།
བག་མེད་ལེ་ལོ་གཉིད་དང་བྲེ་མོའི་གཏམ།།
རྙེད་བཀུར་འདོད་པའི་སྐྱོན་གྱིས་སྦགས་པ་ཡིས།།

A resolve, enthusiasm, power of memory,
meditative concentration, wisdom, deeds of liberation,
all allowing no trace of weakening.
Your attainments, therefore, know none higher.

Unhindered wisdom of existence past, present, and future,
activities of body, speech, and mind pure to perfection—
you, joyfully carrying till the end of time
the heavy load of working for others.

Tremendous qualities honed to perfection,
no room given to even the smallest fault.
I, the object of your great compassion,
cry out for your attention, however brief.

The ship to cross the great ocean of pain
is this endowed and leisured human form
but scarred by mindlessness, indulgent laziness,
sleep, meaningless talk, an eye on fame and reputation,
it is cast aside unused and a great opportunity is wasted.

དོན་མེད་ཕྱོགས་སུ་བཀོལ་བས་དོན་ཆེན་པོ།།
བདེ་ལྡག་སྒྲུབ་པའི་ལུས་བཟང་ཆུད་གསོན་པ།།
མི་ཡི་ཤ་ཚུགས་ཕྱུགས་ཀྱི་འདུ་ཤེས་ཅན།།
བདག་ལ་ཁྱོད་ཀྱིས་ཐུགས་རྗེས་གཟིགས་སུ་གསོལ།།

རྙེད་དཀའ་དོན་ཆེའི་དལ་འབྱོར་ཐོབ་པ་ཡང་།།
སྟོབས་ཀྱིས་མི་བཟློག་འབྲོས་པར་མི་ནུས་པའི།།
སྟོབས་ལྡན་འཆི་བདག་ཕོ་ཉ་བཀྱེ་བ་དང་།།
ན་དང་རྒ་བས་ཟིན་པར་མཐོང་ན་ཡང་།།
ནམ་འཆི་ངེས་མེད་འཆི་བའི་དུས་ཀྱི་ཚེ།།
ཐམས་ཅད་དོར་ནས་འགྲོ་བ་ཤེས་བཞིན་དུ།།

ལོ་ཟླ་ཞག་རྣམས་དོན་མེད་འདའ་བྱེད་པའི།།
རབ་རྨོངས་བདག་ལ་བརྩེ་བའི་དུས་ལ་བབས།།
ངེས་པར་ལེགས་པའི་གོ་འཕང་སྨོས་ཅི་དགོས།།
ལམ་གྱི་རྟེན་དུ་ཐུབ་པས་བསྔགས་པ་ཡི།།

མཐོ་རིས་ཙམ་ཡང་ཐོབ་པའི་གདེང་མེད་པ།།
བདག་ལ་ཁྱེད་ཀྱིས་བཏང་སྙོམས་མཛད་ལགས་སམ།།

I, with the shape of a man but the discrimination of a sheep,
beg you, look to me with compassion.

This rare and valuable opportune form, nevertheless,
lies under the sway of illness and old age,
and in the custody of the inescapable, the unstoppable,
the all-powerful Lord of Death and his messenger hordes.
When unpredictable death arrives,
all will be forsaken and I must travel on.

Yet knowing this to be true,
I still make meaningless my days, months, and years.
Is now not the time for your pity
upon this bewitched and ignorant fool?

Let alone the high echelon that is nirvana,
I cannot be sure of gaining birth in higher realms
praised by Buddha as the basis of the path.
How could you look on me, therefore, with indifference?

མཐོ་རིས་དཔལ་དང་ལྡན་པའི་ལུས་ཐོབ་ཀྱང་།།
གསུང་རབ་ཚུལ་བཞིན་འབྱེད་པའི་ཤེས་རབ་ཀྱིས།།

མ་ནོར་ལམ་བཟང་རྙེད་པར་མ་གྱུར་ན།།
སླར་ཡང་འཁོར་བའི་རྒྱ་མཚོ་ཉིད་དུ་ལྟུང་།།
དེ་ཕྱིར་གཏི་མུག་མུན་པའི་སྨག་ཆེན་གྱིས།།
ཡུན་རིང་དུས་སུ་བསྒྲིབས་པས་བླང་དོར་གནས།།
ཇི་བཞིན་འབྱེད་ལ་ཀུན་ནས་འཐོམས་གྱུར་པ།།
བདག་ལ་ཤེས་རབ་སྒྲོན་མེ་སྤུལ་དུ་གསོལ།།

རབ་འབར་ལྕགས་ཀྱི་ས་གཞིར་མེ་ལྕེས་སྲེག་ཅིང་
ལུས་ལ་མཚོན་ཆའི་ཆར་པ་འབབ།།
གཤིན་རྗེའི་སྐྱེས་བུས་གསལ་ཤིང་ལ་བསྐྱོན་ཟངས་
ཞུན་སྦུད་ཅིང་ཕུར་བུས་ལྕེ་ལ་འདེབས།།
གདངས་རིས་བསྐྱོར་བའི་འཁྲུག་པའི་སྦྲུབས་ཆུད་བུ་ཡུག
འཚུབས་པའི་རླུང་གིས་བཏབ་པ་ཡིས།།
ལ་ལར་ཆུ་བུར་བརྒྱ་བྱུང་ལ་ལར་རྡོལ་ཞིང་
ལུས་ནི་ཚལ་པ་དུ་མར་གས།།

A life graced by blessings of higher realms of existence
but bereft of the true path discovered by wisdom
cutting to the meanings of the Buddha's words
is a life destined to fall once more into samsara's sea.
I, therefore, so long rendered blind by ignorance's
dark shroud,
stand confused about what needs to be cultivated
and what needs to be rooted out.
Hand me, I beg you, the lantern of wisdom.

On the scorching ground of iron
the denizens of hell are burnt alive,
while into their bodies a rain of weapons hurtles.
The guardians of hell hoist them impaled on blazing rods,
pour molten copper down their anguished throats,
and drag them by their tongues driven through with stakes.

Encircled by the icy mountains in frozen wastes,
at all times unsheltered against bitter blizzards,
some break out in blisters, on some the blisters burst,
and their pitiful bodies crack into a million pieces.

གདོང་ནི་སྐྲས་ཁེབས་ཁ་ནི་བསྐོམས་ཤིང་ཆུ་ཀླུང་
མཐོང་སྣེ་གཏུང་ཕྱིར་རྒྱུགས་པ་ན།།
རལ་གྲི་མདུང་རྣམས་ཐོགས་པའི་སྐྱེས་བུས་
འགགས་ཤིང་ཆུ་ཡང་རྣག་ཁྲག་ཉིད་དུ་མཐོང་།།
ཁ་ནི་ཁབ་ཀྱི་མིག་ཙམ་ལྟ་བས་མགྲིན་འགགས་
ཟས་སྐོམ་སྙེད་ཀྱང་སྤྱོད་མི་ནུས།།
ཟྲོས་ཤིང་འཕུང་རྣམས་འབར་ནས་ཞིག་ཅིང་
ཁཤད་གཅིས་འཚོ་ལ་རང་ཤ་བཅད་དེ་ཟ།།

ཕྱོངས་པའི་མུན་ཆེན་འཐིབས་པས་ལམ་དང་
ལམ་མིན་འཁྲིད་ལ་བློ་ཡི་ནུས་པ་བྲལ།།
གཅིག་ལ་གཅིག་གསོད་ལྷ་མིའི་གཞན་དབང་གྱུར་
པས་རྡེག་དང་བཀོལ་བའི་སྡུག་བསྔལ་འབབ།།
ལྷ་རྣམས་དཔལ་ལ་འཁྲུག་པའི་ཕྲག་དོག་མེ་
ཆེན་འབར་བས་ཡིད་བདེའི་གོ་སྐབས་བཅོམ།།
འཐབ་རྩོད་ལས་བྱུང་ལུས་བཅད་དྲལ་ཅིང་
གཡོ་སྒྱུས་བསླད་པས་བདེན་མཐོང་སྐལ་བ་མེད།།

In the desperate realm of ghosts are those
with faces covered by hair, their mouths shriveled by thirst.
Seeing water afar, they run to drink, but their way is blocked
by others brandishing knives and spears,
or else the very water appears as blood or pus.
In some the mouth is as small as a needle's eye,
the throat squeezed tight by goiters,
and food, should they find it, cannot be enjoyed.
In others who eat, the food ignites and burns inside.
Some exist on urine and excrement,
others upon their own flesh.

Hopelessly lost in the vast darkness of stupidity,
animals cannot discern right from wrong,
killing each other, used by gods and men,
bearing sufferings of beatings and servitude.
Consumed by the fires of disturbing jealousy
of the glories of their celestial neighbors,
the demigods destroy all hope of contentment.
Riddled with deception and dishonesty,
their bodies cut and torn by the ravages of war,
they forfeit the chance of ever knowing the truth.

དེ་ལྟར་མཐོང་བ་ལྟ་ཞོག་ཐོས་ན་ཡང་།།
སྙིང་ལ་འཇིགས་སྐྱེད་སྐྱེ་ནི་གཡའ་བ་ཡི།།
དམྱལ་བ་ཡི་དྭགས་དུད་འགྲོ་ལྷ་མིན་གྱི།།
གཡང་ས་ཆེན་པོ་དག་ཏུ་ལྟུང་འགྱུར་བའི།།
དམ་པས་སྨད་པའི་མི་བཟད་སྡིག་པའི་ལས།།
ཐོག་མེད་དུས་ནས་བསགས་ཤིང་གསོག་འགྱུར་བ།།
གཡང་ས་ཆེན་པོར་མངོན་ཕྱོགས་ཉམ་ཐག་བདག །
ངན་འགྲོའི་འཇིགས་ལས་སྐྱོབ་པའི་དུས་ལ་བབ།།

མི་ཡི་གནས་ནའང་ཡོངས་སྤྱོད་དབང་ཕྱུག་གིས།།
མངོན་པར་མཐོ་ན་ཉམས་ཀྱི་དྭོགས་པ་དང་།།
མཐོ་རིས་ཡོན་ཏན་འཁྱེར་བས་ཕོངས་པ་ན།།
འདོད་བདེ་འཚོལ་བར་འགྱུར་བས་ཤ་ཐང་ངོ་།།
བདེ་བར་འདོད་ནས་དེ་ཡི་ཐབས་བསྒྲུབས་པས།།
བདེ་བ་ཐོབ་པ་དེ་ལས་ཆེས་ལྷག་པའི།།
ལུས་ཀྱི་སྡུག་བསྔལ་སེམས་ཀྱི་ཡིད་མི་བདེ།།
རྣམ་པ་དུ་མས་ཀུན་ནས་མནར་བར་འགྱུར།།

Merely hearing of such horrors
sends an icy shiver of fear through the heart.
Plunging to this desperate abyss
of hell, ghosts, animals, and demigods
is by way of inexhaustible unwholesome deeds,
despised by the wise, but built up and performed
since the onset of time, with no end in sight.
Standing here wretched, peering into this abyss,
it is time to save me from these terrors.

Within our human realm also, those enhanced
by wealth, power, and possession
must bear the anxiety of losing it.
Whereas those deprived of the good things in life
are worn down by their search for happiness.
Desiring comfort and well-being,
all means to achieve them are pursued.
Greater, therefore, than the happiness sought
is the torment wrought in different guises
by mental anguish and physical toil.

ལུས་མཛེས་རིན་ཆེན་རྒྱན་གྱིས་རབ་བརྒྱན་ནས།།
ཁང་བཟང་དགའ་བའི་ཚལ་དུ་གནས་བཅས་ཤིང་།།
ཡུན་རིང་འདོད་པའི་བདེ་ལ་ལོངས་སྤྱོད་པ།།
མཐོ་རིས་དཔལ་ལ་རོལ་པའི་ལྷ་རྣམས་ཀྱང་།།
མི་འདོད་འཆི་བའི་ལྟས་ཀྱིས་ཟིན་པ་ན།།
ཡིད་འཕྲོག་སྙིང་ལ་གཅགས་པར་གྱུར་པ་ཡི།།
ལྷ་ཡི་མཛེས་མ་ཡིད་འོང་སྐྱེད་མོས་ཚལ།།
བདུད་རྩིའི་ཁ་ཟས་གོས་བཟང་མཛེས་པའི་རྒྱན།།

ལྷ་བུ་གཞོན་ནུ་རྣམས་དང་མྱུར་དུ་བདག །
མི་འདོད་བཞིན་དུ་འབྲལ་བར་མཐོང་བའི་ཚེ།།
གནས་དེར་སྐྱེས་པའི་ལུས་ཀྱི་བདེ་བ་ལས།།
ཆེས་ཆེར་ལྷག་པའི་ཡིད་ཀྱི་སྡུག་བསྔལ་གྱིས།།
བསྐྱེད་པའི་མྱ་ངན་མེ་ལྕེ་འབར་བས་བསྲེག །
ཚེ་རབས་མང་པོར་ལེགས་པར་སྤྱད་པའི་ལས།།
འབད་པས་བསྒྲུབས་པའི་འབྲས་བུ་སྤྱད་པས་ཟད།།
བག་མེད་དབང་གིས་ངན་འགྲོའི་རྒྱུ་བསྒྲུབས་པས།།

Those dwelling in exalted celestial realms,
of exquisite beauty—bodies bejeweled,
enjoying fine palaces, gardens of delight,
indulging for an eternity in sensual pleasure,
swimming in the luxuries of the gods—
when gripped by signs of unwelcome death,
see their radiantly beautiful goddesses,
stealers of their hearts and minds,
their paradise gardens, their ambrosia-like food,
their eternally young celestial friends
all too soon vanishing forever.

Greater than the pleasures of their celestial life
is the mental agony of those moments,
igniting the fires of anguish and sorrow.
Fruits of wholesome deeds done over many lives
have been enjoyed and are now at an end.
In their indulgent, unthinking lifestyle
they gather causes for an inferior birth
and again must fall to base forms of life.

སླར་ཡང་ངན་སོང་གནས་སུ་ལྷུང་བར་འགྱུར།།
འདོད་ལ་འདུན་པའི་རྣམ་རྟོག་གནོད་སེམས་མེད།།
གཉིད་དང་ཡིད་ལ་གདུང་བའི་རྒྱོད་པ་སྤངས།།
ལུས་དང་སེམས་ལ་གནོད་པའི་སྡུག་བསྔལ་བྲལ།།
ཏིང་འཛིན་སྦྱོར་བས་ཀྱིས་ཡུན་རིང་བདེར་གནས་པ།།
གཟུགས་དང་གཟུགས་མེད་ལྷ་ཡི་གནས་ཐོབ་ཀྱང་།།
འདུ་བྱེད་སྡུག་བསྔལ་འཆིང་ལས་མ་གྲོལ་བས།།
སྔོན་གྱི་ཏིང་འཛིན་འཕེན་པ་ཟད་པ་ན།།

ཕྱིར་ཡང་འོག་ཏུ་ལྷུང་ནས་བརྒྱུད་མར་འཁོར།།
དེ་ལྟར་འཁོར་བའི་གཙོ་བོ་ལྷ་མི་ཡང་།།
སྐྱེ་འཆི་ན་དང་རྒ་ལ་སོགས་པ་ཡི།།
སྡུག་བསྔལ་རྒྱ་བོས་སྲིད་པའི་མཚོར་ཁྱེར་ན།།
སྲིད་པའི་བདེ་ལ་ཆགས་པར་མི་རིགས་སོ།།
འོན་ཀྱང་སྲེད་པས་བློ་མིག་བསྒྲིབས་པ་ཡིས།།
སྡུག་བསྔལ་བདེ་བར་འཛིན་པའི་ལོག་ཤེས་ཅན།།
ཕྱིན་ཅི་ལོག་གི་རྟོག་པས་བསྒྲིབས་པ་བདག །
སྲིད་པའི་རྒྱ་བོ་ཆེ་ལས་བསྒྲལ་དུ་གསོལ།།

Those of the form and formless realms,
shorn of all longing for base pleasure,
lacking in malice, unchained by sleep,
free of regret, shielded from physical harm,
divorced from mental grief, living a long joyful life,
powered by a meditative concentration,
have also not wrenched themselves free
from the chains of innate pervasive suffering,
and once the meditative concentration,
the force behind such exalted states,
begins to fail, they will again fall back
to rejoin the ceaseless circling.

When gods and men, supreme in samsara,
are swept into the sea of existence
by rivers of birth, death, illness, and old age,
what need to point out the folly
of attraction to the pleasures of life.
Yet I, wisdom eyes misted by attachment,
seeing suffering as happiness,
am blindfolded by deluded perception.
Save me from this monstrous sea.

འདོད་པའི་འདམ་དུ་བྱིང་བས་ཐར་པའི་ལམ་ལས་གོལ།།
མ་རིག་ཐིབས་པོར་ཞུགས་པས་ཤེས་རབ་མིག་དང་བྲལ།།
སྲིད་པའི་གཟེབ་དུ་ཚུད་པས་འཁོར་བའི་བཙོན་རྭར་བཅིངས།།
ལས་ཀྱིས་མནར་བ་བདག་ནི་ཁྱེད་ཀྱི་ཐུགས་རྗེའི་གནས།།

འཇིགས་རུང་འཁོར་བའི་གཡང་ས་འགེགས་པ་ལ།།
དྲི་མེད་མང་དུ་ཐོས་ལ་བརྟེན་པ་ཡི།།
ཚུལ་བཞིན་དཔྱོད་པའི་རྣམ་དག་རིགས་སྟོབས་ཀྱིས།།
མཐའ་ཡས་གསུང་རབ་རྣམས་ཀྱི་དྲང་ངེས་ཚུལ།།

ཇི་བཞིན་འབྱེད་ལ་གཞན་དྲིང་མི་འཇོག་པའི།།
མཁས་པའི་གོ་འཕང་ངེས་པར་རྙེད་དགོས་ཀྱང་།།
རྒྱལ་བའི་དགོངས་པ་ཕྲ་མོ་སྨོས་ཅི་དགོས།།
འཛུག་ལྡོག་གནས་ནི་ཤིན་ཏུ་རགས་པ་ལའང་།།
བདག་གི་བློ་མིག་ཆེས་ཆེར་གསལ་མ་གྱུར།།
ད་དུང་རབ་རྨོངས་དགྲ་འདིས་བདག་གི་སྙིང་།།
རིང་དུ་བསྒྲིབས་ནས་གྲོལ་བའི་སྐབས་མེད་པ།།
ཚུལ་འདི་དགོངས་ལ་སྙིང་གི་མུན་པ་སེལ།།

I have strayed from the path to freedom
to sink in the muddy swamp of desire.
Plunged into the ignorance's murkiness,
I am bereft of the eyes of wisdom.
Thrown in the cage of deluded fabrication,
I languish in the prison of samsara.
Tormented by my past deeds
I am truly worthy of your compassion.

Halting the approach of samsara's terrifying abyss
means to rise to the level of the wise
with a vast and unsullied learning
as a foundation for uncontaminated and incisive reasoning,
able to single-handedly distinguish from innumerable works
definitive teachings from those that bear interpretation.

And yet, let alone Buddha's subtler teachings,
even simple points of right and wrong
are obscured and distant from my wisdom eye.
Still this enemy of ignorance envelops my heart,
ruining any opportunity for liberation.
Think on this and clear the darkness of my soul.

རྒྱལ་བ་རྒྱལ་སྲས་སྤྱན་སྔར་རིག་གནས་ལ།།
མང་ཐོས་རྒྱ་མཚོས་སྐྱེ་བ་དུ་མ་རུ།།
ཡང་ཡང་སྦྱངས་པའི་བག་ཆགས་ལེགས་སད་པ།།
འགྲོ་ལ་ལམ་བཟང་མཚོན་པའི་མིག་གཅིག་པུ།།
སྟོན་གྱི་དམ་པ་རྣམས་ཀྱིས་ཡལ་བར་དོར།།
དེ་ཕྱིར་མགོན་དང་བྲལ་བའི་ཕོངས་པ་བདག །
ཕྱོགས་རྣམས་བསླད་པའི་འགྲོན་པོ་བཞིན་གྱུར་པ།།
བརྩེ་ཆེན་ཁྱོད་ཀྱིས་རྗེས་སུ་བཟུང་བའི་དུས།།

ཡང་དང་ཡང་དུ་གུས་པས་བསྟེན་པའི་སྐྱབས།།
བྱམས་པ་བྱམས་པས་འགྲོ་བ་སྒྲོལ་བ་ཁྱོད།།
མྱུར་བ་མྱུར་བར་བྱོན་ནས་བདག་གི་ནི།།
སྐྱེ་བ་སྐྱེ་བར་ཐེག་མཆོག་ཤེས་གཉེན་མཛོད།།

རྟག་ཏུ་བརྩེ་བས་ལུས་ཅན་མཐའ་དག་ལ།།
རྒྱུན་མི་ཆད་པར་གཟིགས་པ་ཁྱེད་དྲུང་དུ།།
གང་གི་ཡོན་ཏན་དྲན་པས་དང་བའི་ཡིད།།
ཉིན་རེ་བཞིན་དུ་སླེབ་པར་བགྱིས་ན་ཡང་།།
གནས་ཀྱིས་བསྐལ་ཞིང་སླར་ཡང་དབེན་པའི་རོ།།

In the presence of buddhas and bodhisattvas
many great beings became oceans of learning in the sciences,
life after life practicing again and again,
their accumulated instincts fully awakened
to become the sole guides of the good path.
Yet I have been ignored by such masters from the past
and am bereft of protection like a tired lost traveler.
It time to be cared for by your compassion.

Again and again, devotedly I turn to you for refuge,
Loving One, who with love liberates living beings.
Come quickly, quickly, and in life after life
be my Mahayana guru.

Remembering your qualities, my mind fills with joy
and thinks each day to come before you
who gazes with constant love on all that lives,
but because of vagaries of place
and a wish to travel far for the taste of solitude,
I cannot make the journey.

རབ་ཏུ་སྨྱོང་ཕྱིར་ཐག་རིང་གནས་སུ་ནི།།
འཇུག་པར་འདོད་པས་ལུས་ཀྱིས་བགྲོད་མི་ནུས།།
དེས་ན་བསོད་ནམས་ཞིང་གི་དམ་པ་ཁྱོད།།

མཉེས་པར་བགྱི་སླད་ལྷག་བསམ་དག་པ་ཡིས།།
རིན་ཆེན་ས་ལེ་སྦྲམ་དང་ལྷ་ཡི་དར།།
དགེ་སྦྱོང་རྣམས་ལ་ཐུབ་པས་བསྔགས་པ་ཡི།།
ཆོས་གོས་གསུམ་དང་གསིལ་བྱེད་དྲང་སྲོང་སྣོད།།

གཞན་ཡང་ཏིང་འཛིན་སྨོན་ལམ་གྱིས་སྤྲུལ་པའི།།
བཀོད་ལེགས་ཡིད་འཕྲོག་མཆོད་པ་ནམ་མཁའི་ཁྱོན།།
ཡོངས་སུ་བཀང་སྟེ་རྐང་གཉིས་གཙོ་བོ་ལ།།
ཞེན་མེད་མ་ཆགས་བློ་ཡིས་དབུལ་བར་བགྱི།།

དེ་ལས་འོངས་པའི་རབ་དཀར་དགེ་བའི་ཚོགས།།
གང་དེས་སྲིད་པར་ཡུན་རིང་འཁྱམས་པ་ན།།
སྡུག་བསྔལ་བྱེ་བས་མནར་ཞིང་བདེ་བས་ཕོངས།།
མ་ལུས་འགྲོ་བའི་སྐྱབས་སུ་བདག་གྱུར་ཅིག །

Therefore, holiest of the spheres of merit,
with the purest of pure minds
I make offerings to please you,
of jewels and gold, celestial cloth,
of the three robes, staff, and begging bowl,
praised by the Buddha as necessities for the ordained.

I make offerings, captivating and beautiful,
created by prayer and by power of meditation
filling the regions of the skies,
and offer them without attachment
to the king of men and gods.

By the virtue that arises from these prayers,
may I become a refuge for those
wandering lost and long in the realms of existence,
tormented by a million sufferings,
bereft of happiness and peace.

འཇིག་རྟེན་འདྲེན་པའི་གོ་འཕང་དམ་པ་ལ།།
རིག་པར་མ་གྱུར་སྐྱེ་བ་ཐམས་ཅད་དུ།།
ཚངས་སྤྱོད་ཡོངས་སུ་དག་པའི་རབ་བྱུང་རྟེན།།
རྙེད་ནས་ཐེག་མཆོག་རིགས་ནི་སད་པར་ཤོག །

བཟོད་ལྡན་དྲང་ཞིང་གྱ་གྱུ་མེད་པ་དང་།།
མ་ཞུམ་སྙིང་སྟོབས་ཤུགས་དྲག་དད་པ་དང་།།
གུས་དང་རྟག་ཏུ་སྦྱོར་བའི་བརྩོན་འགྲུས་དང་།།
རྣམ་དཔྱོད་ཤེས་རབ་ཕུལ་བྱུང་ཐོབ་པར་ཤོག །

རྒྱལ་བའི་དགོངས་པ་རྣམ་དག་རིགས་སྟོབས་ཀྱིས།།
ཇི་བཞིན་རྙེད་ནས་རང་གི་དགོངས་པ་ལྟར།།
བརྩེ་བས་དྲངས་པའི་ཐབས་མཁས་སྤྱོད་པ་ཡིས།།
གཞན་ལ་སྟོན་ལ་མཁས་པའི་མཐར་སོན་པའི།།
བཤེས་གཉེན་བསྟེན་ནས་མང་ཐོས་རྒྱ་མཚོ་ལ།།
རིང་དུ་སྦྱངས་པས་ཐེ་ཚོམ་ཀུན་བཅད་ནས།།
ཐོས་པའི་དོན་རྣམས་ཚུལ་བཞིན་བསྒྲུབས་པ་ཡིས།།
བདེ་བར་གཤེགས་རྣམས་མཉེས་པར་བྱེད་པར་ཤོག །

In all my lives until I have reached
the enlightened existence of a buddha,
may I find myself in the pure lifestyle of a monk
and awaken within me the Mahayana lineage.

May I be patient, honest with others,
neither deceiving nor beguiling,
courageous, undaunted, of strong faith,
of firm and unwavering determination,
and clear and discriminating intelligence.

Having devoted myself in all my lives to teachers
who access Buddha's thoughts by the power of pure reason,
and who travel with consummate skill moved by compassion
to perfection in the art of teaching others,
may I plunge into the ocean of learning to banish all doubts
and, with pure practice born from study,
delight the buddhas.

ཐུབ་པས་བཅས་པའི་མཚམས་ལས་མི་འདའ་ཞིང་།།
རྒྱལ་བའི་གདུང་འཛིན་དགེ་བའི་བཤེས་ལ་གུས།།
དབང་པོ་རབ་རྗེ་ལོག་སྒྲུབ་སྐྱོན་དང་བྲལ།།
ཡོངས་སུ་དག་པའི་འཁོར་དང་ལྡན་པར་ཤོག །

ནག་པོའི་ཕྱོགས་ཀྱིས་ཡིད་ནི་བསྐྱོད་པ་ཡིས།།
ཚོགས་པའི་ཆོས་སྤྱོད་དཀའ་སྟོན་སྦྱོང་བའི་གེགས།།
བདུད་ཀྱི་གཉེན་དུ་གྱུར་པའི་སྡིག་གྲོགས་དང་།།
སྐད་ཅིག་ཙམ་ཡང་ཕྲད་པར་མ་གྱུར་ཅིག །

ཐུབ་དབང་རྗེས་སུ་གུས་པས་སློབ་པའི་ཚེ།།
ཐབས་ཆེན་སྤྱོད་པ་རྫོགས་པར་བྱེད་པའི་གེགས།།
སྐལ་བ་ངན་པའི་རྗེས་འགྲོ་བདུད་ཀྱི་ལས།།
བར་དུ་གཅོད་པའི་མིང་ཡང་མེད་པར་ཤོག །

གང་དང་ལྡན་ན་དམ་པ་དགའ་བྱེད་པ།།
དགེ་སྦྱོང་རྒྱན་དུ་འདྲེན་པས་བསྔགས་པ་ཡི།།
བྱང་ཆུབ་སྤྱོད་པའི་རྗེས་སུ་མཐུན་པའི་རྐྱེན།།
མ་ལུས་ཐོགས་པ་མེད་པར་འགྲུབ་པར་ཤོག །

I pray that I am forever among those
who never breach monastic rules ordained by Buddha,
who hold in reverence spiritual friends
blessed with the lineage of the Conqueror,
and who, with senses sharp,
are free from flawed and faulty behavior.

The head turned by dark forces
hinders experience of the joyful festival
that is the community of a Dharma life.
May I never encounter misleading friends,
in reality the cohorts of Mara.

Practicing devotedly in the wake of mighty Buddha,
I pray there be not even a trace of obstruction,
works of Mara that dog the unfortunate,
hindering fulfillment of bodhisattva practice.

May I possess without hindrance
attitudes conducive to a bodhisattva life,
praised by Buddha as ornaments of practitioners,
and which fill the wise with delight.

བྱང་ཆུབ་སྤྱོད་ཚེ་གདུལ་བྱའི་གནས་ཀུན་ཡང་།།
རྣམ་དག་བསླབ་པས་བསྔམས་པའི་རབ་བྱུང་ལ།།
འགོད་ཅིང་དེ་ལ་འོས་པའི་ཡོ་བྱད་རྣམས།།
བསམས་པ་ཙམ་གྱིས་མ་ལུས་སྩོལ་བར་ཤོག །

དེང་ནས་བརྩམས་ཏེ་ཚེ་རབས་ཐམས་ཅད་དུ།།
ལུས་ངག་ཡིད་ཀྱིས་རྩོམ་པ་གང་བགྱིས་པ།།
དེ་དག་ཐམས་ཅད་མཐའ་ཡས་འགྲོ་བ་ལ།།
གནས་སྐབས་ཀུན་ཏུ་ཕན་པའི་རྒྱུར་གྱུར་ཅིག །

བུ་སྡུག་ཤི་བའི་དུས་ཀྱི་མ་བཞིན་དུ།།
སྡུག་བསྔལ་ཀུན་གྱིས་མནར་བའི་འགྲོ་བ་ཀུན།།
རྟག་ཏུ་ཡིད་ལ་གཅགས་པའི་བརྩེ་བ་ཡིས།།
བདོག་པ་ཐམས་ཅད་དེ་ལ་གཏོང་བར་ཤོག །

When I walk the ways of bodhisattvas,
may I bring monastic life to spirituality
bound by the purest of ethics
and merely by thought, grant it its every need.

From this day on, life after life,
may all that I do, say, and think
be of benefit at all times
to living beings beyond number.

Like a mother at the death of her beautiful child,
may I hold in my heart every living being
tortured and tormented by suffering
and with a mind of love,
give to them all that I own.

མོས་སྤྱོད་ས་ཡི་དྲི་མ་སྦྱོང་བ་ནི།།
འདས་དང་མ་འོངས་ད་ལྟར་བྱུང་བ་ཡི།།
ཚུ་རོལ་མཐོང་བའི་རྒྱལ་སྲས་ནང་ན་བདག །
གསེར་གྱི་ས་འཛིན་དབུས་ན་ལྷུན་པོ་བཞིན།།
སྤྱན་དང་མངོན་ཤེས་མང་དུ་ཐོས་པ་སོགས།།
ཡོན་ཏན་ཀུན་གྱིས་རབ་ཏུ་མཐོ་བ་དང་།།
བྱིས་པའི་རྒྱུད་པ་ཀུན་ལས་འདས་གྱུར་ཏེ།།
གཞན་དྲིང་མི་འཇོག་སྤོབས་པ་ཐོབ་པར་ཤོག །

རྒྱལ་སྲས་འཕགས་པའི་ས་ལ་སློབ་པ་ནི།།
སར་གནས་དཔའ་བོ་དུས་གསུམ་ཐམས་ཅད་དུ།།
ཡོངས་སུ་གཤེགས་པ་རྣམས་ཀྱི་ཁྲིད་ན་བདག །
བྱ་ལམ་བགྲོད་ལ་འདབ་བཟང་དབང་པོ་བཞིན།།
རྒྱལ་སྲས་གཞན་གྱིས་དཔག་པར་དཀའ་བ་ཡི།།
ཤིན་ཏུ་རྒྱ་ཆེའི་ཤེས་བྱའི་གནས་རྣམས་ལ།།
དྲི་མེད་མཁྱེན་པ་ཐོགས་པ་མེད་འཇུག་ཅིང་།།
ཐབས་ཆེན་སྤྱོད་པའི་གཏེར་དུ་འགྱུར་བ་ཤོག །

When ridding myself of faults on *arya* aspirant paths,
among like bodhisattvas of past, present, and future,
may I stand as Meru among the mountains of gold,
made tall by supernatural sight, clairvoyance, learning
to go beyond worldly woes to self-reliant ability.

When I walk on the paths of the *arya* beings
among courageous bodhisattvas of past, present and future,
may I travel like the garuda winging through the skies
into vast realms of knowledge unfathomed by other
  bodhisattvas,
with wisdom pure and unhindered to become
a treasure and source of powerful bodhisattva practice.

དེ་ལྟར་སྤྱད་པའི་འབྲས་བུ་གྲུབ་པ་ན།།
དུས་གསུམ་རྒྱལ་བ་རྣམས་ཀྱི་སྐུ་དང་ཞིང་།།
འཁོར་དང་མཛད་པ་སྐུ་ཚེ་སྨོན་ལམ་རྣམས།།
གང་ཡིན་གཅིག་ཏུ་བསྡོམས་པ་དེ་དག་ཀུན།།
ཐབས་མཁས་སྤྱོད་པས་ཡོངས་སུ་རྫོགས་གྱུར་ནས།།
རིང་ནས་ཡིད་ལ་བརྟགས་པའི་འགྲོ་བ་འདི།།
དམ་ཆོས་བདུད་རྩིའི་ཆར་ཆེན་ཕབ་པ་ཡིས།།
སྐད་ཅིག་གཅིག་ལ་བདག་གིས་སྒྲོལ་བར་ཤོག །།

When such practice bears its fruit,
may I with wise practice accomplish
every form, realm, entourage, deed, lifespan, and prayer
of every buddha gathered together as one
to let fall that great Dharma rain
on every living being long held in my heart
and in an instant set them free.

།རྗེ་བཙུན་གསང་བདག་གི་བསྟོད་པ་བཞུགས་སོ།

གང་གི་མཁྱེན་པ་ནམ་མཁའི་མཐར་སོན་པས།།
དྲི་མེད་མཁྱེན་པའི་གཏེར་དུ་རབ་གྲགས་པ།།
འཇམ་པའི་དབྱངས་དེའི་རྣམ་དཀར་འཕྲིན་ལས་ཀུན།།
ད་དུང་བྱང་ཆུབ་བར་དུ་སྐྱོང་གྱུར་ཅིག །

ལུས་ཅན་ཀུན་གྱི་བླ་མེད་བསོད་ནམས་ཞིང་།།
ཕོངས་པའི་རེ་བ་ཡིད་བཞིན་སྐོང་བའི་གཏེར།།
ཐར་འདོད་རྣམས་ཀྱི་གཙུག་གི་རྒྱན་གྱི་མཆོག །
དཀོན་མཆོག་གསུམ་ལ་གུས་པས་ཕྱག་འཚལ་ལོ།།

འགྲོ་བའི་ཕུན་ཚོགས་ཀུན་ནས་ཉམས་བྱེད་པའི།།
ནག་པོའི་རྩ་ལག་སྡེ་དང་བཅས་པའི་དཔུང་།།
མ་ལུས་རྩད་ནས་གཞོམ་ཕྱིར་རྒྱལ་བ་ཡིས།།
གང་སྐུ་རྡོ་རྗེའི་ལུས་སུ་བྱིན་བརླབས་པ།།
དེ་ནི་གནོད་སྦྱིན་རྣམས་ཀྱི་སྡེ་དཔོན་ཏེ།།
དཔལ་ལྡན་རྣམ་པར་འཇོམས་པ་ཞེས་སུའང་གྲགས།།

In Praise of Vajrapani, Keeper of the Secret Mantra

Wisdom reaching to the ends of space,
famed as a treasury of purest wisdom;
from now until enlightenment
may I be forever nourished
by Manjushri's enlightened presence.

I bow with reverence to Buddha, Dharma, and Sangha,
highest fields of devotion for living beings,
a treasury fulfilling hopes of the impoverished,
crown jewels for those longing for freedom.

To destroy utterly Mara's black hordes,
wreckers of all that is good and joyful,
mighty Buddha blessed your body to be of vajra form.
Lord of Yakshas, Glorious Destroyer, wielder of the
  blazing vajra,
annihilator of whole armies of obstruction,
I prostrate before you.

འབར་བའི་རྡོ་རྗེ་ཕྱག་ན་བསྣམས་པ་ཡིས།།
བགེགས་དཔུང་རྣམ་པར་འཇོམས་ལ་ཕྱག་འཚལ་ལོ།།

སྐལ་བཟང་རྒྱལ་བ་སྟོང་གི་བསྟན་པའི་ཁུར།།
གང་ལ་གཏད་ནས་སྲུང་བར་ཞལ་བཞེས་ཤིང་།།
རིག་སྔགས་འཆང་བ་ཀུན་གྱི་རྗེར་གྱུར་པ།།
རྡོ་རྗེ་གཏུམ་པོ་ཅུང་ཟད་བདག་ལ་གསོན།།

ཉིད་ཀྱི་ཁུར་དུ་བསྣམས་པའི་བསྟན་པ་དེ།།
རིང་དུ་གནས་པ་ཆགས་དང་སྡང་བ་ཡིས།།
ཇི་བཞིན་འཛིན་པ་ཉིད་ལ་རག་ལས་ན།།
འདི་ན་དེ་ལྟར་རྗེས་སུ་སློབ་པ་ལ།།
ནག་ཕྱོགས་འབྱུང་པོས་ལྷག་པར་འཚེ་བར་བྱེད།།
རྒྱལ་འདི་ཡལ་བར་དོར་ན་ཕན་བདེའི་གཏེར།།
བསྟན་པ་རིན་ཆེན་ཕྱོགས་རྣམས་ཐམས་ཅད་དུ།།
སྲུང་བར་མཛད་པའང་ཚིག་ཙམ་སྙིང་པོར་ཟད།།

དེ་སླད་མཐུ་སྟོབས་བདག་པོས་བརྩེར་དགོངས་ལ།།
བདག་ཅག་རྣམས་ཀྱི་ཡིད་ལ་རེ་བའི་དོན།།

The thousand buddhas' teachings of this glorious eon
entrusted to you, guarded under vow by you,
supreme among keepers of mantra.
You of vajra wrath, listen to me.

Preservation of the teachings that you hold by obligation
depends upon their practice and dissemination.
When those, therefore, who practice thus
are being particularly thwarted by dark forces,
to ignore their plight would render your vow to protect
the precious, happiness-bringing teachings—
though they be guarded throughout space—
as nothing but meaningless words.

མངོན་པར་གསོལ་བ་འདི་རྣམས་བདེ་བླག་ཏུ།།
མྱུར་དུ་འབྲས་བུ་མཆིས་པར་མཛད་དུ་གསོལ།།
མ་རུངས་བདུད་སྡེ་འཇོམས་ལ་ཐོགས་མེད་ཅིང་།།
ཕས་ཀྱི་རྒོལ་བས་ཕམ་པར་མི་ནུས་ལ།།
འདོད་དོན་མ་གྲུབ་སྒྲུབ་ཅིང་གྲུབ་པ་རྣམས།།
ཆུད་མི་ཟ་བར་བྱེད་པའི་རིག་སྔགས་མཆོག །
ཚུལ་བཞིན་ཟློས་པས་སྡིག་དང་སྡུག་བསྔལ་སེལ།།
ཚེ་དང་བསོད་ནམས་ཐམས་ཅད་འཕེལ་ལ་སོགས།།
མདོར་ན་འདོད་པ་ཐམས་ཅད་སྦྱིན་ནོ་ཞེས།།
བཅོམ་ལྡན་ཁྱོད་ཀྱིས་ལེགས་པར་བཀའ་སྩལ་པ།།
དེ་ལ་ཡིད་ཆེས་རེ་བ་ཆེར་བཅས་ཏེ།།
ཁྱོད་སྐུ་དྲན་ནས་གཟུངས་སྔགས་ཟློས་པ་ལ།།
སྐལ་ངན་སྐྱེ་བོའི་འཕྲུས་ཀྱི་གནས་མེད་པར།།
ཕན་ཡོན་མངོན་དུ་འགྱུར་བར་མཛད་དུ་གསོལ།།

མ་ནི་ཉམ་ཐག་བུ་ལ་ལྷག་པར་བརྩེ།།
དེ་བཞིན་ཁྱོད་ཀྱི་ཐུགས་རྗེ་དམན་ལ་འཇུག །
བདུད་དཔུང་ཟིལ་གྱིས་གནོན་པའི་ཚུལ་ལ་མཁས།།
མི་མཐུན་འཇོམས་པའི་སྟོབས་ཀྱི་ཕུལ་དུ་བྱུང་།།

Lord of Power, therefore, look on us with compassion,
and bring our hopes expressed in prayer
to quick and easy fulfillment.
Yours is the supreme mantra,
unfettered in destruction of evil forces,
impervious to outside attack, fulfiller of aspiration,
ensuring aspiration fulfilled is never wasted.
Reciting it well puts an end to pain and evil,
augments virtue, lengthens life, and more.
In short, "No wish left ungranted"—
words well spoken by you, Great Conqueror.
With faith and hope in these words,
I bring you to mind to recite the mantra
and beg you, beyond the scorn of the less fortunate,
to make manifest all help and favor.

དེ་སླད་ཁྱོད་ལ་སྐྱབས་སུ་བསྟེན་པ་བདག །
ཉམ་ཐག་ང་རོ་འབོད་པ་འདི་གསོན་པ།།
ཐབས་མཁས་སྤྲུལ་པས་ཇི་ལྟར་རིགས་པ་ཡིས།།
གང་གང་མི་བསྲུན་འབྱུང་པོས་གཅེས་གྱུར་པ།།
དེ་དང་དེ་ཡི་སྐྱབས་ནི་ང་ཡིན་ཞེས།།
གསུང་དེ་ཐོས་ནས་མགོན་དུ་ཁྱོད་བསྟེན་ན།།
བདེན་པ་གསུང་བ་ཁྱོད་ཀྱིས་ཇི་ལྟར་དགོངས།།

ཁྱོད་ཀྱི་ཕྱག་བརྟན་ཐ་མ་ཞིག་གིས་ཀྱང་།།
མང་པོའི་བགེགས་ཚོགས་རྡུལ་དུ་བརླག་མཛད་ན།།
མཐུ་ཆེན་ཁྱོད་ལ་རྟག་ཏུ་བསྟེན་པ་བདག །
ཉམ་ཐག་གྱུར་པ་འདི་ནི་ཀྱེ་མ་མཚར།།
ཁྱོད་ནི་མཐུ་སྟོབས་བདག་པོར་རྒྱལ་བས་བསྔགས།།
ཚུལ་དེ་རིག་ནས་རེ་བ་འཆའ་བ་འདིའི།།
ཟད་བྱུང་དད་པའི་སྨྲུ་གུ་སྤེལ་སླད་དུ།།
ཉིད་ཀྱི་མཐུ་རྩལ་མངོན་སུམ་བསྟན་དུ་གསོལ།།

A mother lavishes greater love on a weakened child,
your compassion similarly finds the lowly.
Forever skilled in overcoming Mara's hordes,
of exceptional power in removing all hindrance,
I turn to you, therefore, for refuge
with cries of help in my despair.

"For those tormented by unrighteous forces,
I will, with skillful manifestation, be their refuge."
If, on hearing your words, I turn to you for my guide,
speaker of the truth, what will you think?

When even the humblest servant of your entourage
can pulverize whole hosts of hindering demons,
is it not astonishing that I, this pathetic soul,
can forever rely upon you,
hailed by Buddha as lord of all power?
I beg you, manifest your skills and powers
to nourish the extraordinary shoots of faith
found in these newborn hopes.

མཚམས་སྦྱིན་གཞོན་ནུས་ཡོངས་སུ་བསྐོར་བ་ཡི།།
རིན་ཆེན་མར་གད་རི་བོ་ཇི་བཞིན་དུ།།
ཡེ་ཤེས་མེ་ཆེན་འབར་བའི་གློང་དཀྱིལ་ན།།
ཁྲོ་འཛུམ་ཉམས་ཀྱིས་བརྗིད་ལ་ཕྱག་འཚལ་ལོ།།

སྦྱོས་བྲལ་ཆོས་སྐུའི་ངང་ལས་མ་གཡོས་པར།།
གྲངས་མེད་སྤྲུལ་པ་ཕྱོགས་བཅུར་སྤྲོས་པ་ཡིས།།
སྒྲུབ་བ་པོ་ལ་དངོས་གྲུབ་མཆོག་སྩོལ་བ།།
དཔག་ཡས་རྡོ་རྗེའི་རིགས་ལ་ཕྱག་འཚལ་ལོ།།

དེ་ལྟར་འཁོར་དང་བཅས་པའི་བཅོམ་ལྡན་གྱིས།།
བགེགས་ཚོགས་རྣམས་ཀྱི་ཉེར་འཚེ་དེ་ཡི་རྒྱུ།།
ལས་ཀྱི་སྒྲིབ་པ་བག་ཆགས་བཅས་པ་ཀུན།།
མྱུར་དུ་བྱང་ཞིང་དག་པར་མཛད་དུ་གསོལ།།
ཚེ་དང་ཚུལ་ཁྲིམས་ཏིང་འཛིན་ཤེས་རབ་སོགས།།
དཀར་ཕྱོགས་ཡར་ངོའི་ཟླ་བཞིན་རྒྱས་པ་དང་།།
སྙིང་རྗེའི་དབང་དུ་བྱས་ནས་ཕན་སྐྱེད་པ།།
དེ་དག་དགུག་པའི་ལས་ཀྱིས་བསྡུ་བར་མཛོད།།
རེ་ཞིག་ངེས་པའི་ལས་ཀྱིས་མི་འདུལ་བའི།།

I prostrate to you, an emerald mountain
encircled by young sunrise clouds,
made brilliant by a wrathful smile
set amid great flames of wisdom.

Never stirring from fabrication-free dharmakaya,
you fabricate myriad manifestation everywhere,
granting practitioners the greatest of powers;
I prostrate to you of the vajra family.

By such manifestation, Great Conqueror and entourage,
free us swiftly from harms of hindering demons
and their causes, karma-created blindness and its imprints.
Long life, morality, meditative powers, wisdom,
every virtue blossoming like the waxing moon,
helping others under the sway of compassion;
gather them in with your summoning powers.

མ་རུངས་སྐྱེ་བོ་དེ་ཡང་བསད་བསྐྱོད་དང་།།
རྨོངས་རེངས་གཞན་པ་ལ་སོགས་ཐབས་མཁས་ཀྱི།།
དྲག་པོའི་འཕྲིན་ལས་རྣམས་ཀྱིས་གཞོམ་པར་མཛོད།།

མདོར་ན་གསང་བའི་བདག་པོ་མགོན་ཁྱོད་ཀྱིས།།
རྗེས་སུ་བཟུང་ནས་བསྟན་པ་སྤེལ་བ་དང་།།
འགྲོ་བའི་དོན་ལ་མཐུ་དང་ལྡན་པ་དང་།།
བསྒྲུབ་པའི་བྱ་བ་ཕ་མཐར་ཕྱིན་པར་ཤོག །

རྒྱལ་བའི་བསྟན་པ་སྤྱི་དང་ཁྱད་པར་དུ།།
རིག་སྔགས་འཆང་བའི་བསྟན་པ་རྒྱས་མཛད་པ།།
བདག་གིས་ཅུང་ཟད་བསྟོད་པས་བསོད་ནམས་ནི།།
གང་ཞིག་སྐྱེད་དེས་འགྲོ་བ་ཁྱོད་འདྲར་ཤོག །
ཁྱོད་ཀྱི་གོ་འཕང་སྒྲོལ་བའི་ལམ་གྱིས་གཙོ།།
བློ་མཆོག་རྣམས་ལ་རྨད་བྱུང་དགའ་སྐྱེད་པ།།
ཐུབ་པའི་ལེགས་བཤད་སྙིང་པོ་གསང་བའི་ལམ།།
ཇི་བཞིན་རྟོགས་ནས་ཚུལ་བཞིན་སྒྲུབ་པར་ཤོག །།

By disposing of evil beings untamed by action
and by thwarting headstrong fools,
at times be destructive with wrathful but skillful means.

To conclude, Great Protector, Keeper of the Secret Mantra,
may I, sustained and nourished by you,
spread and augment the teachings of Buddha,
find power to work for the welfare of others
and journey to the perfection of practice.

May the teachings of the conquering Buddha grow,
in particular doctrines held by keepers of mantra,
and from the merit gained by this meager praise,
may all living beings become like you.

That great highway leading to your exalted state,
source of extraordinary joy to the highest minds,
the secret path, essence of Buddha's glorious teachings,
as I have understood it, so may I practice it.

ལྷག་པའི་ལྷ་མི་གཡོ་མགོན་པོ་ལ་བསྟོད་པ།།

༄༅།། །།སྭསྟི། བདག་གིས་ཚེ་རབས་ཀུན་ཏུ་བསྟེན་པ།།
ལྷག་པའི་ལྷ་མཆོག་མི་གཡོ་མགོན་པོ།།
ཁྱོད་ཀྱིས་མཁྱེན་པར་མཛོད་དུ་གསོལ་གྱིས།།
དྲི་མེད་སྨོན་ལམ་བདག་གིས་གདབ་བོ།།

བདག་ནི་གང་དུ་སྐྱེས་པར་གྱུར་ཀྱང་།།
ལྷ་མཆོག་ཁྱོད་ཀྱི་བསྒོམ་བཟླས་དྲི་མེད།།
སྒོ་གསུམ་གུས་པས་ཉམས་སུ་ལེན་ལ།།
ནམ་ཡང་གཡེལ་བ་མེད་པར་གྱུར་ཅིག །

ལྷག་པའི་ལྷ་ཁྱོད་བསྒྲུབས་པའི་མཐུ་ཡིས།།
མ་ནོར་ལམ་སྟོན་བཤེས་གཉེན་བཟང་པོས།།
བརྩེ་བའི་ཐུགས་ཀྱིས་རྗེས་སུ་བཟུང་སྟེ།།
ཟབ་མོའི་ལམ་རྣམས་སྟོན་པར་གྱུར་ཅིག །

གང་ཚེ་ཤིན་ཏུ་ཟབ་པའི་ཉེ་ལམ།། བདག་གིས་གུས་པས་སྒྲུབ་པ་དེ་ཚེ།།
ཁྲོ་བོའི་རྒྱལ་པོ་ཁྱོད་ཀྱི་མཐུ་ཡིས།། འགལ་བའི་རྐྱེན་རྣམས་ཞི་བར་གྱུར་ཅིག །

In Praise of the Extraordinary Deity Achala

In all my lives I place my trust in you,
extraordinary deity, protector Achala,
hear this pure prayer.

Greatest of deities, wherever I am reborn, may I never stray
from a practice sincere in word, deed, and thought,
of your mantra and meditation.

Extraordinary deity, by the power of meditation upon you,
I pray to be fostered with minds of love
by unerring spiritual masters,
and be taught the profound paths.

When I practice in sincerity the deep and swift path,
I pray, Lord of the Wrathful, that you subdue
all opposing circumstance.

བདག་ནི་བདག་འཛིན་ཞགས་པ་དམ་པོས།།
འཁོར་བའི་བཙོན་རྭར་བསྡམས་པ་དེ་ཚེ།།
བུ་གཅིག་པ་ལ་མ་ཡིས་བརྩེ་བཞིན།།
སྡུག་བསྔལ་མཚོ་ལས་སྒྲོལ་བར་གྱུར་ཅིག །

ལས་ངན་རླུང་གི་ཤུགས་ཀྱིས་བདས་ཏེ།།
ངན་འགྲོའི་གཡང་ལ་ལྷུང་བ་དེ་ཚེ།།
ཐུགས་རྗེའི་ཕྱག་ནི་ལེགས་པར་བརྐྱངས་ནས།།
ངན་འགྲོའི་འཇིགས་ལས་སྐྱོབ་པར་གྱུར་ཅིག །

མདོར་ན་འཕྲལ་དུ་ནད་གདོན་བར་ཆད།།
མ་ལུས་ཞི་ཞིང་མཐར་ཐུག་རྒྱལ་བའི།།
སྐུ་བཞིའི་འབྲས་བུ་དཀའ་བ་མེད་པར།།
མྱུར་དུ་བདག་གིས་ཐོབ་པར་གྱུར་ཅིག །

བཅོམ་ལྡན་མི་གཡོ་མགོན་པོའི་སྒྲོ་ནས།།
སྨོན་ལམ་འདེབས་ཚུལ་ཚིགས་བཅད་བདུན་འདི།།
མྱུར་བ་མྱུར་བར་རྩོམས་ཞེས་བསྐུལ་ཚེ།།
དེ་ལྟ་དེ་ལྟར་བདག་གིས་སྦྲར་རོ།།

Whenever I lie in samsara's prison,
trussed by tight ropes of grasping to self,
I pray that you, like a loving mother to her only child,
pluck me from this ocean of pain.

When carried by cyclones of past unwholesome action,
I am blown over the precipice of suffering realms,
I pray you reach with the hand of compassion
to pull me from these anguished worlds.

To conclude, I pray that along the path
hindrances of sickness and spirits be subjugated,
to reach finally, without hardship, without delay,
my destination of the fourfold buddha form.

This particular seven-versed prayer
to the destroyer and protector Achala,
I was urged to write in haste
and have done so.

དབྱངས་ཅན་ཤེས་རབ་གསལ་བྱེད་མའི་བསྟོད་པ།

༄༅ ། ། ཨོཾ་བདེ་ལེགས་སུ་གྱུར་ཅིག །

ལྷག་བསམ་རྣམ་དག་བྱ་ལམ་ཡངས་པའི་གཞིར།།
སྤེབ་ལེགས་ཚིག་གི་རྒྱུ་སྐར་འཕྲེང་བཀོད་ནས།།
འོད་དཀར་ཅན་ཁྱོད་བདག་གིས་མཛེས་པར་བྱ།།
བདག་བློའི་ཀུ་མུད་ཁྱོད་ཀྱིས་རྒྱས་པར་མཛོད།།

དྲི་མེད་འོད་སྟོང་ལྡན་བཞིན་གསལ་བའི་ཐུགས།།
སྐྱོན་བྲལ་ཚངས་པའི་དབྱངས་ལྟར་སྙན་པའི་གསུང་།།
ལྷུན་སྡུག་གངས་རིའི་རྩེ་འདྲའི་སྐུ་མངའ་བ།།
ལྷག་པའི་ལྷ་མོ་ཁྱོད་ལ་ཕྱག་འཚལ་ལོ།།

མ་རིག་མཚན་མོའི་གྲོགས་ཀྱིས་འགྲོ་རྣམས་ཀྱི།།
བློ་གྲོས་པད་ཚལ་ཟུམ་པར་བྱས་པའི་ཚེ།།
མི་ཤེས་ཟླ་འོད་བསྐྱེད་ཕྱིར་ཁྱོད་ཀྱི་སྐུ།།
སྟོན་མེད་འོད་སྟོང་ལྡན་འདི་བསྟན་ནམ་སྙམ།།

In Praise of Vajra Sarasvati, Light of Wisdom

May there be happiness!

In the vast openness of the purest of skies
I write these stars of well-chosen words.
Goddess of the moon, I beautify you.
Open the night flowers of my mind.

Your mind bright as a million beams of pure light,
speech sweet as the unblemished melody of Brahma,
body as beautiful as snowy mountain peaks.
Extraordinary goddess, I bow before you.

When the dark night of ignorance has closed
the lotus petals of wisdom of living beings,
I think on your form as an unparalleled brilliance
that transforms such unknowing into the light of the moon.

འབུམ་ཕྲག་གློག་འཕྲེང་འཁྲུས་འདྲའི་སྤྲིན་ཚ་དམར།།
གངས་རི་ཚར་དུ་དངར་ལྷའི་མཆེ་བ་གཙིགས།།
གནམ་ལྕགས་འབར་བ་ལྷ་བུའི་འོད་འཕྲོ་བ།།
དཔའ་མོ་ཁྲོད་ཀྱིས་སྲིད་གསུམ་གཡོ་བར་མཛད།།

རྣམ་པ་དུ་མར་སྣང་བའི་ཀུན་རྫོབ་དང་།།
རང་བཞིན་ཅི་ཡང་མི་དམིགས་དོན་དམ་སྟེ།།
ཆོས་ཀུན་བདེན་པ་གཉིས་སུ་འདོམས་པའི་ཕྱིར།།
མཛེས་པའི་སྤྱན་གཉིས་ལྡན་ལ་ཕྱག་འཚལ་ལོ།།

བདག་ལྷའི་སྡིག་པ་སྡུག་པོས་ཀུན་ནས་བསྐོར།།
མ་རིག་ཐིབས་པོས་བར་མཚམས་མེད་པར་དཀྲིགས།།
འཁོར་བའི་ཁང་བཟང་བྲིས་པ་འབྲིད་པའི་གནས།།
ཀུན་ནས་འཇིག་ཕྱིར་གཡས་ན་རྡོ་རྗེ་བསྣམས།།

སྲིད་པའི་བཙོན་རྭར་འགྲོ་འདི་ཐར་མེད་པའི།།
མངོན་ཞེན་ལྕགས་སྒྲོག་དམ་པོས་འཆིང་བྱེད་པ།།
ཉོན་མོངས་བདུད་ཀྱི་མགོ་བོ་སྤྱོན་མེད་པའི།།
ཡེ་ཤེས་མཚོན་གྱིས་བཅད་ནས་གཡོན་ན་འཛིན།།

Red eyes blaze like a million lightning darts,
fangs glisten like a range of snowy peaks,
light spills out like thunderbolts flaming.
Warrior goddess, you move the three worlds.

I bow to you, two beautiful eyes revealing
all phenomena to be of two truths,
the conventional appearing in a myriad of forms,
the final of no self-nature anywhere.

Enclosed by thick walls of notions of self,
shrouded always by the darkest ignorance,
this beguiling mansion of samsara,
destroyed by the vajra in your right hand.

The head of the demon delusion,
securing those in the prison of existence
with the unbreakable chains of grasping
hanging from your left hand,
severed by the sword of wisdom.

རྒྱལ་དཀའ་སྲིད་པའི་མཚོ་ལས་སྒྲོལ་བའི་གྲུ།།
བདེ་ཆེན་ཐར་པའི་ཐང་ལ་བགྲོད་པའི་ཐབས།།
ཐབས་ཤེས་རང་བཞིན་བརྒྱད་བསྐུམ་ཞབས་གཉིས་ཀྱིས།།
པད་ཉིའི་སྟེང་དུ་གདུག་པའི་རོ་ལ་བརྫིས།།

ཉེས་བྲལ་ཁྱོད་སྐུ་ཀུན་ནས་མཛེས་པ་ནི།།
ཆ་ཤས་ཡོངས་སུ་རྫོགས་པའི་ཟླ་རྒྱས་སམ།།
ཉི་ཤར་འོད་ཀྱིས་མཛེས་པའི་གངས་རི་བཞིན།།
རིན་ཆེན་དུ་མའི་འོད་ཀྱིས་ལྷམ་མེ་བ།།

རིན་ཆེན་རུས་པའི་རྒྱན་གྱིས་མཛེས་པ་ཁྱོད།།
མཁའ་ལ་ཆུ་འཛིན་ཕྲེང་བ་འཁྲིགས་པའམ།།
རྣམ་པ་དུ་མས་བཀྲ་བའི་འཇའ་ཚོན་ལྟར།།
མ་འདྲེས་གསལ་བར་སྣང་ཡང་ངོས་གཟུང་བྲལ།།

དཔག་མེད་ཡོན་ཏན་དུ་མའི་དཔལ་གྱིས་མཐོ།།
ལྟ་བས་མི་ངོམས་བརྗིད་པ་ཁྱོད་ཀྱི་སྐུ།།
མཐོང་བར་གྱུར་ཚེ་ལྷུན་པོ་ངོ་ཚ་ནས།།
གཏིང་ཡངས་རྒྱ་མཚོའི་ནང་དུ་ཞུགས་པ་འདྲ།།

Of the nature of wisdom and method,
the boats to cross the perilous sea of existence,
path to the plains of bliss in freedom,
your legs, one stretched, the other bent,
crush a hideous corpse upon sun and lotus disc.

Faultless goddess, body as supremely beautiful
as the perfectly complete full moon,
as exquisite snow mountains in the sun,
resplendent in the light of your jewels.

Adorned by precious bone ornaments,
you are as garlands of clouds in the sky,
as a rainbow of many and varied colors,
evidently manifest, yet elusive.

To gaze insatiably upon your lustrous form,
exalted by glorious and unbelievable qualities,
is to see Mount Meru, and by comparison,
sink shamefully into the deepest ocean.

འགྲོ་བའི་ཉེས་ཚོགས་ལྷན་ལྷིན་འཁྲུད་པའི་ཆུ།།
ཡན་ལག་དྲུག་ཅུའི་དཔལ་མངའ་ཁྱོད་ཀྱི་གསུང་།།
འདི་ཐོས་གྱུར་ཚེ་གཏྣ་ཡིད་ཞུམ་ནས།།
ངལ་བ་མེད་པར་རྒྱ་མཚོར་སྙེགས་སམ་སྙམ།།

ཇི་སྙེད་ཤེས་བྱའི་གནས་རྣམས་མ་ལུས་པ།།
ཇི་བཞིན་མ་འདྲེས་གསལ་བ་ཁྱོད་ཐུགས་ལ།།
ཇི་ཙམ་འབད་ཀྱང་འགྲན་པར་མ་བཟོད་ནས།།
ཏ་ལྡང་ཅན་དེ་ཕྱོགས་རྣམས་ཀུན་ཏུ་བྲོས།།

བདག་གི་ལྷག་པའི་ལྷ་མོ་རྗེ་བཙུན་མ།།
ཁྱོད་ཀྱི་ཡོན་ཏན་མ་ལུས་སུས་བརྗོད་ནུས།།
དེ་ལྟ་ན་ཡང་ཡོན་ཏན་རྒྱ་མཚོ་ལས།།
ཆུ་ཐིགས་ཙམ་ཞིག་བླངས་ཏེ་ཁྱོད་ལ་བསྟོད།།

དེ་ལྟར་ལྷག་པའི་ལྷ་མོ་ཁྱོད་བསྟོད་པས།།
དོན་མཐོང་བློ་གྲོས་མིག་དང་བྲལ་བའི་མཐུས།།
སྲིད་པའི་བཙོན་རྭར་ལྷུང་བའི་མགོན་མེད་བདག །
ཐར་པའི་གྲོང་ཁྱེར་མཆོག་ཏུ་བཀྲི་བར་མཛོད།།

Your voice, adorned with sixty illustrious qualities,
is water to wash away all faults.
When heard, do not the waters of the Ganges
shrink and hasten to the sea?

All existence is clearly illuminated by your mind.
Indra, unable to challenge it, try as he might,
turned and fled through the heavens.

My extraordinary goddess, exalted lady,
who could describe your qualities in full?
From your ocean of excellence, nevertheless,
I take a drop and offer this eulogy to you.

By such praise, extraordinary goddess,
lead me to the great city of liberation,
away from the prison of existence
where I lie protectorless,
jailed by a blindness unseeing of reality.

ལྟ་ངན་དབང་གིས་ཡང་དག་ལམ་སྟོར་བས།།
འཁོར་བའི་གཙོང་རོང་གཏིང་ཟབ་དག་ཏུ་ལྟུང་།།
ཐར་པའི་གནས་འདིར་འཁོད་པའི་ལུས་ཅན་རྣམས།།
སྟོབས་ལྡན་ཁྱོད་ཀྱིས་བརྩེ་བས་བསྒྲལ་དུ་གསོལ།།

ལས་ཉོན་མི་མཐུན་རླུང་གིས་དྲག་ཏུ་བདས།།
སྡུག་བསྔལ་རྩ་བ་སྐྱེ་བའི་ཆུ་སྲིན་ཁར།།
རང་དབང་མེད་པར་འཕེན་པའི་མ་རིག་པ།།
བརྩེ་ལྡན་ཁྱོད་ཀྱིས་རྩད་ནས་བཅད་དུ་གསོལ།།

དམིགས་མེད་ཐུགས་རྗེའི་ཆུ་གཏེར་ཆེན་པོས་བརླན།།
འགྲོ་བའི་བདེ་ལེགས་མ་ལུས་འབྱུང་བའི་གཞི།།
བློ་ཡི་རྒུད་པ་སེལ་བའི་ཡིད་བཞིན་ནོར།།
ཀུན་ལ་བུ་སྡུག་ལྟར་དགོངས་མ་ཁྱོད་ཀྱིས།།
དམ་པའི་འབྱོར་བ་ཤེས་རབ་ནོར་གྱིས་དབུལ།།
མཁས་པའི་མདུན་སར་འགྲོད་པའི་བདེ་བས་ཕོངས།།
མ་རིག་སྦུབས་སུ་ཚུད་པའི་ཉམ་ཐག་ལ།།
རབ་འབྱམས་ཡེ་ཤེས་སྣང་བ་བསྐྱེད་དུ་གསོལ།།

With your compassion, powerful goddess,
help those misled by wrong views,
cast into the deep pit of samsara.

Goddess of compassion, wipe out the ignorance
that violently drives the ill winds of karma and delusion,
to throw us helplessly into the gaping jaws
of the sea monster of birth, root of suffering.

Moistened by great waters of objectless compassion,
you are a source of every happiness and joy,
a wish-fulfilling jewel dispelling poverty of the mind,
gazing upon others as a mother upon her only child.
Manifest now a million displays of wisdom
for those bereft of the sacred possession of the jewel of
knowledge,
lacking the joy of sitting in the presence of the wise,
languishing in dark confines of ignorance.

ཟུག་རྔུ་ཀུན་སེལ་སྒྲོན་མེད་སྨན་པ་ཁྱོད།།
མ་རིག་ཡིང་ཏོག་སྡུག་པོས་འགྲོ་རྣམས་ཀྱི།།
བློ་གྲོས་མིག་བསྒྲིབས་ཡལ་བར་འདོར་གྱུར་ན།།
ཁྱོད་ཐུགས་ཀུན་ལ་བརྩེ་བའང་མིང་དུ་ཟད།།

འོན་ཏེ་གཞན་བློའི་རབ་རིབ་སེལ་བའི་ཐབས།།
མི་ཤེས་ཤེས་ཀྱང་སེལ་བར་མི་ནུས་ན།།
ད་ནི་ཁྱོད་ཀྱིས་མ་ལུས་མཁྱེན་པ་དང་།།
འཕྲིན་ལས་ནུས་པའི་རྩལ་དེའང་བདག་གིས་འཁུམས།།

གང་ཚེ་བུ་སྡུག་ཉམ་ངའི་ལམ་འགྲོ་བ།།
བརྩེ་བའི་མ་ཡིས་བཟློག་པར་མི་བྱེད་ན།།
དེ་ཚེ་དེ་ལ་དེ་བས་བརྩེ་བའི་མགོན།།
གཞན་པ་གང་གིས་དེ་ལ་སྐྱོབ་པར་བྱེད།།

བློ་ལྡན་གང་གིས་ཁྱོད་སྐུ་དྲན་བྱེད་ཅིང་།།
གདུང་བའི་ཤུགས་ཀྱི་རྩལ་འདིས་བསྐྱོད་བྱེད་པ།།
དེ་ཡི་མི་ཤེས་མུན་པ་སྐད་ཅིག་ལ།།
ཁྱོད་ཀྱི་ཐུགས་རྗེའི་ཤུགས་ཀྱིས་མཐར་བྱེད་ཤོག །

Were you, peerless physician curing all pain,
to ignore those whose eyes of wisdom
are covered by thick cataracts of ignorance,
you would be compassionate to all in name only.

But if you did not know the ways
to dispel confusion in the minds of others,
or you knew but you could not do,
then now I would shrink from your omniscience
and from the powers of your ability.

If a child strays down a dangerous path
and his loving mother does nothing,
what guardian more loving than her
could protect that child?

May those with intelligence bring your form to mind
and praise you with emotion as strong as this,
and may their darkness of unknowing
be brought instantly to an end
by the power of your compassion.

རྣམ་པར་རྒྱལ་མའི་བསྟོད་པ་ས་གསུམ་རེ་སྐོང་མ།

༄༅། །ས་གསུམ་འགྲོ་བའི་རེ་སྐོང་དངོས་གྲུབ་གཏེར།།
ལེགས་ཚཤད་འོད་སྟོང་འཕྲོད་པའི་ཉིན་མོར་བྱེད།།
ཡོན་ཏན་ཆ་ཤས་ཀུན་རྫོགས་འོད་དཀར་ཅན།།
དཔལ་ལྡན་ཟླ་མ་ལུས་ཅན་གཙུག་ན་རྒྱལ།།

གང་ལ་བརྟེན་ན་བློ་གྲོས་མཆོག་སྟེར་ཞིང་།།
འཆི་བདག་བེ་ཅོན་རི་མོའི་དགྲུག་པ་ལྟར།།
གང་གིས་མཛད་པའི་ལྷ་མོ་འགྲོ་བའི་སྐྱབས།།
གཙུག་ཏོར་རྣམ་རྒྱལ་ཅུང་ཟད་བསྟོད་པར་བགྱི།།

མིག་བྲལ་སྐྱེ་བོས་སྣ་ཚོགས་གཟུགས་ལ་བཞིན།།
ཁྱོད་ཀྱི་ངང་ཚུལ་བདག་ལ་རིང་དུ་བསྐལ།།
འོན་ཀྱང་དམ་ཆོས་ཡང་དག་སྟུད་པའི་ཕྱུག །
བདེ་བ་ཅན་གྱི་ཁང་བཟང་མཆོག་ཉིད་ན།།
འཇིག་རྟེན་རྣམ་འདྲེན་ཚེ་དཔག་མེད་མགོན་གྱིས།།
ཁྱོད་ལ་རྒྱ་ཆེར་བསྔགས་པ་ཐོས་པ་ལས།།

In Praise of Goddess Namgyalma

Fulfilling hopes of living beings, a veritable treasury of powers,
sun of a million rays of well-spoken words,
its brilliant white light of every virtue perfected,
glorious lama, victorious upon the heads of sentient beings.

To rely upon her is to gain the highest acumen,
is to reduce Yama's club to a mere picture,
goddess, guardian of living creatures,
you of Buddha's crown, I offer this meager praise.

A sightless man groping at forms,
I am at a loss to describe you,
yet from that hermitage of *Sacred Dharma Perfectly Compiled*,
in the paradise of Sukhavati,
the teacher Amitayus, guardian of the world,
has lavished praise upon you, and from its study,

འཕགས་མའི་ཞབས་ཟུང་རིང་ནས་བསྟེན་པ་བདག །
འདི་སྐད་གླེང་བའི་གོ་སྐབས་ཙུང་ཟད་ལྷེད།།

ཡིད་འཕྲོག་འོད་ཟེར་སྟོང་གི་དྲ་བ་ཅན།།
ཕུལ་བྱུང་ཆུ་ཞེང་གབ་པ་ཁྲོད་ཀྱི་སྐུ།།
འོ་མའི་ཆུ་གཏེར་དབུས་ན་གནས་རི་བཞིན།།
པད་ཟླའི་སྟེང་ན་མཛེས་ལ་ཕྱག་འཚལ་ལོ།།

ཆུ་ཤེལ་བཙོ་མའི་གསེར་དང་ཨིནྡྲ་ནཱི་ལ།།
ཡོངས་སུ་དག་པའི་འོད་ལྟར་རབ་གསལ་བའི།།
དབུས་དང་གཡས་གཡོན་ཞལ་བཟང་རྒྱས་པ་ནི།།
སྒེག་དང་ཞི་དང་ཁྲོ་ལ་ཕྱག་འཚལ་ལོ།།

གདུགས་མཛེས་ཏོག་ལ་ཨིནྡྲ་ནཱི་ལ་བཞིན།།
རབ་རྒྱས་དབུ་ལ་རལ་པའི་ཐོར་ཅོག་ཅན།།
དྲི་བྲལ་མཁའ་ལ་འཁྲིག་པའི་འཇའ་ཚོན་ལྟར།།
མཐོན་མཐིང་སྤྱན་མཆོག་སྨིན་མ་རིང་པོས་མཛེས།།

bowing my head to your feet from afar,
I have found opportunity, albeit brief, to say these words.

Radiant in its captivating latticework of light,
I prostrate to your perfectly symmetrical form,
a snow mountain amid an ocean of milk,
beautifully seated upon a lotus-moon circle.

I prostrate to you of three full and noble faces,
aglow with the luminosity of crystal, gold, and sapphire,
the elegant middle, the peaceful right, the wrathful left.

Like the sapphire that crowns the canopy,
your plaited hair crowns your broad head.
Like rainbows shimmering in clear sky,
long eyebrows adorn your dark eyes.

དབྱིབས་ལེགས་ཤངས་ཀྱི་རྒྱུད་ནི་ཡིད་དུ་འོང་།།
མཆུ་སྒྲོས་མཛེས་པའི་ཞལ་ནི་ལྷ་ན་སྡུག །
མཉེན་ལེགས་སྙན་གྱི་བུག་པར་རིན་ཆེན་འཕྱང་།།
རྨད་བྱུང་ཉམས་ཀྱིས་ཡིད་འཛིན་ཁྱོད་ལ་འདུད།།

སྐར་འཕྲེང་བཀྲ་བའི་མདངས་ལྟར་རབ་གསལ་བའི།།
དོ་ཤལ་མཆོག་གིས་མགྲིན་པར་རབ་ཏུ་འབྲུད།།
འོ་མའི་རྒྱུན་འཛིན་ནུ་འབུར་ཟུང་གཅིག་གིས།།
རབ་ཡངས་བྲང་ལ་ངང་པས་པད་མཚོར་བཞིན།།

རིན་ཆེན་རྒྱན་གྱིས་མཛེས་པའི་འཇམ་མཉེན་ཕྱག །
པད་མའི་རྩ་བ་ལྟར་དཀར་ཟུང་བཞི་ཡི།།
དང་པོ་རྡོ་རྗེ་སྡིགས་མཛུབ་ཞགས་པ་སྣེ།།
གཉིས་པ་འོད་དཔག་མེད་དང་མི་འཇིགས་སྦྱིན།།
གསུམ་པས་མདའ་གཞུ་བཞི་པའི་ཕྱག་ཟུང་གིས།།
མཆོད་སྦྱིན་བུམ་པ་བཟུང་ནས་འགྲོ་བ་ལ།།
འཆི་མེད་ཚེ་ཡི་དཔལ་སྟེར་བཅོམ་ལྡན་མ།།
ཚེ་དཔག་མེད་པ་ཁྱོད་ལ་ཕྱག་འཚལ་ལོ།།

Attractive lines of a well-formed nose,
exquisite lips on a graceful mouth,
soft, silky ears hung with precious stones,
I prostrate before you of captivating elegance.

Like sparkling colors of a beautiful string of stars,
the finest necklace embraces your body.
The nipples of your milk-bearing breasts
upon a broad chest like swans on a lotus lake.

Your soft hands in four pairs,
adorned by precious jewels, white as lotus roots,
the first holding crossed vajra and lasso in threatening
gesture,
the second Amitabha's statue and mudra of protection,
the third a bow and arrow, fourth the mudra of offering
and the ambrosia vase granting power over life and death.
Conquering warrior, longevity goddess, I prostrate to you.

ཡིད་བཞིན་མཚོ་ཡི་ངོགས་ཀྱི་པད་སྡོང་བཞིན།།
དྲང་ཞིང་ལྡེམ་པའི་སྙེད་སྙབས་གསལ་བ་ཅན།།
འཇའ་ཚོན་གུར་ཕུབ་ཤེལ་གྱི་མཆོད་སྡོང་ལྟར།།
དྲི་མེད་མཛེས་སྐུ་བཀྲ་བའི་གོས་ཀྱིས་སྤྲུད།།

མི་ཕྱེད་སྐྱིལ་ཀྲུང་མཆོག་གིས་ལེགས་གནས་ཤིང་།།
བརྒྱད་གཉིས་ལང་ཚོའི་དཔལ་འཛིན་རྒྱལ་བའི་ཡུམ།།
མི་འདྲའི་རྣམ་འཕྲུལ་དུ་མས་རྣམ་རོལ་བ།།
འགྲོ་བའི་ཡིད་བཞིན་འཇུག་ལ་ཕྱག་འཚལ་ལོ།།

ཛ་ཡབ་དཀར་པོ་བསྣུམས་པའི་རྒྱལ་བའི་སྲས།།
ཕྱག་ན་པད་མ་རྡོ་རྗེ་འཛིན་པ་གཉིས།།
གཡས་གཡོན་གནས་ནས་ཁྱོད་སྐུར་མདོན་ཕྱོགས་ཏེ།།
རྟག་ཏུ་བསྒྲིམས་ཏེ་བལྟས་ཀྱང་ངོམས་པ་མེད།།

རལ་གྲི་ལྕུགས་ཀྱུ་དབྱུག་པ་རྡོ་རྗེ་གཡས།།
གཡོན་པ་མ་རུངས་འདུལ་བའི་སྡིགས་མཛུབ་ཅན།།
མི་གཡོ་འདོད་རྒྱལ་དབྱུག་སྔོན་སྟོབས་པོ་ཆེ།།
ཁྱོད་ཀྱི་ཕྱོགས་བཞིར་གནས་ནས་བགེགས་དཔུང་འཇོམས།།

Like lotus stems on the wish-granting ocean shore,
your radiant waist grows straight yet curved.
Like a crystal shrine encased in a rainbow's tent,
your beautiful perfect body clothed in elegant silk.

Agreeably seated in the adamantine lotus pose,
the mother of buddhas as a glorious sixteen-year-old,
I prostrate to you who manifests in multitudinous forms
to realize hopes and wishes of living beings.

Two bodhisattvas holding white fans,
Avalokiteshvara, lotus in hand, Vajrapani, vajra clasped,
are absorbed in insatiable gaze upon your form.

On your four sides destroying all hindrance,
sword, hook, club, vajra, in their right hands,
their left with threatening finger to tame the wicked,
Achala, Takiraja, Niladanda, Mahabala in wrathful form.

འཆི་མེད་བདུད་རྩིའི་ཆར་གྱི་རྒྱུན་འབེབས་པའི།།
གཙང་མའི་གནས་ཀྱི་ལྷ་ཡི་བུ་གཉིས་ནི།།
སྟེང་གི་ཕྱོགས་ནས་རིན་ཆེན་བུམ་པ་ཡིས།།
དག་པའི་ཆུ་རྒྱུན་འབེབས་ལ་མངོན་པར་བརྩོན།།

མ་ལུས་ཤེས་བྱ་མཐའ་དག་མངོན་དུ་གྱུར།།
སྨུ་མེད་འགྲོ་ལ་རྒྱུན་ཆད་མེད་པར་བརྩེ།།
མེ་མཚོན་དུག་སོགས་འཇིགས་པ་ཀུན་ལས་སྐྱོབས།།
མི་དང་ལྷ་ཡི་རྣམ་འདྲེན་ཁྱོད་ལ་འདུད།།

ཤེས་བྱ་ཀུན་ལ་རྨོངས་པའི་དྲི་བ་བཅད།།
སེམས་ཅན་ཀུན་ལ་སྙོམས་པའི་ཐུགས་དང་ལྡན།།
གནས་སྐབས་ཀུན་ཏུ་ཕན་དང་བདེ་སྟེར་བ།།
འཇིག་རྟེན་ཀུན་གྱི་སྐྱབས་ལ་ཕྱག་འཚལ་ལོ།།

དེ་ལྟར་འགྲོ་བའི་སྐྱབས་གྱུར་རྗེ་བཙུན་མ།།
བསྒོམ་བཟླས་མཆོད་བསྟོད་ལས་བྱུང་དགེ་བ་དེས།།
འཕགས་མའི་གོ་འཕང་མཆོག་དེ་མྱུར་ཐོབ་ནས།།
ཉམ་ཆུང་ལུས་ཅན་ཀུན་གྱི་མགོན་བགྱིད་ཤོག །

Above, two young gods from their pure celestial realm
earnestly pour pure waters from jeweled vases,
falling as the ambrosia rain of immortality.

All existence manifest before you,
love unending for beings beyond number,
giving shelter from fire, poisons, and weapons,
leader of men and gods, I bow before you.

Entanglements of ignorance toward all existence cut away,
mind spread equally to every living being,
bringer of joy and succor at all times, all places,
guardian of all worlds, I prostrate to you.

By virtue of meditation, offering, recitation, and praise
upon this noble lady, protector of living beings,
may I soon attain to your exalted state
to become savior of every needy creature.

མི་བསྲུན་ཡིད་ཀྱི་བྲན་དུ་གྱུར་པའི་མཐུས།།
མི་འདོད་འབྲས་བུ་སྐྱེར་བའི་གནག་པའི་ལས།།
མི་ཤེས་དབང་གིས་བགྱིས་པ་གང་ཡིན་པ།།
མ་ལུས་བདེ་བླག་ཉིད་དུ་ཞི་གྱུར་ཅིག །

མཆོག་གི་ཚེ་དང་ལྷབས་ཆེན་རྣམ་དཔྱོད་དང་།།
དད་དང་སྙིང་རྗེ་བརྩོན་འགྲུས་ཏིང་འཛིན་སོགས།།
ལུས་དང་རྟོགས་པའི་ཡོན་ཏན་ཇི་སྙེད་པ།།
མཐའ་དག་གོང་ནས་གོང་དུ་རྒྱས་པར་ཤོག །

བྱང་ཆུབ་སྒྲུབ་པའི་རྗེས་སུ་རབ་གཞོལ་བ།།
བདེ་གཤེགས་དགྱེས་པའི་རབ་འབྱམས་དབང་གི་ལས།།
དེ་དག་ཐམས་ཅད་ཇི་ལྟར་སྨོན་པ་བཞིན།།
འདོད་པ་ཙམ་གྱིས་རྗེས་སུ་བྱེད་པར་ཤོག །

ཐོས་བསམ་སྒོམ་པས་བདག་རྒྱུད་འདུལ་བའི་ཚེ།།
ཡང་དག་ལམ་གྱི་གེགས་ལ་མངོན་བརྩོན་པ།།
ནག་པོའི་རྩ་ལག་རྣམས་ཀྱི་སྟོབས་དང་དཔུང་།།
མངོན་སྤྱོད་ལས་ཀྱིས་ཐམས་ཅད་ཚར་གཅོད་ཤོག །

May I dissolve with ease pernicious deeds
born from slavery to an intractable mind,
destined to lead to unwished-for results,
all performed under the sway of ignorance.

A full life, great ability, intelligence, faith,
compassion, determination, meditative concentration;
may all such qualities of body and mind
flourish and go from strength to strength.

Absorbed in the practice of enlightenment,
may I perform by mere wish, in accord with my prayers,
infinitely powerful deeds pleasing to the buddhas.

When shaping my mind with study, contemplation,
  and meditation,
I meet obstruction upon enlightenment's path,
may I destroy utterly with wrathful action
the power of all dark forces.

མཐོང་ཐོས་དྲན་དང་རེག་པ་ཙམ་གྱིས་ཀྱང་།།
འགྲོ་བ་ཀུན་གྱི་རེ་བ་གང་ཡིན་པ།།
མཐའ་དག་ཡོངས་སུ་རྫོགས་པར་བྱེད་པ་ལ།།
ཡིད་བཞིན་ནོར་དང་དཔག་བསམ་ཤིང་བཞིན་ཤོག །

མདོར་ན་བཤེས་གཉེན་དམ་པ་མཉེས་བྱས་ནས།།
ཐུབ་པའི་དགོངས་པ་རྙེད་པའི་མང་ཐོས་ཀྱིས།།
སྒྲུབ་པའི་བྱ་བ་ལེགས་པར་མཐར་ཕྱིན་ནས།།
རྒྱལ་བའི་བསྟན་པ་ཕྱོགས་བཅུར་རྒྱས་བྱེད་ཤོག །

By being seen, heard, or remembered,
or by mere contact with me,
may I satisfy fully, like a wish-fulfilling jewel or
wish-granting tree,
every hope of every living being.

In short, having delighted my spiritual masters,
and armed with study leading to the thoughts of the Buddha,
may I travel to the perfection of practice
to unfurl the Buddha's teachings in the ten directions.

ཐོག་མཐའ་མ་བཞུགས་སོ།

༄༅ །། །།ཕྱོགས་བཅུའི་རྒྱལ་བ་སྲས་དང་བཅས་པ་
ཐམས་ཅད་ལ་ཕྱག་འཚལ་ལོ།།

མཐའ་ཡས་འགྲོ་བ་སྲིད་ལས་བསྒྲལ་བྱའི་ཕྱིར།།
མཐའ་མེད་སྨོན་ལམ་ལྷག་བསམ་དག་པས་གདབ།།
བསླུ་མེད་དཀོན་མཆོག་གསུམ་དང་མཐུ་སྟོབས་ཅན།།
དྲང་སྲོང་མཐུ་ཡིས་བདེན་ཚིག་འགྲུབ་གྱུར་ཅིག །

བདག་ནི་སྐྱེ་ཞིང་སྐྱེ་བ་ཐམས་ཅད་དུ།།
ངན་སོང་ངན་འགྲོ་ལོག་པར་ལྷུང་བ་ཡི།།
སྐྱེ་གནས་རྣམས་སུ་ནམ་ཡང་མི་སྐྱེ་ཞིང་།།
དལ་འབྱོར་ཚང་བའི་མི་ལུས་ཐོབ་པར་ཤོག །

སྐྱེས་མ་ཐག་ནས་སྲིད་པའི་བདེ་བ་ལ།།
ནམ་ཡང་མ་ཆགས་ཐར་པ་ཐོབ་བྱའི་ཕྱིར།།
ངེས་འབྱུང་བསམ་པས་ཚངས་སྤྱོད་འཚོལ་བ་ལ།།
བརྩོན་འགྲུས་ལྷོད་པ་མེད་པར་འཇུག་པར་ཤོག །

A Prayer for the Beginning, Middle, and End of Practice

I bow before the conquering buddhas, bodhisattvas, and arhats of all directions and of all times.

I offer this boundless prayer with the purest of minds
to free countless beings from cycles of existence.
By the power of the unfailing Three Jewels
and of great *rishis* possessed of the force of truth,
may these sincere words bear fruit.

Life after life, may I never be born into realms
of great suffering or unfavorable circumstance
but gain always a precious human form
blessed with every conducive provision.

From the moment of birth may I never
be lured by the pleasures of existence,
but, guided by renunciation intent on freedom,
be resolute in seeking the pure life.

བདག་ནི་རབ་ཏུ་འབྱུང་བར་བྱེད་པ་ལ།།
འཁོར་དང་ཉེ་དུ་ལོངས་སྤྱོད་གང་གིས་ཀྱང་།།
གེགས་བྱེད་མེད་པར་མཐུན་པའི་རྐྱེན་རྣམས་ཀུན།།
ཇི་ལྟར་བསམས་པ་ཇི་བཞིན་འགྲུབ་པར་ཤོག །

རབ་ཏུ་བྱུང་ནས་ཇི་སྲིད་འཚོ་ཡི་བར།།
མཁན་སློབ་སྤྱན་སྔར་ཇི་ལྟར་ཁས་བླངས་བཞིན།།
བཅས་དང་རང་བཞིན་ཁ་ན་མ་ཐོ་བའི།།
ཉེས་པས་ནམ་ཡང་གོས་པར་མ་གྱུར་ཅིག །

ཚངས་སྤྱོད་རྟེན་ལ་ཐེག་པ་ཆེན་པོ་ཡི།།
ཟབ་ཅིང་རྒྱ་ཆེའི་ཆོས་རྣམས་ཇི་སྙེད་པ།།
མ་རྣམས་དོན་དུ་དཀའ་བ་དུ་མ་ཡིས།།
བསྐལ་པ་དཔག་ཏུ་མེད་པར་སྒྲུབ་པར་ཤོག །

ལུང་རྟོགས་ཡོན་ཏན་དུ་མས་རྒྱུད་གཏམས་ཤིང་།།
དབང་པོ་ཞི་ཞིང་རབ་དུལ་སྙིང་བརྗེར་བཅས།།
གཞན་དོན་སྐྱོ་མེད་སྒྲུབ་པའི་སྙིང་སྟོབས་ཅན།།
བཤེས་གཉེན་དམ་པས་རྗེས་སུ་འཛིན་པར་ཤོག །

May there be no hindrance to becoming a monk,
from friends, family, or possessions,
and for every conducive circumstance,
by mere thought may it appear.

Once a monk, may I be untainted as long as I live,
by breech of vow or natural fault,
as promised in the presence of my preceptor.

I pray that on such pure foundation,
and for every mother sentient being,
I devote myself with hardship for countless eons
to every aspect, profound and vast, of the Mahayana.

May I be cared for by true spiritual friends,
filled with knowledge and insight,
senses stilled, minds controlled, loving, compassionate,
and with courage untiring in working for others.

རྟག་ཏུ་ངུ་ཡིས་ཆོས་འཕགས་བསྙེན་པ་ལྟར།།
ལུས་སྲོག་ལོངས་སྤྱོད་ཀུན་གྱིས་གཡོ་མེད་པར།།
བཤེས་གཉེན་དམ་པ་ལེགས་པར་མཉེས་བྱས་ནས།།
མི་མཉེས་སྐད་ཅིག་ཙམ་ཡང་མི་བྱེད་ཤོག །

ཟབ་ཞི་སྤྲོས་དང་བྲལ་བའི་ཤེར་ཕྱིན་དོན།།
ལོག་རྟོག་དྲི་མའི་རྒྱུ་ཡིས་མ་བསླད་པར།།
ཇི་ལྟར་རྟག་ཏུ་ངུ་ལ་བསྟན་པ་ལྟར།།
དེ་ལྟར་བདག་ལ་རྟག་ཏུ་འདོམས་པར་ཤོག །

ཐུབ་པའི་དགོངས་པའི་དོན་ལས་ཕྱིར་ཕྱོགས་པའི།།
རྟག་ཆད་ལྟ་བ་སྟོན་པར་བྱེད་པ་པོ།།
མི་དགེའི་བཤེས་གཉེན་སྡིག་པའི་གྲོགས་རྣམས་ཀྱི།།
དབང་དུ་ནམ་ཡང་འགྲོ་བར་མ་གྱུར་ཅིག །

ལྷག་བསམ་རྣམ་པར་དག་པའི་དར་ཆེན་འཕྱུར།།
བརྩོན་འགྲུས་ལྷོད་པ་མེད་པའི་རླུང་གིས་བསྐྱོད།།
ཐོས་བསམ་སྒོམ་པའི་གྲུ་གཟིངས་ལེགས་བསྡུམས་ནས།།
ལུས་ཅན་འཁོར་བའི་མཚོ་ལས་སྒྲོལ་བར་ཤོག །

As Sada Prarudita devoted himself to Dharma Arya,
may I sincerely please my spiritual master
with body, life, and wealth,
never disappointing him for an instant.

I pray that the Perfection of Wisdom, forever profound,
a bringer of peace, unbound by identification,
be taught to me as taught to Sada Prarudita,
unsullied by the muddy waters of false views.

May I never fall under the sway
of false teachers and misleading friends,
their flawed views of existence and nonexistence
well outside the Buddha's intention.

With sail hoisted of the sincerest of minds,
driven by winds of unflagging effort,
on this well-built ship of study, thought, and meditation,
may I bring living beings from samsara's ocean.

ཇི་ཙམ་མང་དུ་ཐོས་དང་ལྷག་པར་གཏོང་།།
རྣམ་དག་ཚུལ་ཁྲིམས་རྣམ་དཔྱོད་ཤེས་རབ་ཀྱིས།།
བདག་རྒྱུད་ལྷག་པར་གྱུར་པ་དེ་ཙམ་དུ།།
ཕྱི་ཕྱིར་ཁེངས་པ་ཀུན་དང་བྲལ་བར་ཤོག །

རྣམ་དག་རིགས་པའི་སྤོབས་ཀྱིས་གསུང་རབ་དོན།།
ཇི་བཞིན་འབྱེད་ལ་གཞན་དྲིང་མི་འཇོག་པའི།།
མཁས་པའི་གམ་དུ་མཐའ་ཡས་གསུང་རབ་ལ།།
ངོམས་པ་མེད་པའི་ཐོས་པ་བྱེད་པར་ཤོག །

ཇི་ལྟར་ཐོས་པའི་དོན་ལ་རིགས་པ་བཞིས།།
ཉིན་དང་མཚན་དུ་ཚུལ་བཞིན་རབ་བརྟགས་ནས།།
བསམ་བྱའི་གནས་ལ་བསམས་ལས་བྱུང་བ་ཡི།།
རྣམ་དཔྱོད་བློ་ཡིས་ཐེ་ཚོམ་ཆོད་པར་ཤོག །

གང་ཚེ་ཤིན་ཏུ་ཟབ་པའི་ཆོས་ཚུལ་ལ།།
བསམ་བྱུང་བློ་ཡིས་ངེས་ཤེས་སྐྱེད་པའི་ཚེ།།
ཚེ་འདིའི་འཁྲི་བ་ཆོད་པའི་བརྩོན་འགྲུས་ཀྱིས།།
དབེན་པ་བསྟེན་ནས་ཚུལ་བཞིན་སྒྲུབ་པར་ཤོག །

As much as I excel in learning,
as much as I give to others,
as pure as my morality grows,
as much as I become wise,
by as much may I be empty of pride.

I pray that I listen insatiably
to countless teachings at the feet of a master,
single-handedly with logic unflawed,
prizing open scriptures' meanings.

Having examined day and night
with fourfold logic all that I have heard,
may I banish every doubt
with the discerning understanding
that arises from such contemplation.

With conviction on dharmas profound
gained from understanding born of contemplation,
I pray that I retreat to solitude
with a perseverance severing life's attachments
to devote myself to proper practice.

དེ་ལྟར་ཐོས་བསམ་སྒོམ་པས་རྒྱལ་བ་ཡི།།
དགོངས་པའི་གནད་རྣམས་རྒྱུད་ལ་བསྒྲུན་པའི་ཚེ།།
སྲིད་ལ་བཀྲམ་པའི་ཚེ་འདིའི་སྣང་བ་དང་།།
རང་བདེ་འདོད་པའི་བློ་རྣམས་མི་འབྱུང་ཤོག །

བདག་གིས་བདོག་པའི་དངོས་པོ་ཐམས་ཅད་ལ།།
མ་ཆགས་བློ་ཡིས་སེར་སྣ་བཅོམ་བྱས་ཏེ།།
ཐོག་མར་ཟང་ཟིང་སྦྱིན་པས་སེམས་ཅན་རྣམས།།
འཁོར་དུ་བསྡུས་ནས་ཆོས་ཀྱིས་ཚིམ་བྱེད་ཤོག །

ཇི་ལྟར་ནོད་པའི་བསླབ་པ་ཕྲ་བ་ཡང་།།
ངེས་འབྱུང་བསམ་པས་བྱང་ཆུབ་ཐོབ་ཀྱི་བར།།
སྲོག་གི་ཕྱིར་ཡང་གཏོང་བར་མི་བྱེད་པའི།།
ཐར་པའི་རྒྱལ་མཚན་རྟག་ཏུ་འཛིན་པར་ཤོག །

བདག་ལ་བརྡེག་འཚོག་མཆང་འབྲུ་སེམས་ཅན་རྣམས།།
མཐོང་དམ་ཐོས་སམ་ཡིད་ལ་དྲན་པའི་ཚེ།།
ཁོང་ཁྲོ་བྲལ་ཞིང་སླར་ཡང་དེ་དག་གི །
ཡོན་ཏན་བརྗོད་ཅིང་བཟོད་པ་སྒོམ་པར་ཤོག །

When the Buddha's thoughts dawn upon me
through study, thought, and meditation,
I pray that things of this life forever bonded to samsara
and thoughts of my happiness alone
never arise in my mind.

Unattached to my possessions
I pray that I destroy parsimony,
gathering disciples around me
by giving first of material wealth
to satisfy them with Dharma.

With a mind renounced may I never transgress
even the smallest precept, though it may cost my life,
flying forever, therefore, the flag of freedom.

When I see, hear, or think of those
who struck, beat, or maligned me,
may I be without anger, speak of their virtues,
and meditate upon patience.

དཀར་པོའི་ཆོས་རྣམས་མ་ཐོབ་ཐོབ་པ་དང་།།
ཐོབ་རྣམས་གོང་ནས་གོང་དུ་འཕེལ་བ་ལས།།
ཉམས་པར་བྱེད་པའི་ལེ་ལོ་རྣམ་པ་གསུམ།།
ཀུན་ནས་སྤངས་ཏེ་བརྩོན་འགྲུས་རྩོམ་པར་ཤོག །

སྲིད་མཐའ་གནོན་པའི་ལྷག་མཐོང་སྟོབས་དང་བྲལ།།
ཞི་མཐའ་གནོན་པའི་སྙིང་རྗེའི་རླན་གྱིས་དབེན།།
ཕལ་ཆེར་སྲིད་པར་འཕེན་པར་བྱེད་པ་ཡི།།
ཞི་གནས་སྤངས་ཏེ་ཟུང་འབྲེལ་སྒོམ་པར་ཤོག །

གནས་ལུགས་ཟབ་མོའི་དོན་ལ་སྐྲག་གྱུར་ནས།།
བློས་བྱས་ཉི་ཚེའི་སྟོང་པ་མཆོག་འཛིན་པའི།།
ལོག་པའི་ལྟ་ངན་མཐའ་དག་རབ་སྤངས་ཏེ།།
ཆོས་ཀུན་གདོད་ནས་སྟོང་པར་རྟོགས་པར་ཤོག །

རྣམ་དག་བསླབ་པ་ཁྲེལ་མེད་སེམས་ཀྱིས་བྲལ།།
དམ་པས་སྨད་པའི་ལས་ལ་འཇིགས་མི་བྱེད།།
ཁྲིམས་འཆལ་དགེ་སྦྱོང་ཤ་ཚུགས་ཅན་རྣམས་ཀྱང་།།
བདག་གིས་སྐྱོན་མེད་ཁྲིམས་ལ་སྦྱོར་བར་ཤོག །

I pray I will apply myself to enthusiasm,
achieving virtues unachieved, improving those attained,
banishing utterly threefold debilitating laziness.

I pray to abandon the meditative absorption
that lacks the power of insight to quell samsara,
that is divorced from the moist compassion to quash
nirvana's passivity,
and that mostly throws one back to cycles of existence,
but develop instead the meditative absorption
that unites compassion and insight.

I pray that I banish false views of emptiness,
mentally fabricated and partially known,
born from fear of the most profound truth, cherished as
supreme,
and that I realize all phenomena to be forever empty.

May I bring to faultless morality
those so-called practitioners with their wayward ethics,
shamelessly empty of pure practice,
rashly pursuing paths shunned by the wise.

ཡང་དག་ལམ་དོར་ལོག་པའི་ལམ་ངན་ཞུགས།།
མི་དགེའི་ཆ་ཤེས་གཉེན་སྡིག་གྲོགས་དབང་དུ་སོང་།།
གང་ཡིན་དེ་ཡང་བདག་གིས་བདེ་བླག་ཏུ།།
རྒྱལ་བས་བསྔགས་པའི་ལམ་ལ་འགོད་པར་ཤོག །

བདག་གི་འཆད་རྩོད་རྩོམ་པ་སེང་གེའི་སྒྲས།།
ལོག་སྨྲའི་ཤ་ཚོགས་སྤོབས་པ་འཕྲོག་བྱས་ནས།།
གང་གིས་འདུལ་བའི་ཐབས་ཀྱིས་རྗེས་བཟུང་སྟེ།།
མི་ནུབ་བསྟན་པའི་རྒྱལ་མཚན་འཛིན་པར་ཤོག །

བདག་ནི་གང་དུ་སྐྱེ་ནས་ཐུབ་པ་ཡི།།
གསུང་གི་བདུད་རྩི་འཐུང་བ་དེ་ཡི་ཚེ།།
རིགས་གཟུགས་འབྱོར་དང་དབང་ཕྱུག་ཤེས་རབ་དང་།།
ཚེ་རིང་ནད་མེད་བདེ་དང་ལྡན་པར་ཤོག །

བདག་གིས་ལུས་དང་སྲོག་དང་ལོངས་སྤྱོད་ལ།།
རྒྱུན་དུ་འཚེ་བའི་བསམ་པ་དང་བྲལ་ཞིང་།།
བདག་ལ་མི་སྙན་བརྗོད་པ་དེ་དག་ལའང་།།
བདག་ནི་ལྷག་པར་མ་བཞིན་བྱམས་གྱུར་ཅིག །

May I bring to the path praised by buddhas
those lost and fallen onto wrong paths,
swayed by deluded teachers and misleading friends.

I pray that my lion-like roar
of teaching, argument, and composition
flattens the pride of fox-like false orators,
and, gathering well-trained disciples about me,
I fly the banner of the teachings forever.

In whatever life I may drink the nectar of Buddha's teachings,
I pray to be born into a good family
and be of handsome build, wealthy, powerful, and wise,
blessed with long life and sound health.

May I develop the unique love of a mother
for those who malign me
and harbor ill designs upon my life,
my body, or my possessions.

བདག་གིས་དེ་དག་རིང་པོར་མི་ཐོགས་པར།།
བདག་པས་གཞན་གཅེས་སྒོམ་པའི་བྱང་ཆུབ་སེམས།།
ལྷག་བསམ་དག་པ་རྒྱུད་ལ་བསྐྱེད་བྱས་ནས།།
བླ་མེད་བྱང་ཆུབ་གོ་འཕང་སྟེར་བར་ཤོག །

སྨོན་ལམ་འདི་དག་གང་གིས་མཐོང་ཐོས་དྲན་ཐོས།།
ཡིད་ལ་དྲན་པར་བྱེད་པ་དེ་དག་ཀྱང་།།
རྒྱལ་སྲས་རྣམས་ཀྱི་སྨོན་ལམ་རླབས་པོ་ཆེ།།
མ་ལུས་སྒྲུབ་ལ་ཞུམ་པ་མེད་པར་ཤོག །

ལྷག་བསམ་དག་པའི་སྟོབས་ཀྱིས་ལེགས་བསྒྲུབས་པའི།།
རྒྱ་ཆེན་སྨོན་ལམ་བཏབ་པ་འདི་ཡི་མཐུས།།
སྨོན་ལམ་ཕ་རོལ་ཕྱིན་པ་ཡོངས་རྫོགས་ནས།།
ལུས་ཅན་ཀུན་གྱི་རེ་བ་སྐོང་བར་ཤོག །།

By growing within myself
the pure and extraordinary bodhi-mind
whose nature is to cherish others more than self,
may I soon give them unsurpassable enlightenment.

Whoever hears, sees, or calls these verses to mind,
may they be undaunted in fulfilling
the powerful prayers of the bodhisattvas.

By the power of these vast prayers
made with the purest intention,
may I attain the perfection of prayer
and fulfill the hopes of every living being.

དལ་རྟེན་ལ་སྙིང་པོ་ལེན་པར་བསྐུལ་བའི་ཚིགས་བཅད་བཞུགས་སོ།

༄༅། །ན་མོ་གུ་རུ་མཉྫུ་གྷོ་ཥཱ་ཡ།

འགྲོ་བ་ཀུན་གྱི་བདེ་དང་ལེགས་པའི་དཔལ།།
གང་ཞིག་སྐྱབས་སུ་བཟུང་བས་སྩོལ་མཛད་མ།།
སྡུག་བསྔལ་ཅན་རྣམས་སྐྱོབ་པའི་ཁུར་འཁྱེར་བའི།།
རྗེ་བཙུན་སྒྲོལ་མ་དེ་ལ་གུས་ཕྱག་འཚལ།།

གང་དག་སྡུག་བསྔལ་རྒྱ་མཚོ་ཆེར་ལྷུང་བ།།
དེ་དང་དེ་དག་ང་ཡིས་བསྒྲལ་ལོ་ཞེས།།
ཐབས་ཆེན་དམ་བཅའ་རྗེས་སུ་སྒྲུབ་མཛད་པའི།།
བརྩེ་ལྡན་མ་དེའི་ཞབས་ཀྱི་ཆུ་སྐྱེས་ནི།།

གང་གིས་གུས་པས་སྤྱི་བོར་རབ་མཆོད་པ།།
དལ་བའི་རྟེན་བཟང་རྙེད་པའི་བཞིན་བཟང་ཁྱོད།།
ཁོ་བོས་ཕན་པ་སྨྲས་པའི་རྗེས་འབྲང་ན།།
མདོ་ཙམ་ཤད་ཀྱི་བསམ་པ་ཐག་པས་ཉོན།།

The Essence of a Human Life
Words of Advice for the Lay Practitioner

Homage to my guru, the youthful Manjushri!

To those within her refuge, every happiness and joy,
for those beset by suffering, every assistance.
Noble Tara, I bow before you.

"Those adrift on great seas of suffering I will save"—
a powerful vow made good.
To your lotus feet, compassionate goddess,
I offer this bowed head.

You of fine features, you have gained
this opportune and leisured human form.
If you follow me who speaks to help others,
listen well, I have something to say.

ངེས་པར་འོང་ཞིང་མྱུར་དུ་འོང་ངེས་པའི།།
འཆི་བའི་བསམ་པ་ཡང་ཡང་མ་སྦྱངས་ན།།
དགེ་བའི་བསམ་པ་མི་སྐྱེ་སྐྱེས་ན་ཡང་།།
ཚེ་འདིའི་ཕུན་ཚོགས་ལྷུར་ལེན་ཙམ་དུ་ཟད།།

དེ་ཕྱིར་གཞན་དག་འཆི་བ་མཐོང་ཐོས་རྣམས།།
ཡིད་ལ་སོམས་ལ་བདག་ལ་འདི་འདྲ་ཞིག །
མྱུར་དུ་འོང་ངེས་ནམ་ཡོང་ཆ་མེད་ལ།།
དེ་ཚེ་ལུས་དང་ལོངས་སྤྱོད་མཛའ་བཤེས་རྣམས།།
ཀུན་དང་འབྲལ་ཞིང་དགེ་དང་སྡིག་པའི་ལས།།
གྲིབ་མ་བཞིན་དུ་རྗེས་སུ་འབྲང་བ་དང་།།
སྡིག་པའི་ལས་ལས་རྒྱུན་རིང་ཤུགས་དྲག་པའི།།

ངན་སོང་གསུམ་གྱི་སྡུག་བསྔལ་འབྱུང་བ་དང་།།
རྒྱལ་བའི་ལམ་ལས་བདེ་འགྲོ་བརྒྱུད་ནས་ནི།།
མྱུར་དུ་དགེ་བའི་གོ་འཕང་འཐོབ་པའི་ཚུལ།།
ཤེས་པར་གྱིས་ལ་ཉིན་རེ་བཞིན་དུ་སོམས།།

Death will definitely come and will quickly come.
Should you neglect to train your thoughts
again and again on such certainties
you will grow no virtuous mind,
and even if you do, it will be spent
on enjoyment of the glories of this life.

Think, therefore, upon seeing and hearing of others' deaths,
"I am no different, death will soon come,
its certainty in no doubt, but no certainty as to when.
I must say farewell to body, wealth, and friends,
but good and bad deeds will follow like shadows.

"From bad will come the long and unbearable pain
of the three lower realms;
from good the higher, happier realms
from which to swiftly enter the echelons of enlightenment."
Know this and think upon it day after day.

དེ་ལྟར་བསམས་ནས་སྐྱབས་སུ་འགྲོ་ལ་འབད།།
ཐུབ་པས་ཁྱིམ་པའི་རྟེན་ལ་བསྔགས་པ་ཡི།།
གཏན་ཁྲིམས་ལྔ་ལ་བློ་དང་འཚམ་པར་སློབ།།
དུས་མཚམས་ཉི་མར་གསོ་སྦྱོང་ཡན་ལག་བརྒྱད།།
ལེགས་པར་བླངས་ནས་སྲུང་བ་ཤིན་ཏུ་གཅེས།།

ལྷག་པར་འཇིག་རྟེན་གཉིས་སུ་ཕུང་བྱེད་པའི།།
སྨྱོས་འགྱུར་འཐུང་བ་དམ་པ་རྣམས་ཀྱིས་སྨད།།
དེ་ཕྱིར་བཞིན་བཟང་ཁྱོད་ཀྱིས་སྨད་པའི་གནས།།
ལས་འདི་ལ་ནི་གཏན་དུ་ལོག་ན་ལེགས།།

གང་ལ་སྤྱད་པས་ཕུགས་སུ་སྡུག་བསྔལ་ན།།
འཕྲལ་དུ་བདེ་བར་སྣང་ཡང་བསྟེན་མི་བྱ།།
དུག་དང་འདྲེས་པའི་ཁ་ཟས་གཡོས་ལེགས་རྣམས།།
ཀུན་གྱིས་སྤྱོད་པར་བྱེད་པ་མ་མཐོང་ངམ།།

With such thoughts make efforts in refuge,
live as best you can in the five lifelong vows,
praised by Buddha as the basis of lay life.
Take sometimes the eight daylong vows
and guard them dearly.

Drunkenness, particularly, is the ruin of the world,
held in contempt by the wise.
Therefore, my fine-featured ones,
it is good to turn from such despised behavior.

If what you do brings on suffering eventually,
though it may appear in the moment as happiness,
then do not do it.
After all, food beautifully cooked but mixed with poison
is left untouched, is it not?

ཉིན་རེ་ཞིང་ཡང་དཀོན་མཆོག་མཆོད་པ་སོགས།།
དགེ་ལ་འབད་ཅིང་སྤྱར་བྱས་སྡིག་པ་ཚཤགས།།
སླན་ཆད་སྡོམ་པ་ཇི་དྲག་ཇི་དྲག་བྱ།།
གང་བསགས་དགེ་བ་སངས་རྒྱས་རྒྱུ་རུ་སྔོས།།

མདོར་ན་སྐྱེ་དང་འཆི་བའི་དུས་རྣམས་སུ།།
གཅིག་པུ་སྐྱེ་ཞིང་གཅིག་པུ་འཆི་བས་ན།།
གྲོགས་དང་ཉེ་དུ་ལ་སོགས་ཀུན་གྱིས་བསླུ།།
སླུ་བ་མེད་པའི་མཆོག་ནི་དམ་ཆོས་ཡིན།།

ཚེ་ཐུང་འདི་ནི་གློག་བཞིན་ཡུད་ཙམ་པ།།
གང་ལྟར་བྱས་ཀྱང་ཕྱིད་ཀྱི་གཏན་བདེ་གཅིག །
སྒྲུབ་དུས་ད་རེ་ཡིན་ནོ་ལེགས་པར་སེམས།།
དལ་འབྱོར་རིན་ཆེན་སྟོང་ལོག་མ་བྱེད་ཅིག །

དེ་ལྟར་གདམས་ལས་བསོད་ནམས་གང་ཐོབ་དེས།།
སྐྱིད་ཀྱང་མི་འཚོང་སྡུག་ཀྱང་མི་ཕུང་བའི།།
ཚེ་འདིའི་བུན་ལོང་བསྒྲུབ་པའི་བློ་ལོག་ནས།།
འགྲོ་ཀུན་ཆོས་ཀྱི་དགའ་བས་འཚོ་བར་ཤོག །

To the Three Jewels make prayers and offerings each day,
work hard to be wholesome, confess previous wrongs,
strengthen your vows again and again,
dedicating all merit for enlightenment.

To conclude: you are born alone, die alone,
friends and relations are therefore unreliable;
Dharma alone is the supreme reliance.

This short life is over, gone in a flash.
Realize that, come what may, now is the time
to find happiness everlasting.
Do not leave this precious human life empty-handed.

By the virtue of this advice,
may living beings turn from the bustle of this life,
whose happiness is never enough,
whose suffering never runs out,
to live instead by the great joy of Dharma.

རྟེན་འབྲེལ་བསྟོད་པ་བཞུགས་སོ།

༄༅ ། ། །ན་མོ་གུ་རུ་མཉྫུ་གྷོ་ཥཱ་ཡ།

གང་ཞིག་གཟིགས་ཤིང་གསུང་བ་ཡིས།།
མཁྱེན་དང་སྟོན་པ་བླ་ན་མེད།།
རྒྱལ་བ་རྟེན་ཅིང་འབྲེལ་བར་འབྱུང་།།
གཟིགས་ཤིང་འདོམས་པ་དེ་ལ་འདུད།།

འཇིག་རྟེན་རྒུད་པ་ཇི་སྙེད་པ།།
དེ་ཡི་རྩ་བ་མ་རིག་སྟེ།།
གང་ཞིག་མཐོང་བས་དེ་ལྡོག་པ།།
རྟེན་ཅིང་འབྲེལ་བར་འབྱུང་བ་གསུངས།།

དེ་ཚེ་བློ་དང་ལྡན་པ་ཡིས།།
རྟེན་ཅིང་འབྲེལ་བར་འབྱུང་བའི་ལམ།།
ཁྱོད་ཀྱི་བསྟན་པའི་གནད་ཉིད་དུ།།
ཇི་ལྟར་ཁོང་དུ་ཆུད་མི་འགྱུར།།

Dependent Arising
A Praise of the Buddha

Homage to my guru, the youthful Manjushri!

Seeing and speaking of dependent arising,
He was wisdom supreme, teacher supreme.
I bow to him who knew and taught
the all-conquering dependent arising.

Of the suffering existing in the world,
its root is none other than ignorance.
The understanding to kill this root
you said is none other than dependent arising.

How could those of intelligence not see
dependent arising as the heart of your doctrine.
Where is greater praise of you, therefore,
than in praise of dependent arising?

དེ་ལྟ་ལགས་ན་མགོན་ཁྱོད་ལ།།
བསྟོད་པའི་སྒོར་ནི་སུ་ཞིག་གིས།།
བརྟེན་ནས་འབྱུང་བ་གསུང་པ་ལས།།
ངོ་མཚར་གྱུར་པ་ཅི་ཞིག་རྙེད།།
གང་གང་རྐྱེན་ལ་རག་ལས་པ།།
དེ་དེ་རང་བཞིན་གྱིས་སྟོང་ཞེས།།
གསུང་བ་འདི་ལས་ཡ་མཚན་པའི།།
ལེགས་འདོམས་ཚུལ་ནི་ཅི་ཞིག་ཡོད།།

གང་དུ་བཟུང་བས་བྱིས་པ་རྣམས།།
མཐར་འཛིན་འཆིང་བ་བརྟན་བྱེད་པ།།
དེ་ཉིད་མཁས་ལ་སྤྲོས་པ་ཡི།།
དྲ་བ་མ་ལུས་གཅོད་པའི་སྒོ།།

བསྟན་འདི་གཞན་དུ་མ་མཐོང་བས།།
སྟོན་པ་ཞེས་བྱ་ཁྱོད་ཉིད་དེ།།
ཝ་སྐྱེས་ལ་ནི་སེང་གེ་བཞིན།།
མུ་སྟེགས་ཅན་ལའང་གཙམ་བུའི་ཚིག །

"Whatever depends on circumstance is empty of nature."
What greater teaching is there than this!
The foolish, however, seize on it
and only tighten chains of extreme views,
while for the wise it cuts entangled nets of fabrication.

This teaching is not seen in the works of others,
the title of Teacher, therefore, is yours alone.
Given to others it is but the hollow flattery
of a fox being hailed a lion.

ཨེ་མའོ་སྟོན་པ་ཨེ་མའོ་སྐྱབས།།
ཨེ་མའོ་སྨྲ་མཆོག་ཨེ་མའོ་མགོན།།
རྟེན་ཅིང་འབྲེལ་འབྱུང་ལེགས་གསུང་བའི།།
སྟོན་པ་དེ་ལ་བདག་ཕྱག་འཚལ།།

ཕན་མཛད་ཁྱོད་ཀྱིས་འགྲོ་བ་ལ།།
སྨན་པའི་སླད་དུ་བཀའ་སྩལ་པ།།
བསྟན་པའི་སྙིང་པོ་སྟོང་པ་ཉིད།།
ངེས་པའི་རྒྱུ་མཚན་ཟླ་མེད་པ།།

རྟེན་ཅིང་འབྲེལ་བར་འབྱུང་བའི་ཚུལ།།
འགལ་བ་དང་ནི་མ་གྲུབ་པར།།
མཐོང་བ་འདི་ཡིས་ཁྱོད་ཀྱི་ལུགས།།
ཇི་ལྟར་ཁོང་དུ་ཆུད་པར་ནུས།།

ཁྱོད་ནི་ནམ་ཞིག་སྟོང་པ་ཉིད།།
རྟེན་འབྱུང་དོན་དུ་མཐོང་བ་ན།།
རང་བཞིན་གྱིས་ནི་སྟོང་པ་དང་།།
བྱ་བྱེད་འཐད་པའང་མི་འགལ་ཞིང་།།

Greatest of teachers! Greatest protector!
Speaker supreme! Guide supreme!
I bow to the teacher of dependent arising!

Benevolent teacher, you taught to help all living beings.
Emptiness is the essence of those teachings,
its highest proof dependent arising.

Those claiming it proves the opposite,
those denying its very existence,
how will they grasp your teachings?

For you, emptiness seen as dependent arising
does not render as contradictory
emptiness of self-nature and ability to function.

དེ་ལས་བཟློག་པར་མཐོང་བ་ན།།
སྟོང་ལ་བྱ་བ་མི་རུང་ཞིང་།།
བྱ་དང་བཅས་ལ་སྟོང་མེད་པས།།
ཉམ་ངའི་གཡང་དུ་ལྷུང་བར་བཞེད།།

དེའི་ཕྱིར་ཁྱོད་ཀྱི་བསྟན་པ་ལ།།
རྟེན་འབྱུང་མཐོང་བ་ལེགས་པར་བསྔགས།།
དེ་ཡང་ཀུན་ཏུ་མེད་པ་དང་།།
རང་བཞིན་གྱིས་ནི་ཡོད་པས་མིན།།

ལྟོས་མེད་ནམ་མཁའི་མེ་ཏོག་བཞིན།།
དེས་ན་མ་བརྟེན་ཡོད་མ་ཡིན།།
ངོ་བོས་གྲུབ་ན་དེ་གྲུབ་པ།།
རྒྱུ་དང་རྐྱེན་ལ་ལྟོས་པ་འགལ།།

དེའི་ཕྱིར་བརྟེན་ནས་འབྱུང་བ་ལས།།
མ་གཏོགས་ཆོས་འགའ་ཡོད་མིན་པས།།
རང་བཞིན་གྱིས་ནི་སྟོང་པ་ལས།།
མ་གཏོགས་ཆོས་འགའ་མེད་པར་གསུངས།།

To hold to the opposite, however—
that with emptiness there can be no function
and with function, no emptiness—
is to fall into a dangerous trap.

In your teachings, therefore,
knowledge of dependent arising is highly praised,
but it will not be known
to views of self or nonexistence.

Nondependence, you have said, is like the sky flower.
Nondependence, therefore, does not exist.
Anything existent by its own nature
contradicts existence by cause and circumstance.

Nothing is not dependently arising;
nothing, therefore, is not empty of self-nature.

རང་བཞིན་ལྡོག་པ་མེད་པའི་ཕྱིར།།
ཆོས་རྣམས་རང་བཞིན་འགག་ཡོད་ན།།
མྱ་ངན་འདས་པ་མི་རུང་ཞིང་།།
སྤྲོས་ཀུན་ལྡོག་པ་མེད་པ་གསུངས།།

དེ་ཕྱིར་རང་བཞིན་རྣམ་བྲལ་ཞེས།།
སེང་གེའི་སྒྲ་ཡིས་ཡང་ཡང་དུ།།
མཁས་པའི་ཚོགས་སུ་ལེགས་གསུངས་པ།།
འདི་ལ་སུ་ཡིས་འགོང་པར་ནུས།།

རང་བཞིན་འགག་ཡང་མེད་པ་དང་།།
འདི་ལ་བརྟེན་ནས་འདི་འབྱུང་བའི།།
རྣམ་གཞག་ཐམས་ཅད་འཐད་པ་གཉིས།།
མི་འགལ་འདུ་བར་སྨོས་ཅི་དགོས།།

བརྟེན་ནས་འབྱུང་བའི་རྒྱུ་མཚན་གྱིས།།
མཐར་ལྟ་བ་ལ་མི་བརྟེན་ཞེས།།
ལེགས་གསུངས་འདི་ནི་མགོན་ཁྱོད་ཀྱི།།
སྨྲ་བ་བླ་ན་མེད་པའི་རྒྱུ།།

Self-nature, you said, cannot be destroyed.
Phenomena, therefore, possessed of nature,
would render nirvana impossible.
Samsara likewise would have no end.

You spoke, therefore, with the roar of a lion
again and again on this absence of nature,
and amid the assemblies of the wise,
who dared to challenge you?

The absence of self-nature anywhere,
this arising because of that,
both presentations are true,
and what need to say that both come together
without contradiction.

Moreover, by reason of dependent arising,
one will not depend on extreme views.
This is the excellent teaching, my protector,
that renders you orator supreme.

འདི་ཀུན་ངོ་བོས་སྟོང་པ་དང་།།
འདི་ལས་འདི་འབྲས་འབྱུང་བ་ཡི།།
ངེས་པ་གཉིས་པོ་ཕན་ཚུན་དུ།།
གེགས་མེད་པར་ནི་གྲོགས་བྱེད་པ།།
འདི་ལས་ངོ་མཚར་གྱུར་པ་དང་།།
འདི་ལས་རྨད་དུ་བྱུང་བ་གང་།།
ཚུལ་འདིས་ཁྱོད་ལ་བསྟོད་ན་ནི།།
བསྟོད་པར་འགྱུར་གྱི་གཞན་དུ་མིན།།

རྨོངས་པས་བྲན་དུ་བཟུང་བ་ཡིས།།
གང་ཞིག་ཁྱོད་དང་ཞེ་འགྲས་པ།།
དེ་ཡིས་རང་བཞིན་མེད་པའི་སྒྲ།།
མི་བཟོད་གྱུར་ལ་མཚར་ཅི་ཡོད།།

ཁྱོད་ཀྱི་གསུང་གི་གཅེས་པའི་མཛོད།།
བརྟེན་ནས་འབྱུང་བར་ཁས་བླངས་ནས།།
སྟོང་ཉིད་ང་རོ་མི་བཟོད་པ།།
འདི་ལ་ཁོ་བོ་ངོ་མཚར་གྱུར།།

All this by nature is empty, and this arises from that.
Such realizations do not hinder but mutually complement.
What is more wonderful, more astonishing than that?
Praising you this way is praise indeed;
all other praise is lesser.

That some, hostile to you,
held as the slaves of ignorance,
are unable to bear the sounds of no self-nature
comes as no surprise.

That others, accepting dependent arising,
the crown jewel of your teaching,
are unable to tolerate the roar of emptiness
does surprise me.

རང་བཞིན་མེད་ལ་བཀྲི་བའི་སྒྲོ།།
བླ་མེད་རྟེན་ཅིང་འབྲེལ་འབྱུང་གི།
མིང་ཉིད་ཀྱིས་ནི་རང་བཞིན་དུ།།
འཛིན་ན་ད་ཀོ་སྐྱེ་བོ་འདི།།
འཕགས་མཆོག་རྣམས་ཀྱིས་ལེགས་བགྲོད་པའི།།
འཇུག་ངོགས་བླ་དང་བྲལ་གྱུར་པ།།
ཁྲོད་དགྲེས་གྱུར་པའི་ལམ་བཟང་དེར།།
ཐབས་གང་གིས་ནི་བཀྲི་བར་བྱ།།

རང་བཞིན་བཅོས་མིན་ལྟོས་མེད་དང་།།
རྟེན་འབྲེལ་ལྟོས་དང་བཅོས་མ་གཉིས།།
ཇི་ལྟ་བུར་ན་གཞི་གཅིག་ལ།།
མི་འགལ་འདུ་བ་ཉིད་དུ་འགྱུར།།

དེ་ཕྱིར་བརྟེན་ནས་འབྱུང་བ་གང་།།
རང་བཞིན་གྱིས་ནི་གདོད་མ་ནས།།
རྣམ་པར་དབེན་ཡང་དེར་སྣང་བས།།
འདི་ཀུན་སྒྱུ་མ་བཞིན་དུ་གསུངས།།

If by the very name of dependent arising,
gateway supreme to no self-nature,
self-nature is asserted, how will they be led
to that noble path that pleases you,
that incomparable highway well-traveled by exalted beings?

Self-nature—real and nondependent;
dependent arising—unreal and of dependent nature;
how, without contradiction, could these two ever
  come together?

Consequently, that which dependently arises
has forever been empty and void of nature.
Things, however, do not appear that way.
All this, you have said, is therefore like an illusion.

ཁྱོད་ཀྱིས་ཇི་ལྟར་བསྟན་པ་ལ།།
རྒོལ་བ་འགས་ཀྱང་ཆོས་མཐུན་དུ།།
གླགས་མི་རྙེད་པར་གསུངས་པ་ཡང་།།
འདི་ཉིད་ཀྱིས་ནི་ལེགས་པར་ཁུམས།།
ཅི་སྐད་ཅེས་ན་འདི་ཆཤད་པས།།
མཐོང་དང་མ་མཐོང་དངོས་པོ་ལ།།
སྒྲོ་འདོགས་པ་དང་སྐུར་འདེབས་ཀྱི།།
གོ་སྐབས་རིང་དུ་མཛད་ཕྱིར་རོ།།

ཁྱོད་ཀྱི་སྨྲ་བ་བླ་མེད་པར།།
མཐོང་བའི་རྒྱུ་མཚན་རྟེན་འབྱུང་གི །
ལམ་འདི་ཉིད་ཀྱིས་གསུང་གཞན་ཡང་།།
ཚད་མར་གྱུར་པར་ངེས་པ་སྐྱེ།།

དོན་བཞིན་གཟིགས་ནས་ལེགས་གསུངས་པ།།
ཁྱོད་ཀྱི་རྗེས་སུ་སློབ་པ་ལ།།
རྒུད་པ་ཐམས་ཅད་རིང་དུ་གྱུར།།
ཉེས་ཀུན་རྩ་བ་ལྡོག་ཕྱིར་རོ།།

"Others may attack your teaching
but they will never be any match."
Such claims are validated by dependent arising.
How? Because its explanation casts away all possibility
of flawed assertion and faulty denial
of all phenomena evident or hidden.

This very path of dependent arising,
the reason for seeing your words as unparalleled,
generates conviction in the validity of other teachings.

Having seen the truth, you taught it.
Those following you will leave all troubles far behind,
for they will cut to the root of every fault.

ཁྱོད་ཀྱི་བསྟན་ལས་ཕྱིར་ཕྱོགས་པས།།
ཡུན་རིང་ངལ་བ་བསྟེན་བྱས་ཀྱང་།།
ཕྱི་ཕྱིར་སྐྱོན་རྣམས་བོས་པ་བཞིན།།
བདག་ཏུ་ལྟ་བ་བརྟན་ཕྱིར་རོ།།

ཨེ་མ་རྗེ་མཁས་པས་འདི་གཉིས་ཀྱི།།
ཁྱད་པར་ཁོང་དུ་ཆུད་གྱུར་པ།།
དེ་ཚེ་རྐང་གི་ཁོང་ནས་ནི།།
ཁྱོད་ལ་ཅི་ཕྱིར་གུས་མི་འགྱུར།།

ཁྱོད་གསུང་དུ་མ་ཅི་ཞིག་སློས།།
ཆ་ཤས་རེ་ཡི་དོན་ཙམ་ལའང་།།
འོལ་སྤྱི་ཙམ་གྱི་ངེས་རྙེད་པ།།
དེ་ལའང་མཆོག་གི་བདེ་བ་སྟེར།།

ཀྱི་ཧུད་བདག་བློ་རྨོངས་པས་བཅོམ།།
འདི་འདྲའི་ཡོན་ཏན་ཕུང་པོ་ལ།།
རིང་ནས་སྐྱབས་སུ་སོང་གྱུར་ཀྱང་།།
ཡོན་ཏན་ཆ་ཙམ་མ་འཚལ་ཏོ།།

Those, however, outside your teachings,
though they practice long and hard,
are those who beckon back faults,
for they are welded to views of self.

Ah! When the wise see the difference,
how could they not revere you
from the very depths of their hearts!

What need to talk of many teachings!
The simplest conviction in just a single part
brings on the greatest of joy!

Alas! My mind is ruined by ignorance!
For so long have I gone for refuge
to this great store of meritorious qualities,
yet not a single one do I possess.

འོན་ཀྱང་འཆི་བདག་ཁར་ཕྱོགས་པའི།།
སྲོག་གི་རྒྱུན་ནི་མ་ནུབ་བར།།
ཁྱོད་ལ་ཅུང་ཟད་ཡིད་ཆེས་པ།།
དེ་ཡང་སྐལ་པ་བཟང་སྙམ་བགྱིད།།
སྟོན་པའི་ནང་ན་རྟེན་འབྲེལ་སྟོན་པ་དང་།།
ཤེས་རབ་ནང་ན་རྟེན་འབྲེལ་ཤེས་པ་གཉིས།།
འཛིག་རྟེན་དག་ན་རྒྱལ་བའི་དབང་པོ་བཞིན།།
ཕུལ་བྱུང་ལེགས་པར་ཁྱོད་མཁྱེན་གཞན་གྱིས་མིན།།

ཁྱོད་ཀྱིས་ཇི་སྙེད་བཀའ་སྩལ་པ།།
རྟེན་འབྲེལ་ཉིད་ལས་བརྩམས་ཏེ་འཇུག །
དེ་ཡང་མྱ་ངན་འདའ་ཕྱིར་ཏེ།།
ཞི་འགྱུར་མིན་མཛད་ཁྱོད་ལ་མེད།།

ཀྱེ་མའོ་ཁྱོད་ཀྱི་བསྟན་པ་ནི།།
གང་གི་རྣ་བའི་ལམ་སོང་བ།།
དེ་དག་ཐམས་ཅད་ཞི་འགྱུར་ཕྱིར།།
ཁྱོད་བསྟན་འཛིན་པར་སུ་མི་གུས།།

As yet, however, my life has not slipped
between the jaws of the Lord of Death
and, having a modicum of faith in you,
I do consider myself fortunate.
Among teachers, the teacher of dependent arising,
among knowledge, knowledge of dependent arising.
These two, like a mighty conqueror in the world,
you know to be supreme, where others do not.

All that you have taught
proceeds from dependent arising;
its purpose, the transcending of suffering.
Nothing you do, therefore, is not for peace.

Ah! Your teachings!
Those whose ears they fall upon will all find peace.
Who, therefore, would not hold them dear?

ཕས་རྒོལ་མཐའ་དག་འཇོམས་པ་དང་།།
ལྟག་འོག་འགལ་འདུས་སྟོང་པ་དང་།།
སྐྱེ་རྒུའི་དོན་གཉིས་སྟེར་བྱེད་པ།།
ལུགས་འདིར་ཁོ་བོ་སྤྲོ་བ་འཕེལ།།

འདི་ཡི་ཕྱིར་དུ་ཁྱོད་ཀྱིས་ནི།།
ལ་ལར་སྐུ་དང་གཞན་དུ་སྒྲོག །
སྡུག་པའི་གཉེན་དང་ལོངས་སྤྱོད་ཚོགས།།
གྲངས་མེད་བསྐལ་པར་ཡང་ཡང་བཏང་།།

གང་གི་ཡོན་ཏན་མཐོང་བ་ཡིས།།
ལྕགས་ཀྱུས་ཉ་ལ་ཇི་བཞིན་དུ།།
ཉིད་ཀྱི་ཐུགས་དྲངས་ཆོས་དེ་ནི།།
ཁྱོད་ལས་མ་ཐོས་སྐལ་བ་ཞན།།

དེ་ཡི་མྱ་ངན་ཤུགས་ཀྱིས་ནི།།
སྡུག་པའི་བུ་ལ་མ་ཡི་ཡིད།།
རྗེས་སུ་སོང་བ་ཇི་བཞིན་དུ།།
བདག་གི་ཡིད་ནི་གཏོང་མི་བྱེད།།

Across their breadth, no contradiction;
opponents' arguments all destroyed—
fulfilling the two aims of living beings.
My joy in these teachings grows and grows.

For this knowledge you gave away—
over countless eons again and again—
your loved ones, your possessions,
sometimes your body, other times your life.

Seeing such qualities
I am drawn by your mind
like a fish on the hook.
Not hearing your Dharma from you in person,
such misfortune!

By the pain of such sorrow,
my mind will never give you up,
like the mind of a mother for her precious child.

འདི་ལའང་ཁྱོད་གསུང་བསམ་པ་ན།།
མཚན་དཔེའི་དཔལ་གྱིས་རབ་ཏུ་འབར།།
འོད་ཀྱི་དྲ་བས་ཡོངས་བསྐོར་བའི།།
སྟོན་པ་དེ་ཡི་ཚངས་དབྱངས་ཀྱིས།།
འདི་ནི་འདི་ལྟར་གསུངས་སྙམ་དུ།།
ཡིད་ལ་ཐུབ་པའི་གཟུགས་བརྙན་ནི།།
ཤར་བ་ཙམ་ཡང་ཚ་བ་ཡིས།།
གདུངས་ལ་ཟླ་ཟེར་བཞིན་དུ་སྨན།།

དེ་ལྟར་རྨད་དུ་བྱུང་བ་ཡི།།
ལུགས་བཟང་དེ་ཡང་མི་མཁས་པའི།།
སྐྱེ་བོས་བལ་པ་ཛ་བཞིན་དུ།།
རྣམ་པ་ཀུན་ཏུ་འཛིངས་པར་བྱས།།
ཚུལ་འདི་མཐོང་ནས་བདག་གིས་ནི།།
འབད་པ་དུ་མས་མཁས་པ་ཡི།།
རྗེས་སུ་འབྲངས་ནས་ཁྱོད་ཀྱི་ནི།།
དགོངས་པ་ཡང་དང་ཡང་དུ་བཙལ།།

And yet as I think on your words,
hearing you talk of this and that,
teacher with a voice melodic as Brahma,
resplendent with features of perfection
encircled by garlands of light,
your enlightened form reflects in my mind,
like the cool light of the moon,
medicine for my feverish torment.

Those unwise in this wonderful doctrine
were confused and entangled like plaited grass.
Seeing this, I followed with diligence the great scholars,
seeking again and again your thoughts,
poring over many works of our and others' tradition,
yet still my mind was torn by doubts.

དེ་ཚེ་རང་གཞན་སྡེ་པ་ཡི།།
གཞུང་མང་དག་ལ་སྦྱངས་པ་ན།།
ཕྱི་ཕྱིར་ཐེ་ཚོམ་དྲ་བ་ཡིས།།
བདག་གི་ཡིད་ནི་ཀུན་ཏུ་གདུངས།།
ཁྱོད་ཀྱི་བླ་མེད་ཐེག་པའི་ཚུལ།།
ཡོད་དང་མེད་པའི་མཐའ་སྤངས་ཏེ།།
ཇི་བཞིན་འགྲེལ་པར་ལུང་བསྟན་པ།།
ཀླུ་སྒྲུབ་གཞུང་ལུགས་ཀུན་དའི་ཚལ།།
དྲི་མེད་མཁྱེན་པའི་དཀྱིལ་འཁོར་རྒྱས།།
གསུང་རབ་མཁའ་ལ་ཐོགས་མེད་རྒྱུ།།
མཐར་འཛིན་སྙིང་གི་མུན་པ་སེལ།།
ལོག་སྨྲའི་རྒྱུ་སྐར་ཟིལ་གནོན་པ།།
དཔལ་ལྡན་ཟླ་བའི་ལེགས་བཤད་ཀྱི།།
འོད་དཀར་ཕྲེང་བས་གསལ་བྱས་པ།།
བླ་མའི་དྲིན་གྱིས་མཐོང་བའི་ཚེ།།
བདག་གི་ཡིད་ཀྱིས་ངལ་གསོ་ཐོབ།།

When, with the kindness of my lamas, I saw
this unsurpassed vehicle of yours leaving behind
extremes of existence and nonexistence,
elucidated by the prophesized Nagarjuna,
his lotus grove illuminated by the moonlight
of the glorious Chandrakirti's teachings,
whose globe of stainless wisdom moved
freely through the sky of your words,
dispelling the darkness that holds to extremes,
outshining the stars of false speakers—
it was then that my mind found its peace.

མཛད་པ་ཀུན་ལས་གསུང་གི་ནི།།
མཛད་པ་མཆོག་ཡིན་དེ་ཡང་ནི།།
འདི་ཉིད་ཡིན་ཕྱིར་མཁས་པ་ཡིས།།
འདི་ལས་སངས་རྒྱས་རྗེས་དྲན་བྱོས།།

སྟོན་དེའི་རྗེས་སུ་རབ་ཏུ་བྱུང་གྱུར་ཏེ།།
རྒྱལ་བའི་གསུང་ལ་སྦྱངས་པ་མི་དམན་ཞིང་།།
རྣལ་འབྱོར་སྤྱོད་ལ་བརྩོན་པའི་དགེ་སློང་ཞིག །
དྲང་སྲོང་ཆེན་པོ་དེ་ལ་དེ་ལྟར་གུས།།

སྟོན་པ་བླ་ན་མེད་པའི་བསྟན་པ་དང་།།
མཇལ་བ་འདི་འདྲ་བླ་མའི་དྲིན་ཡིན་པས།།
དགེ་བ་འདི་ཡང་འགྲོ་བ་མ་ལུས་པ།།
བཤེས་གཉེན་དམ་པས་འཛིན་པའི་རྒྱུ་རུ་བསྔོ།།

ཕན་མཛད་དེ་ཡི་བསྟན་པའང་སྲིད་པའི་མཐར།།
ངན་རྟོག་རླུང་གིས་རྣམ་པར་མི་གཡོ་ཞིང་།།
བསྟན་པའི་ངང་ཚུལ་ཤེས་ནས་སྟོན་པ་ལ།།
ཡིད་ཆེས་བརྙེད་པས་རྟག་ཏུ་གང་བར་ཤོག །

Of all Buddha's deeds his words were the greatest,
and they were words of dependent arising.
Let the wise, therefore, remember him this way.

Becoming ordained into the way of the Buddha
by not being lax in study of his words,
and by yoga practice of great resolve,
this monk devotes himself to that great purveyor of truth.

Due to the kindness of my lamas,
I have met the teachings of the greatest of teachers.
I dedicate this virtue, therefore, for every living being
to be nourished by true spiritual friends.

I pray that the teachings of he who is solely benevolent
remain unscattered by the winds of false views until the end
of time,
and with faith in the Buddha gained from understanding
their essential nature, may they pervade forever.

བརྟེན་ནས་འབྱུང་བའི་དེ་ཉིད་གསལ་མཛད་པ།།
ཐུབ་པའི་ལུགས་བཟང་སྐྱེ་བ་ཐམས་ཅད་དུ།།
ལུས་དང་སྲོག་ཀྱང་བཏང་ནས་འཛིན་པ་ལ།།
སྐད་ཅིག་ཙམ་ཡང་ལྷོད་པར་མ་གྱུར་ཅིག །

འདྲེན་པ་མཆོག་དེས་དཀའ་བ་དཔག་མེད་ཀྱིས།།
ནན་ཏན་སྙིང་པོར་མཛད་ནས་བསྒྲུབས་པ་འདི།།
ཐབས་གང་ཞིག་གིས་འཕེལ་བར་འགྱུར་སྙམ་པའི།།
རྣམ་པར་དཔྱོད་པས་ཉིན་མཚན་འདའ་བར་ཤོག །

ལྷག་བསམ་དག་པས་རྒྱལ་དེར་བརྩོན་པ་ན།།
ཚངས་དང་དབང་པོ་འཇིག་རྟེན་སྐྱོང་བ་དང་།།
ལེགས་ལྡན་ནག་པོ་ལ་སོགས་སྲུང་མས་ཀྱང་།།
གཡེལ་བ་མེད་པར་རྟག་ཏུ་གྲོགས་བྱེད་ཤོག །

In all my births, even at the cost of my life,
may I never falter nor shrink from working
for the wonderful doctrine of the mighty Buddha,
who showed clearly the nature of dependent arising.

I pray that I pass my days and nights
in thinking how I might spread this Dharma,
born from the heroic perseverance
in the face of countless hardships
of this supreme guide.

When I pursue these endeavors wholeheartedly and sincerely,
may I be supported constantly by Brahma, Indra, Mahakala,
the four guardians of the world, and all other protectors.

ཤེར་ཕྱིན་གྱི་མདོ་པར་འདེབས་ཀྱི་སྨོན་ཚིགས།།

༄༅ །། །།རྒྱལ་བ་དཔག་མེད་རྣམས་ཀྱི་ཚངས་དབྱངས་ཀྱིས།།
ཟབ་ཅིང་རྒྱ་ཆེའི་འཁོར་ལོ་བསྐོར་བའི་ཁུར།།
གང་གིས་བཟུང་བའི་རི་ཡི་དབང་པོ་ནི།།
དཔལ་ལྡན་བྱ་རྒོད་ཕུང་པོ་ཞེས་སུ་གྲགས།།

རྨད་བྱུང་ས་འཛིན་མཆོག་དེར་མངོན་གཤེགས་ནས།།
ཕྱོགས་བཅུའི་ཞིང་དུ་འོད་ཀྱིས་རབ་འགེངས་ཤིང་།།
ས་ཆེན་རྣམ་པ་དྲུག་ཏུ་གཡོ་མཛད་པའི།།
ཤཱཀྱ་སེང་གེའི་ཞབས་ལ་མགོས་ཕྱག་འཚལ།།

དེར་ནི་ཐུབ་པའི་དཔལ་གྱི་མགུར་ནས་ནི།།
ཕུན་ཚོགས་འཁོར་ལ་ལེགས་པར་བཀའ་སྩལ་པ།།
ལེགས་བཤད་ཀུན་གྱི་རབ་དང་ཕུལ་ཉིད་ནི།།
ལེགས་བཤད་བླ་མེད་ཤེས་རབ་ཕ་རོལ་ཕྱིན།།

Verses of Benediction

On Publication of a New Edition of Perfection of Wisdom Sutras

The turning of Dharma wheels, profound and vast,
in melodic tones of buddhas beyond number
was hosted by that most powerful of mountains
renowned as Glorious Vulture's Peak.

On that awesome peak he came,
worlds of every direction brimming with light,
the very earth shaking in six ways,
to the Lion of the Shakyas I bow.

On that peak, from the mighty Buddha,
exquisitely delivered to exemplary listeners,
the choicest, the finest of all fine speech,
the incomparable Perfection of Wisdom.

དེ་ནི་ལྷ་མིའི་འདྲེན་པས་ལན་གསུམ་དུ།།
རྒྱལ་བས་གསུངས་པའི་ཆོས་མཛོད་ཀུན་འཛིན་པ།།
ཆོས་འཛིན་ཀུན་དགའ་བོ་ལ་གཏོད་པ་ན།།
ང་ཡིས་བཤད་པའི་ཆོས་ཀྱི་རྣམ་གྲངས་གཞན།།
མ་ལུས་བོར་ཏམ་ཆུད་གཟོན་གྱུར་ཀྱང་བློའི།།
རྒྱལ་བའི་ཡུམ་འདི་ཙུང་ཟད་ཆུད་གཟན་ན།།
དེ་ཚེ་ཁྱོད་ལ་སྐྱོན་དུ་བཟང་ངོ་ཞེས།།
ནན་ཏན་ཆེན་པོས་བཀའ་སྩལ་མཛད་པ་དང་།།

མདོ་སྡེ་མཆོག་འདི་གང་དུ་བཞུགས་པའི་ཡུལ།།
དེར་ནི་རྒྱལ་བའི་དབང་པོ་བཞུགས་སོ་ཞེས།།
སྟོན་པ་ཉིད་དང་ཁྱད་པར་མ་མཆིས་པར།།
ཉིད་ཀྱི་ཞལ་ནས་རྣམ་པ་དུ་མར་བསྔགས།།

འདི་བྲིས་པ་དང་ཀློག་དང་མཆོད་ལ་སོགས།།
གསུང་རབ་གཞན་ལས་ཆེས་ཆེར་ཁྱད་ཞུགས་པར།།
ཡང་དང་ཡང་དུ་གཏན་ཚིགས་དང་བཅས་ཏེ།།
གསུངས་ཕྱིར་འདི་ལ་འཇུག་རྣམས་སྐལ་བ་བཟང་།།

When preservation of the conqueror's words
was entrusted to Ananda, keeper of Dharma,
three times the Buddha emphasized,
"Were all other words spoken by me
to be lost or left to waste, then so be it,
but if merely a fraction of the Perfection of Wisdom,
Mother of all Buddhas, were to be lost,
Ananda you would be at fault."

Furthermore, you have said,
"Where these, the greatest of sutras, are found,
there too is found the power of the Buddha."
In various ways, therefore, you hailed the Perfection of
  Wisdom
as being indistinguishable from the Buddha.

It has been often said, supported by reason,
that to read, write, and honor the Perfection of Wisdom
is of greater merit than that gained from other sutras.
Those that do this, therefore, are fortunate indeed.

ཚུལ་འདི་གཟིགས་ནས་མཁས་པ་དུ་མ་ཡིས།།
འབད་པ་ཆེན་པོས་ཡང་ཡང་བསྔགས་མཛད་པས།།
དད་ལྡན་རྣམས་ལ་བཟང་པོའི་སྤྲོ་བ་བསྐྱེད་པ།།
ད་དུང་བར་དུ་ཉམས་པར་མ་གྱུར་ཏེ།།
དེ་ཕྱིར་མངོན་མཐོའི་དཔལ་གྱིས་རབ་ཏུ་མཛེས།།
སྐྱབས་གསུམ་བླ་མ་གཙུག་གི་རྒྱན་དུ་འཛིན།།
རང་སྲིད་ཚུལ་བཞིན་སྐྱོང་བའི་ཁུར་ཁྱེར་བ།།
བསྟན་པའི་སྦྱིན་བདག་ནམ་མཁའ་བཟང་པོ་དང་།།
བསྟན་ལ་གུས་ཤིང་གཏོང་ལ་རབ་ཏུ་དགའ།།
མི་དབང་ཆེན་པོའི་ལྕམ་མོ་རིན་ཅེན་སྒྲོན།།
གཞོན་ཡང་རྒན་པོའི་བློ་གྲོས་ཅན་གྱུར་པ།།
གྲགས་པ་དབང་ཕྱུག་ཡབ་ཡུམ་སྲས་གསུམ་ནི།།

དགེ་ལེགས་འབུམ་ཕྲག་དུ་མའི་གཞིར་གྱུར་པ།།
ལམ་བཟང་འདི་ལ་ཤིན་ཏུ་མོས་གྱུར་ཏེ།།
སྟོང་ཕྲག་བརྒྱ་པ་ལ་སོགས་ཤེར་ཕྱིན་དང་།།
ཏིང་འཛིན་རྒྱལ་པོ་དམ་ཆོས་པད་མ་དཀར།།
རྒྱ་ཆེ་རོལ་པ་གཟུགས་མཆོག་གྲུ་ལྔ་དང་།།
ཡངས་པའི་གྲོང་འཇུག་བསྐལ་པ་བཟང་པོ་སྟེ།།

Knowing this, the wise, with great pains,
have lauded again and again such practice
and in doing so have initiated for the faithful
a noble tradition continued to this day.
Because of this, Namkha Zangpo, Dharma patron,
handsome with the splendor of high birth,
holding his triple-refuge lamas as crown jewels,
tending dutifully his worldly affairs,
his wife, Rinchen Dron, devoted to the teachings,
delighting in the practice of giving,
their son, Dragpa Wangchuk, young in years, old in wisdom,
all three—mother, father, son—have laid the groundwork
for an abundance of all that is virtuous and good.

With great faith in a noble practice,
using binders as flawless as lapis and ink of natural gold,
they have created to the inspiration of all
a visual feast without parallel, pure nectar to the eyes,
including among twenty-nine sutras

མདོ་སྡེའི་རྣམ་གྲངས་ཉི་ཤུ་རྩ་དགུ་ནི།།
པེ་ཏྟུ་ལྷར་དག་པའི་གླེགས་བམ་ལ།།
རིན་ཆེན་ས་ལེ་སྦྲམ་གྱིས་ལེགས་བྲིས་པ།།
མིག་ལ་བདུད་རྩིའི་དགའ་སྟོན་འགྱེད་པའི་མཆོག །
ངོ་མཚར་གནས་སུ་གྱུར་པ་འདི་དག་བཞེངས།།

དེ་ནི་ལྷ་དང་བཅས་པའི་འཇིག་རྟེན་གྱི།།
འཕྲལ་དང་ཡུན་གྱི་ཕན་དང་བདེ་བའི་གཞི།།
རྒྱལ་བའི་བསྟན་པ་ལུང་དང་རྟོགས་པའི་ཆོས།།
ཕྱོགས་དུས་ཀུན་ཏུ་རྒྱས་པའི་ཕྱིར་དུ་ཡིན།།
མཁས་པར་སྦྱངས་པའི་ཡི་གེ་པ་རྣམས་ལ།།
སྙེད་དང་བཀུར་སྟི་མཆོག་གིས་མཆོད་པ་དང་།།
ཞུས་གཉེན་མཁས་པ་དག་གིས་གྲོགས་མཛད་པས།།
གླེགས་བམ་འདི་རྣམས་གཞན་ལས་ཕུལ་དུ་བྱུང་།།
སྙིགས་དུས་འགྲོ་བའི་བསོད་ནམས་ཞིང་གཅིག་པུ།།

the *Hundred-thousand-versed Perfection of Wisdom,*
the *Samadhi Raja, Saddharma Pundarika,*
Lalita Vistara, Bhadrakalpa, and others.

This is done to spread to all corners of the world
scripture and insight of Buddha's holy teaching,
source of all good—transient or long-lasting
in the worlds of men and gods.
The scribes being men wisely taught,
richly served with material need and respect,
aided by masters wise and scholarly,
this publication outshines all others.

ཤཱཀྱའི་རྒྱལ་པོའི་ཕོ་བྲང་ལྷ་ས་ཡི།།
ཉེ་འཁོར་གནས་སུ་གྱུར་པའི་ས་ཡི་ཆ།།
ཕུན་ཚོགས་དཔལ་གྱི་དགེ་མཚན་རབ་འཛིན་པ།།
བཀྲ་ཤིས་ཆུ་བོ་དལ་གྱིས་འབབ་པའི་ངོགས།།
ཡིད་འཛིན་སྐྱེད་ཚལ་ཕྲེང་བས་བསྐོར་བ་ལ།།
ས་ཡི་ཐིག་ལེར་གནས་པའི་གཞིས་ཀ་ནི།།
སྣེའུ་ཞེས་གྱུར་བདེ་སླག་ཉིད་དུ་གྲུབ།།

བདེ་གཤེགས་ཀུན་གྱི་ལམ་གཅིག་པུ།།
རྒྱལ་བ་སྲས་བཅས་སྐྱེད་པའི་ཡུམ།།
རབ་ཟབ་བསྟན་པའི་སྙིང་པོ་མཆོག །
གཞུང་བཟང་སྟོང་ཕྲག་བརྒྱ་པ་སོགས།།
བསྒྲུབས་ལས་བསོད་ནམས་གང་ཐོབ་དེས།།
རྐང་གཉིས་གཙོ་བོ་སངས་རྒྱས་སུ།།
རིང་པོར་མི་ཐོགས་བདག་གྱུར་ཏེ།།
འགྲོ་ཀུན་སངས་རྒྱས་སར་འདྲེན་ཤོག །

Not far from Lhasa, city palace of our Shakya king,
sole field of merit in degenerate times,
this land, delightfully endowed with every gift,
surrounded by groves pleasing to the mind,
alongside the gently moving bountiful river
in this peaceful settlement, nestled in the earth,
known as the region of Neu,
has this come to be.

By the virtue sown through practice of
the *Hundred-thousand-versed* and other Perfection of
  Wisdom sutras,
the sole path walked by those gone to bliss,
essence of a great and profound doctrine,
mother giving birth to buddhas and bodhisattvas,
may I soon become a buddha, a lord among men,
leading living beings to such an exalted state.

ཇི་སྲིད་དེ་མ་ཐོབ་པ་ཡི། །
སྐྱེ་བ་གཞན་དང་གཞན་དག་ཏུ། །
ཐེག་མཆོག་རིགས་སུ་སྐྱེ་བ་དང་། །
བཤེས་གཉེན་དམ་པ་རྙེད་པར་ཤོག །

དེ་ལས་ཤེས་རབ་ཕ་རོལ་ཕྱིན། །
ལེགས་པར་ཐོས་ཤིང་སེམས་པ་དང་། །
དེ་དོན་ཚུལ་བཞིན་སྒྲུབ་པ་ཡིས། །
རྒྱལ་རྣམས་མཉེས་པར་བྱེད་པར་ཤོག །

སེམས་ནི་ཉོན་མོངས་དབང་སོང་བས། །
ལུས་དང་ངག་དང་ཡིད་ཀྱིས་ནི། །
སྡིག་པ་གང་དག་བགྱིས་པ་རྣམས། །
དེ་དག་ཐམས་ཅད་བྱང་གྱུར་ཅིག །

སངས་རྒྱས་བྱང་ཆུབ་སེམས་དཔའ་དང་། །
རྣམ་པ་ཀུན་ཏུ་མི་འབྲལ་ཞིང་། །
དེ་ཡིས་བསྟན་པའི་ལམ་བཟང་ལ། །
ལྷག་བསམ་ཆེན་པོ་བརྩོན་འགྲུས་རྩོམ་པར་ཤོག །

For as long as I fall short of that destination,
may I be born life after life of Mahayana lineage
and never fail to find a precious teacher.

In his presence may I hear and study the Perfection of
Wisdom
and by faultless application of its meanings,
delight the conquering buddhas.

May I purify myself of every error
committed in body, speech, and thought
through a mind under the sway of delusion.

May I, in every way, forever be together
with the buddhas and bodhisattvas,
and on the noble path taught by them,
may I be of undaunted perseverance.

རིགས་མགོ་གཟུགས་མཛེས་གཟི་བརྗིད་ཆེ།།
ཚེ་མཐར་ཕྱིན་དང་ནད་མེད་དང་།།
ཆོས་ལྡན་འབྱོར་པ་ཕུན་ཚོགས་ཤིང་།།
ཤེས་རབ་རྒྱ་ཆེན་ཐོབ་པར་ཤོག །

ཡུལ་ཕྱོགས་ཀུན་ཏུ་དཔལ་འབར་ཞིང་།།
དགེ་ལེགས་རྒྱུན་མི་འཆད་པ་་དང་།།
དཀར་ཕྱོགས་སྐྱོང་བའི་ལྷ་རྣམས་ཀྱིས།།
རྟག་ཏུ་བརྩེ་བས་སྐྱོང་གྱུར་ཅིག །

འདི་ཡི་ཆེད་དུ་ལུས་དང་ངག །
ཡིད་ཀྱིས་མཐུན་པའི་རྐྱེན་རྣམས་ནི།།
ཅུང་ཟད་ཙམ་རེ་བྱས་པ་རྣམས།།
ཀུན་ཀྱང་བྱང་ཆུབ་མཆོག་ཐོབ་ཤོག །

ཤིན་ཏུ་རྒྱས་པའི་མདོ་སྡེ་འདི།།
གང་དང་གང་དུ་བཞུགས་གྱུར་པ།།
དེ་དང་དེར་ནི་མི་མཐུན་ཕྱོགས།།
ཞི་ཞིང་བདེ་ལེགས་རྒྱས་གྱུར་ཅིག །

May I be endowed with high birth, a handsome form,
charisma, wealth, and prosperity on a spiritual base,
of great intelligence and a long life bereft of illness.

May fortune shine in every corner of the world,
may virtue and goodness know no end,
and may those protectors of all that is good
forever guard with love.

Toward that end, may all those who,
with body, speech, and thought, create
even one solitary opportune moment
attain the highest enlightenment.

Wherever these vast scriptures reside,
there may all misfortune subside
and happiness and joy flourish.

དེ་ལྟར་ངོ་མཚར་ཡོན་ཏན་ཀུན་གྱི་གཞི།།
དམ་ཆོས་རིན་ཆེན་འདི་ཡི་བྱིན་རླབས་ཀྱིས།།
ཚེ་རབས་འདིར་ཡང་བར་ཆད་ཀུན་ཞི་ནས།།
སྨོན་ལམ་ཐམས་ཅད་ཆོས་བཞིན་འགྲུབ་པར་ཤོག །

By the blessings of the precious Dharma,
source of every remarkable quality,
may every obstruction in this life melt away
and every prayer come true.

ཆོས་རྒྱལ་ནང་སྒྲུབ་ཀྱི་བསྟོད་པ་བཞུགས་སོ།

༄༅ ། ། ན་མཿ ཤྲཱི་བཛྲ་བྷཻ་ར་ཝཱ་ཡ།།

བརྒྱངས་བསྐུམས་ཞབས་ནི་ཙུང་ཟད་བརྡབས་པ་ཙམ་གྱིས་དཀྱིལ་
འཁོར་བཞིར་བཅས་རི་དབང་ཤིག་ཤིག་པོར་འགྱུར་ཞིང་།།
གཏུམ་དྲག་མ་ཧེའི་ཞལ་ནི་རབ་ཏུ་གདངས་པས་བསྒྲགས་པའི་གད་
རྒྱངས་ཆེན་པོས་ས་གསུམ་ཀུན་འགེངས་པ།།
རྒྱལ་བའི་ཡབ་གཅིག་འཇམ་པའི་དབྱངས་གང་མ་རུངས་འདུལ་ཕྱིར་
དྲག་པོའི་སྐུར་བསྟན་བཅོམ་ལྡན་གཤིན་རྗེའི་གཤེད།།
གང་དེར་གུས་པས་བཏུད་ནས་གཤིན་རྗེའི་རྒྱལ་པོ་བསྟོད་ཀྱིས་ད་ནི་
བགེགས་རྣམས་བག་ཡོད་དུས་ལ་བབས།།

རི་བོ་རལ་ཞིང་ཆུ་གཏེར་འཁྲུགས་པ་ལྷ་བུར་ཙུར་ཙུར་
ཞེས་པའི་སྒྲ་ཆེན་བརྒྱུད་མར་རབ་སྒྲོགས་པ།།
དྲག་པོའི་མེ་ལྕེ་གནག་པའི་དུ་བས་འཁྲུད་པའི་ཚོགས་རྣམས་འབུམ་
ཕྲག་གློག་ཕྲེང་ཆར་སྤྲིན་ནང་འཁྲུག་བཞིན།།
ཤིན་ཏུ་བཟོད་དཀའི་རེག་བྱ་ཚ་བའི་ངར་ལྡན་ཁ་དོག་ལྷ་ཡི་ཕྲེང་བས་
ཀླུམ་པོར་བསྐོར་བའི་དབུས།།

Praise of the Protector Dharmaraja

Homage to blessed Vajra Bhairava!

One leg outstretched, the other drawn in,
the merest tap sending shudders through
mighty Meru and the four mandalas of the earth,
rapacious and wide-open buffalo mouth,
its thundering laugh filling the three worlds,
Manjushri, father of buddhas in wrathful form
as ferocious Yamantaka taming the dissolute.
Those prostrating devotedly before him
should offer praise to Dharmaraja.
Now is the time to beware of hindrance.

An incessant thunder of sound,
like mountains splitting apart, like the sea in tumult,
raging tongues of fire enveloped in black smoke,
like a million lightning flashes within a rain cloud,
standing amid unbearable heat encircled by five colors,
upon a black demon prostrate on a mandala circle of the sun,

སྨུན་པ་བྲེ་བས་བྲུགས་ལྟར་གནག་པའི་ཆོས་འབྱུང་ཆལ་ཆིལ་གཡོ་བའི་
ཁྲག་ཞག་རྒྱ་མཚོས་གང་བའི་སྟེང་།།

རྟ་བདུན་བདག་པོའི་གདན་ལ་གནོད་བྱེད་ནག་པོ་གན་རྐྱལ་བསྒྱེལ་བའི་
སྟེང་ན་གཤིན་རྗེའི་རྒྱལ་པོ་ནི།།

མི་སྨན་ལྟར་གནག་ཐུང་ལ་སྦོམ་པའི་ལུས་ཅན་གཡས་བརྐྱངས་གཡོན་
བསྐུམས་ས་ཆེན་གཡོ་བའི་གོམས་སྟབས་ཅན།།

སེར་སྐྱའི་རལ་པ་གྱེན་དུ་འཛིངས་པའི་དབུ་ལ་ཐོད་སྐམ་ལྔས་བརྒྱན་དྲག་
པོའི་རྡོ་རྗེ་སྤྱི་བོར་འཛིན།།

ཁྲག་གིས་སྦགས་པའི་མགོ་རློན་ཕྲེང་བ་མགྲིན་པར་འཕྱང་ཞིང་སྤྱན་
གསུམ་བགྲད་པའི་སྡང་མིག་གཡོ་བ་ཅན།།

མཆེ་བ་རྣོན་པོར་གཙིགས་པའི་བགྲད་པའི་ཞལ་ནས་དབུགས་ཕྲེང་གཡོ་
བ་གཏུག་པའི་སྤྲུལ་གྱི་ཁ་རླངས་བཞིན།།

གཡས་པས་འབར་བའི་གྲི་གུག་བདུད་དཔུང་ཀླད་ལ་འཕྱུར་ཞིང་ཁྲག་
ལྡན་ཐོད་པ་གཡོན་གྱིས་བཟུང་ལ་རོལ།།

སྟག་ལྤགས་སྨད་གཡོགས་བགོས་པའི་གཏུམ་ཆེན་ཁྲོད་ཀྱིས་གཤིན་རྗེའི་
གཤེད་ལ་ཇི་ལྟར་ཞལ་བཞེས་དེ་བཞིན་དུ།།

མ་གཡེལ་མ་གཡེལ་མྱུར་དུ་དྲན་པར་མཛོད་ལ་རྣལ་འབྱོར་བདག་གིས་
གང་ཞིག་བསྒོ་བ་ཐམས་ཅད་སྒྲུབས།།

atop a sacred triangle black as a billionfold darkness,
brimming with a rolling ocean of blood and fat,
Yamaraja, king of the Lords of Death,
jet-black body, short and not slender,
stretched to the right with a gait to shake the earth,
yellowish spiky hair nestling five dried skulls
ornamenting the wrathful vajra upon your crown,
fresh and bloody human heads garlanding your neck,
three bulging eyes roving wrathfully,
a fanged snarl about your open mouth,
the vaporous breath of a venomous snake,
a blazing curved knife in your right hand
brandished at the brains of Mara's armies,
in the left a blood-filled skull to enjoy,
a tiger skin draped about your waist—
ferocious protector, do not be distracted,
quickly bring to mind promises made to Yamantaka
and carry out this yogi's commands.

གཞན་ཡང་ཁྱོད་ཀྱི་ཕྱོགས་བཞིར་རྦ་དང་རྨིག་པ་རབ་ཏུ་རྙོ་བའི་མ་ཧེའི་དྲག་པོའི་གདན་སྟེང་ན།།
དཀར་དང་སེར་དང་དམར་དང་གནག་པོའི་གཤིན་རྗེ་ཆེན་པོ་དྲག་ཏུ་ཁྲོས་པའི་མ་ཧེའི་གདོང་པ་ཅན།།
བརྐྱངས་བསྐུམས་སྟབས་ཀྱིས་རབ་ཏུ་འགྱིང་ཞིང་དུར་ཁྲོད་ཆས་ཀྱིས་ལེགས་བརྒྱན་ཞལ་གདངས་མིག་རྩ་ཀུན་ཏུ་དམར།།
བགེགས་དཔུང་འཇོམས་ལ་རྡོ་རྗེའི་ཐོག་ལྟར་བསྔགས་པ་དེ་དག་གིས་ཀྱང་ཞི་རྒྱས་དབང་དྲག་ལས་ཀུན་སྒྲུབས།།

མདོར་ན་རྒྱལ་བ་ཀུན་གྱིས་ཡང་དང་ཡང་བསྔགས་འཇམ་པའི་དབྱངས་ཞེས་ས་སྟེང་ཀུན་ཏུ་གྲགས་པ་དེའི།།
ཕུན་ཚོགས་གོ་འཕང་མཆོག་དེ་མཁའ་མཉམ་ལུས་ཅན་ཀུན་གྱི་དོན་དུ་ཇི་སྲིད་བདག་གིས་མ་མཐན་པ།།
དེ་སྲིད་གཤིན་རྗེ་གཤེད་ཀྱི་བཀའ་ནི་གུས་པས་ལྷུར་ལེན་ཆོས་རྒྱལ་གཤིན་རྗེ་འཁོར་དང་བཅས་པ་ཡིས།།
ཡང་དག་ལམ་གྱི་ནོར་མཆོག་འཕྲོག་ལ་བརྩོན་པའི་ནག་པོའི་རྩ་ལག་སྡེ་དང་བཅས་པ་གཞོམ་པར་མཛོད།།

On either side, in front and behind,
standing on sharp-horned, sharp-hoofed fierce buffaloes,
four yama demons—white, yellow, red, and black—
each horribly wrathful with buffalo face,
one leg stretched, the other drawn in,
striking an extremely arrogant pose,
all garbed in graveyard array,
open-mouthed, eyeballs wholly red,
hailed as vajra thunderbolts
in their destruction of hindrance and obstruction.
You too, discharge your deeds,
peaceful, wrathful, powerful, or vast.

To conclude;
so long as I have not yet walked
for living beings as vast as space
upon the glorious land of Manjushri,
famed on earth, severally praised by every Buddha,
then for so long, I ask you Dharmaraja and entourage,
who gladly and devotedly execute Yamantaka's will,
destroy the consort of darkness and his legions
who strive to steal the jewel that is the true path!

ཕྲེང་བའི་གསོལ་འདེབས་ཚིགས་བཅད་ཉེར་གཅིག་མ།།

ན་མོ་གུ་རུ་མཉྫུ་གྷོ་ཥཱ་ཡ།

དཔག་ཡས་བསྐལ་པར་རྨད་བྱུང་སྤྱོད་པ་ཡིས།།
མ་ལུས་འགྲོ་བ་སྒྲོལ་བའི་ཁུར་ཁྱེར་བ།།
ཕྱོགས་བཅུའི་ཞིང་ན་ཇི་སྙེད་བཞུགས་པ་ཡི།།
ཐུབ་དབང་སྲས་དང་བཅས་རྣམས་དགོངས་སུ་གསོལ།།

འདིར་ནི་རླབས་ཆེན་སྤྱོད་ལ་འཇུག་པའི་ཕྱིར།།
རྒྱལ་སྲས་རྣམས་ཀྱི་ཐབས་ལ་འཇུག་པའི་སྒོ།།
རབ་འབྱམས་ཚོགས་གཉིས་སྡུད་པའི་གཏེར་ཆེན་པོ།།
དྲི་མེད་སྨོན་ལམ་ཕྲེང་བ་གདབ་པར་བགྱི།།

གང་གང་གུས་པས་ཇི་ལྟར་གསོལ་བྱེད་པ།།
དེ་དང་དེ་ཡི་འདོད་པ་བསྐང་རོ་ཞེས།།
ཉིན་མཚན་ཀུན་ཏུ་འགྲོ་ལ་གཟིགས་རྣམས་ཀྱིས།།
བདག་གི་སྨོན་པ་བདེ་བླག་འགྲུབ་པར་མཛོད།།

Twenty-one Verse Rosary Prayer

Homage to my guru, the youthful Manjushri!

With awe-inspiring deeds over eons beyond number
you assumed the mantle of freeing all living beings,
mighty buddhas and bodhisattvas of all worlds,
of all directions, hear these words.

⁂

To partake of great bodhisattva practice,
I make this pure rosary prayer
for unending wealth of dual spiritual merit,
entrance to the way of the bodhisattva.

"Those that pray with devotion, their prayers will be
fulfilled."
You who gaze both night and day upon all living beings,
swiftly and painlessly answer my prayer.

བདག་གིས་ལེགས་པར་སྤྱད་པའི་ཚོགས།།
བགྱིས་དང་བགྱིད་འགྱུར་ཅི་མཆིས་པ།།
གཞན་ཡང་དགེ་ཚོགས་གང་ཡིན་པ།།
དེ་དག་གཅིག་ཏུ་བསྡོམས་པ་ཡིས།།

འཇིག་རྟེན་རྣམ་པར་འདྲེན་པ་ཡི།།
གོ་འཕང་དམ་པ་མངོན་བགྱིས་ནས།།
སྡུག་བསྔལ་མཚོར་ལྷུང་ཉམ་ཐག་ཀུན།།
སྲིད་ལས་མྱུར་དུ་སྒྲོལ་བར་ཤོག །

གོ་འཕང་མཆོག་ལ་མ་རེག་པར།།
སྐྱེ་ཞིང་སྐྱེ་བར་རྒྱལ་བ་ཡི།།
བསྟན་ལ་རབ་ཏུ་འབྱུང་བ་དང་།།
ཚུལ་ཁྲིམས་ཡོངས་སུ་དག་པར་ཤོག །

དམ་པའི་མགོན་ལ་བརྟེན་ནས་ནི།།
དེ་ཡི་རྗེས་སུ་བསྟན་པ་ལ།།
ཐོས་དང་བསམ་དང་སྒོམ་པ་ཡིས།།
རྣམ་པ་ཀུན་ཏུ་སློབ་པར་ཤོག །

I pray that by gathering together the good I have done
and will continue to do, and by every other virtue,
I arrive at the sacred state of a buddha.

When I become an enlightened guide for the world,
may I rescue quickly from samsara the weak and helpless
who flounder in the vast ocean of suffering.

Until I reach that exalted state
I pray that I am ordained life after life,
into the teachings of the conquering Buddha,
to keep the purest of pure morality.

I pray that I rely upon a true spiritual guide
and grow learned in every possible way
through study, thought, and meditation.

ཟབ་པ་དང་ནི་རྒྱ་ཆེ་བའི།།
ལེགས་བཤད་དཔག་མེད་ཐོས་པ་དང་།།
ཇི་བཞིན་འབྱེད་པའི་རྣམ་དཔྱོད་དང་།།
དེ་དག་ཆུད་མི་ཟ་བའི་རྒྱུ།།

མི་བརྗེད་པ་ཡི་གཟུངས་རྣམས་དང་།།
གཏུགས་པ་མེད་པའི་སྤོབས་པ་དང་།།
རྟག་ཏུ་སྦྱོར་བའི་བརྩོན་འགྲུས་དག །
ཟླ་དང་བྲལ་བ་ཐོབ་པར་ཤོག །

དེ་ཚེ་བཟང་པོའི་རྩོམ་པ་ལ།།
བར་དུ་གཅོད་པ་མེད་པ་དང་།།
རྗེས་སུ་མཐུན་པའི་རྐྱེན་རྣམས་ནི།།
བདེ་བླག་ཉིད་དུ་འབྱོར་པར་ཤོག །

རྒྱ་ཆེའི་ཞིང་ནི་སྦྱོང་བ་དང་།།
རྒྱལ་བ་མཆོད་དང་སེམས་ཅན་ཁམས།།
གྲངས་མེད་སྨིན་པར་བགྱིད་པ་ལ།།
འཇམ་པའི་དབྱངས་བཞིན་བདག་གྱུར་ཅིག །

I pray that I attain, to unparalleled degrees,
knowledge gleaned from listening to
countless explanations of the profound and vast,
and insight gained from unerring analysis.

To ensure such qualities are not wasted,
I pray to attain dharani powers of memory
as well as confidence unbound by limitation
and a perseverance constantly applied.

At such times, I pray never to meet
obstacle or hindrance to virtue-led endeavor
but be blessed by conducive circumstance.

I pray that, in the manner of noble Manjushri,
I purify vast realms, offer to buddhas,
and ripen countless worlds of living beings.

ལུས་དང་ངག་དང་ཡིད་ཀྱིས་ནི།།
སྤྱོད་པ་ཅི་དང་ཅི་སྤྱད་པ།།
ཐམས་ཅད་མཐའ་ཡས་འགྲོ་བ་ལ།།
ཕན་བདེ་དཔག་ཏུ་མེད་པར་ཤོག །

རྣམ་པ་ཀུན་ཏུ་སྡིག་གྲོགས་དང་།།
བདུད་ཀྱིས་བསླུ་བར་མི་ནུས་ཤིང་།།
བཤེས་གཉེན་བཟང་པོའི་རྗེས་ཞུགས་ནས།།
བྱང་ཆུབ་སྤྱོད་པ་རྫོགས་བྱེད་ཤོག །

དབེན་པའི་ཡོན་ཏན་མཐོང་བ་ཡིས།།
རྣམ་གཡེང་མ་ལུས་སྤོང་བ་དང་།།
རྟག་ཏུ་བག་དང་ལྡན་པ་ཡིས།།
སྒྲུབ་པ་སྙིང་པོར་བྱེད་པར་ཤོག །

འཇིག་རྟེན་ཆོས་བརྒྱད་དག་ལ་ནི།།
ཡིད་ནི་མཉམ་པ་ཉིད་ཐོབ་ཅིང་།།
རྟག་ཏུ་ཟང་ཟིང་མེད་པ་ཡི།།
ཆོས་ཀྱི་དགའ་བདེས་འཚོ་བར་ཤོག །

I pray every deed that I have done
in body, speech, and thought
brings happiness beyond limit
to living beings beyond number.

I pray that in no way I be misled
by unwholesome friends and deceiving Mara
but in the care of true spiritual friends,
complete the enlightened way of life.

I pray to see the benefits of solitude
and rid myself of mental wandering
and being forever mindful and attentive,
remain at the heart of my practice.

I pray that I develop equanimity
concerning the eight worldly attitudes
and find my joy in the Dharma,
forever free of the busy life.

ཐུབ་བསྟན་འཛིག་ཏུ་ཉེ་བའི་ཚེ།།
བསྟན་པ་འབའ་ཞིག་འགྲོ་ཀུན་གྱི།།
ཕན་བདེའི་རྒྱུ་བར་མཐོང་ནས་ནི།།
རྒྱལ་བའི་ཆོས་ཚུལ་འཛིན་གྱུར་ཅིག །

ཡིད་ནི་སྙིང་རྗེའི་དབང་གྱུར་ཏེ།།
ཇི་ལྟར་བགྲིས་ན་སེམས་ཅན་རྣམས།།
རྣམ་པར་གྲོལ་བར་འགྱུར་སྙམ་པའི།།
བསམ་པ་དེ་དང་འབྲལ་མ་གྱུར།།

རྒྱལ་བའི་ཡོན་ཏན་ཇི་བཞིན་དུ།།
ཤེས་པའི་དད་པ་སྐྱེད་གྱུར་ཏེ།།
བཀའ་དྲིན་གཟོ་བས་དེ་དག་གི །
དགོངས་པ་ཡོངས་སུ་སྐྱོང་བར་ཤོག །

ལུས་སེམས་སོ་སོར་འབྲལ་བ་ན།།
གནད་གཅོད་སྡུག་བསྔལ་མེད་པ་དང་།།
རྒྱལ་བའི་རྒྱལ་ཚབ་མི་ཕམ་མགོན།།
འཁོར་དང་བཅས་པ་མཐོང་བར་ཤོག །

As his teachings draw to a close,
and seeing his doctrine alone to be
the basis of happiness for all that lives,
I pray that I sustain the Dharma of the Buddha.

I pray that my mind, moved by compassion,
be never divorced, come what may,
from thoughts of liberating living beings.

I pray that I find the faith
that knows the qualities of buddhas,
and by repaying their kindness
I pray to fulfill their aspirations.

When body and mind come to part,
I pray to be spared the sufferings of death
and behold regent Maitreya and entourage.

དེ་ནས་དགའ་ལྡན་གནས་སུ་ནི།།
སྐྱེས་མ་ཐག་ཏུ་འཁོར་དབུས་སུ།།
མི་ཕམ་མགོན་ལ་བྱང་ཆུབ་ཏུ།།
ལུང་བསྟན་བདག་གིས་ཐོབ་གྱུར་ཅིག །

དེ་ཡི་མོད་ལ་ཡོན་ཏན་ཚོགས།།
དཔག་མེད་མངོན་དུ་གྱུར་ནས་ནི།།
གྲངས་མེད་ཞིང་དུ་རྒྱལ་སྲས་ཀྱི།།
རླབས་ཆེན་སྤྱོད་པ་རྫོགས་པར་ཤོག །

རྒྱལ་བ་རྒྱལ་སྲས་རྒྱ་མཚོ་ཡི།།
བདེན་པ་དང་ནི་བདག་ཅག་གི །
གཡོ་མེད་བསམ་པའི་སྟོབས་ཀྱིས་ནི།།
སྨོན་པ་བདེ་བླག་འགྲུབ་གྱུར་ཅིག །

Reborn in the sacred realm of Tushita,
I pray to be at once in his disciple circle,
there to receive prophecy of enlightenment.

There may I gain qualities beyond number,
journeying on to countless worlds
to accomplish powerful bodhisattva endeavors.

By the power the buddhas, bodhisattvas, and their
  ocean-like truths,
and by the force of our unwavering minds,
may this prayer be quickly fulfilled.

ཛི་སྲིད་ཐུབ་མཆོག །

༄༅ ། །ཛི་སྲིད་ཐུབ་མཆོག་གོ་འཕང་དམ་པ་དེ།།
བདག་གིས་མངོན་དུ་མ་བྱས་དེ་སྲིད་དུ།།
རྣམ་དག་ལམ་བཟང་སྒྲུབ་པའི་རྟེན་རྙེད་ཅིང་།།
རབ་ཏུ་འབྱུང་ཞིང་ཚེ་རབས་དྲན་པར་ཤོག །

གཟུངས་སྤོབས་ཏིང་འཛིན་མངོན་ཤེས་རྫུ་འཕྲུལ་སོགས།།
མཐའ་ཡས་ཡོན་ཏན་དུ་མའི་མཛོད་འཛིན་ཅིང་།།
མཁྱེན་བརྩེ་ནུས་པ་ཟླ་དང་བྲལ་ཐོབ་ནས།།
བྱང་ཆུབ་སྤྱོད་པ་མྱུར་དུ་མཐར་ཕྱིན་ཤོག །

དུས་མིན་འཆི་བའི་མཚན་མ་མཐོང་བ་ན།།
དེ་ཡི་མོད་ལ་ཚེ་དཔག་མེད་མགོན་སྐུ།།
གསལ་བར་མཐོང་ནས་འཆི་བདག་དཔའ་བཅོམ་སྟེ།།
འཆི་མེད་རིག་འཛིན་མྱུར་དུ་ཐོབ་པར་ཤོག །

For As Long As

For as long as I have not actualized
the enlightened state of a mighty buddha,
I pray that I gain a form capable of walking
this pure and noble path,
that I become ordained
and remember past lives.

The powerful dharani memory, confidence,
meditative concentration, clairvoyance, miraculous creation:
I pray that I become a mine of limitless qualities,
and with incomparable wisdom, compassion, and power,
I pray that I swiftly complete the tasks for enlightenment.

Should I see the signs of untimely death,
I pray that I may clearly behold my protector Amitayus,
to destroy the Lord of Death, and to swiftly gain
the vidyadhara power over life and death.

ཚེ་རབས་ཀུན་ཏུ་ཚེ་དཔག་མེད་པ་ཡིས།།
ཐེག་མཆོག་ཤེས་གཉེན་དངོས་སུ་མཛད་པའི་མཐུས།།
རྒྱལ་བས་བསྔགས་པའི་ལམ་བཟང་དེ་ཉིད་ལས།།
སྐད་ཅིག་ཙམ་ཡང་ལྡོག་པར་མ་གྱུར་ཅིག །

སེམས་ཅན་ཡལ་བར་དོར་ནས་རང་དོན་ལ།།
རེ་བའི་བློ་ནི་ནམ་ཡང་མི་སྐྱེ་ཞིང་།།
གཞན་དོན་སྒྲུབ་པའི་ཚུལ་ལ་མ་སྦྱོངས་པའི།།
ཐབས་ལ་མཁས་པས་གཞན་དོན་ལྷུར་ལེན་ཤོག །

བདག་གི་མིང་ཙམ་བརྗོད་དང་དྲན་པས་ཀྱང་།།
སྡིག་པའི་ལས་ཀྱི་འབྲས་བུས་མནར་བ་ཀུན།།
ཕུན་ཚོགས་བདེ་བའི་དཔལ་རབ་འབྱོར་གྱུར་ནས།།
ཐེག་མཆོག་བགྲོད་པའི་ཐེམ་སྐས་འཛེག་གྱུར་ཅིག །

རྒྱལ་བའི་སྲས་ཀྱི་རྣམ་ཐར་ཕྱོགས་ཙམ་ཞིག །
མཚོན་པར་བྱས་པས་རྒྱལ་སྲས་སྤྱོད་པའི་གེགས།།
མ་ལུས་ཞིང་ཞིང་མཐུན་པའི་ཚོགས་ཆོས་ཀུན།།
ཡིད་ལ་བསམས་པ་ཙམ་གྱིས་འགྲུབ་པར་ཤོག །

In all my lives I pray that Amitayus
is manifest as my Mahayana master, and that by his power
I never turn, even for a moment,
from the noble path praised by the buddhas.

I pray that I never give up on others
to nourish thoughts of my own hopes
but work joyfully, with skill and wisdom,
in fulfilling the needs of others.

By merely speaking or hearing my name
may those tormented by the fruition of evil deeds
be blessed with the greatest joy and happiness,
and may they climb the steps of the great Mahayana.

By revealing a mere fragment of bodhisattva life,
may there be no hindrance to the bodhisattva way
and may every circumstance conducive and harmonious
appear by mere thought.

ཤཱཀྱའི་དབང་པོ་འདྲེན་པ་འོད་དཔག་མེད།།
མི་ཕམ་འཇམ་དབྱངས་གསང་བདག་སྤྱན་རས་གཟིགས།།
བདེ་གཤེགས་འཁོར་བཅས་རྟེན་འབྲེལ་མི་བསླུ་བའི།།
བདེན་པའི་སྨོན་ལམ་འདི་དག་མྱུར་འགྲུབ་ཤོག །

By the truth of the mighty Shakyamuni, of the guide
Amitabha,
of Maitreya, Manjushri, Vajrapani, Avalokiteshvara,
and of infallible dependent arising,
may these prayers be swiftly fulfilled.

Notes and Comments on the Poems

Praise of the Buddha

This beautiful poem reveals Tsongkhapa's immense devotion to the Buddha. It mentions several unique qualities of the Buddha as well as incidents illustrative of those qualities. The account of Buddha appearing in the skies refers to the story of Magadha Zangmo, daughter of Anathapindika, a great patron of the Buddha. She lived in Gorakhpur, far from where Buddha was staying. One night, moved by great faith, she climbed to the roof of the house and prayed for the Buddha to appear. At once the skies became filled with the miraculous sights the poem describes.

Other verses speak of Buddha's conquering of Mara (see glossary) while under the bodhi tree in Bodhgaya and of his ability to manifest at a time, a place, and in a form according to the recipient's perception.

The mention of Buddha as being compared to a white lotus refers to an event long before he appeared on this earth when, as a disciple of Buddha Ratnabhadra, he chose this world as the realm for his activity. Other disciples had decided against our world because of its degenerative state. Buddha Shakyamuni therefore was praised for his courage and was likened to the white lotus, the supreme of all lotuses.

Generally the poem stresses the compassion and impartiality of the Buddha and, consequentially, that our inability to benefit from the powers of the Buddha is an obstruction within us, not within the Buddha.

In the first verse, *Indra* is the ruler of the gods of the desire realm, an *asura* is a class of demon, sometimes known as demigods; they are insanely jealous of the happiness and luxury of the gods and often wage war upon them. *Pramudita* is the king of the *gandharva,* or celestial musicians. For *naga* and *rishi,* see glossary. For five remains, see glossary entry under *degenerate times.*

The translation follows the commentary of Changkya Ngawang Losang Choden (1642–1714), second incarnation in the unbroken line of Changkya lamas.

Prayer to Sarasvati

Sarasvati is a goddess strongly affiliated with wisdom and the arts, especially language and poetry. Her skin is white, and she is extraordinarily beautiful and often pictured playing the Indian sitar-like vina. Tsongkhapa held a close relationship with this goddess.

Om sarasiddhi hring hring is one of the mantras of Sarasvati. *Hring* echoes the sound of the vina. The mantra is recited in conjunction with a practice for the increase of wisdom.

Praise of Manjushri

Manjushri is the personification of the Buddha's wisdom. Because such wisdom is an indispensable cause of a buddha, Manjushri is regarded as the sole father of every buddha. Tsongkhapa has come to be regarded as a manifestation of Manjushri.

From another aspect, Tsongkhapa was regarded as a great practitioner who eventually gained direct spiritual access to Manjushri, able to approach him for teachings. It is said that some of Tsongkhapa's poems, including *Prayer for Rebirth in Sukhavati,* were dictated to Tsongkhapa by Manjushri.

The *nyagrodha* tree is the Indian fig, the *utpala* is the fabled blue lotus, while the *bimba* is a bright red berry, possibly *Connicia indica.* The *celestial wish-fulfilling tree* grows in the lands of the gods of the desire realm. From its branches come all wished-for material possessions. The *gandharvas* are celestial musicians who play for the delight of the gods. The *kalapinga* bird lives on ocean islands and has the sweetest of songs.

In the third section of this poem, the ordinary mind is compared to an elephant because of its tendency to blunder through life causing untold damage. However, once tamed it becomes a most useful asset.

Dharmadhatu is the "sphere of reality" and refers to emptiness, the final nature of all phenomena, whereas *dharmakaya* is the "truth body" of a buddha and here refers to the mind of Manjushri in union with the dharmadhatu. The *eighteen realms of phenomena* are the six types of consciousness, their six kinds of object, and the six sensory powers. The *fearless lion pose* refers to meditative equipoise concentrated upon emptiness that knows no fear.

This translation accords with the commentary of the Seventh Dalai Lama, Kalzang Gyatso (1708–57).

Praise to Amitayus

Amitayus together with the goddesses Namgyalma and White Tara comprise the three main longevity deities of the Vajrayana tradition. His name means "Immeasurable Life." Amitayus is often indistinguishable from Amitabha. Tantric practices focused on Amitayus can result in acquiring power over one's life and death. This power is symbolized by the nectar of immortality in the bowl he holds on his lap.

Sindhura, literally "blood of the ocean," is a red pigment used in painting, medicine, and as a cosmetic. For Sukhavati, see notes to *Prayer for Rebirth in Sukhavati*.

This translation follows the commentary of Kirti Losang Trinlae (1849–1904).

Praise to Amitabha

Amitabha is the Buddha of Sukhavati, the realm of bliss. The *Sukhavati Vyuha Sutra*, in its description of this pure realm and its buddha, calls him Amitabha, "Immeasurable Light," when praising his all-encompassing radiating light, and Amitayus, "Immeasurable Life," when describing the lifespan of Sukhavati's inhabitants. Tsongkhapa, too, refers to him as Amitayus in the first verse.

The *five realms* are the three lower realms of existence—the hell realms, the realm of hungry ghosts, and the realm of animals—plus the higher realms of humans and gods.

Prayer for Birth in Sukhavati

Sukhavati is a heavenly paradise somewhere in the west that was formed by the billion prayers made by Amitabha on his long path to enlightenment.

Advanced practice is not necessary for rebirth in Sukhavati. Faith, strong prayers, and a calm mind at death are sufficient causes for a future life in this realm.

The *bardo* is the intermediate state between death and rebirth. One can remain in the bardo for up to forty-nine days. The *seven desirable features of higher realms* are: birth in a good family, attractive features, a long life, good health, good fortune, wealth, and intelligence. *Shurangama samadhi* translates as the "meditative concentration that goes boldly."

This prayer is said to have been spoken by Manjushri through Tsongkhapa.

Praise of an Unnamed Sakya Lama

The unnamed lama is the Sakya master Rendawa, who Tsongkhapa regarded as the kindest of all his teachers. It was to him that Tsongkhapa dedicated his famous "Migtsema" prayer, which Rendawa then rededicated to Tsongkhapa. The refusal here to mention his name is an indication of how sacred Tsongkhapa held this master to be.

A Prayer to My Precious Dharma Master

Tsongkhapa served many lamas during his search for the Buddha's Dharma. He held guru devotion to be of the utmost importance both at the beginning of practice and especially during the advanced practices of tantra. Although his insights and spiritual development soon outpaced his masters, he continued humbly to regard them with great devotion.

The *two stages* are the generation and completion stages of tantra.

A Harvest of Powerful Attainment

It is common practice to petition for blessings from lineage masters of a particular tradition or teaching, beginning with the Buddha up to one's present teacher. There are many lineages in Tibet and consequently many lineage prayers. Such a prayer would be accompanied by a visualization of the lineage masters.

This prayer focuses on Pawo Dorje, who was one of Tsongkhapa's main teachers and who, as the poem states, had direct visions of Manjushri.

Vajra-holder (Skt. *Vajradhara*) is the Buddha in the form of the teacher of tantra and therefore originator of every tantric lineage.

In Praise of Maitreya

Maitreya, the buddha of the future, lives in the sacred realm of Tushita, where he will remain until he becomes the fifth universal teacher of this eon to appear on the earth. For that reason he is often pictured with legs uncrossed ready to rise.

Tsongkhapa had a special connection with Maitreya. One of his teachers, the Kadampa Lhodrag Namkha Gyaltsen (1326–1401) regarded Tsongkhapa as an emanation of Maitreya as well as of Manjushri. Once on his travels Tsongkhapa and his disciples came across a rundown statue of Maitreya. Saddened by the neglect, he set about gathering money and materials to repair the statue. To accomplish this task they sold all their possessions and made many prayers. Tsongkhapa thinks of the statue in this prayer, referring to it as Maitreya himself, and laments that he was unable to go there to pay homage.

Maitreya is given the title *Crown of Brahma* to indicate that he is revered by the great god Brahma, who places him upon his head as a mark of great respect. *Kama* is the lustful god who sought to distract the Buddha with alluring manifestations as he sat striving for enlightenment under the bodhi tree.

Supernatural sight refers to the first two of the five supernatural sights (see glossary).

This translation follows the commentary of the nineteenth-century lama Khalka Ngawang Palden (b. 1797) of Drepung monastery.

In Praise of Vajrapani

From one aspect, Vajrapani is the personification of Buddha's great power, especially the power to thwart the hindrance and obstruction that so often accompanies spiritual practice. The vajra symbolizes indestructibility. The secret and advanced practices of tantra bring their own wrathful forms of obstruction, and often wrathful means are required to deal with them, a point alluded to by Tsongkhapa in this poem.

From another aspect, Vajrapani is the bodhisattva entrusted with the preservation of the teachings, especially tantra. He is known, therefore, as a *keeper of mantra*. "Mantra" here refers to the tantras. Other references to *mantra* refer to powerful syllables uttered in invocation of Vajrapani.

A *yaksha* is a class of nature spirit, demon, or cannibal. Vajrapani is known as the *king of yakshas* because he was said to have been a yaksha before his conversion by the Buddha. His form certainly appears demonic, like that of a yaksha.

The *fabrication-free dharmakaya* is the enlightened mind freed from the entanglements of holding to the true existence of phenomena.

Lhodrag Namkha Gyaltsen, one of Tsongkhapa's teachers, had a special affiliation with Vajrapani, and thus through him Tsongkhapa received teachings from Vajrapani himself.

In Praise of the Extraordinary Deity Achala

Achala is a meditation deity of the lower tantras. This praise appears to have been composed extemporaneously. The last verse mentions, somewhat wryly, its great haste, and the colophon records it as having been "spoken" by Tsongkhapa, rather than composed.

In Praise of Vajra Sarasvati

Vajra Sarasvati is Sarasvati in wrathful form, with three faces, six arms, and a red body. Her two legs symbolize *wisdom* and *method*—the two essentials for attaining complete enlightenment. *Wisdom* is the path of understanding and knowing the final nature of all phenomena, while *method* is the development and practice of bodhi mind. Her voice is *adorned with sixty illustrious qualities,* detailed in *Praise of Manjushri*.

In Praise of Goddess Namgyalma

Namgyalma (Skt. *Ushnishavijaya*) is a goddess of longevity who emanated from the Buddha's crown protuberance (Skt.

ushnisha). With Amitayus and White Tara she makes up the most popular trinity of longevity deities in Himalayan Buddhism. She possesses three *full and noble faces,* each showing a different aspect. The middle face is elegant, the right is peaceful, and the left, wrathful.

Tsongkhapa describes Namgyalma as she is depicted in traditional Tibetan paintings with her four attendant wrathful deities sitting around her. These four belong to the family known as the *eleven wrathful ones.*

It is said that Sarasvati, goddess of wisdom, told Tsongkhapa that he would not live past the age of fifty-seven. To remedy this he made many prayers to Namgyalma.

A Prayer for the Beginning, Middle, and End of Practice

This is a prayer for circumstances conducive to a pure unhindered practice in future lives. The prayer moves through the various stages of the Mahayana path, from being born into the kind of family conducive to becoming a monk, to meeting with spiritual friends and masters, to maintaining unflagging enthusiasm for study and practice, to renouncing the pleasures of this life, and finally to manifesting the perfection of the bodhisattva path. As well as being a prayer of great devotion, it is somewhat autobiographical in that it maps out Tsongkhapa's own life and practice.

Mother sentient beings refers to the practice of regarding every living being as possessing the kindness of our mothers and to the logical probability that, over the duration of beginningless reincarnations, every living being has at one time in the past actually been our mother. *Sada Prarudita* was an exemplary practitioner of guru devotion in ancient India. His name means "always crying," for he was often in tears during his search for his teacher, *Dharma Arya.* Tsongkhapa was very impressed by his devotion and wrote a biography of him.

Threefold laziness comprises attachment to useless activities, procrastination, and self-denigration.

Perfection of prayer refers to the following prayer: "Wherever I may be born, may I never be apart from the bodhi mind, and for the sake of all living beings may I unceasingly practice the perfections."

The Essence of a Human Life

According to the colophon, Tsongkhapa was asked by an artist called Palden for words of advice on living a lay life. His response is this eloquent poem on not wasting the precious opportunity that human life affords. Although this poem is essentially a sermon, Tsongkhapa is never preachy. There is real care and compassion in his voice.

It is not clear if Tsongkhapa is addressing Palden alone. He addresses his audience as "my fine-featured ones." This may be a comment on Palden's looks or on the fact that lay men and women, unlike the ordained, often place great value on their looks.

The *five lifelong vows* are to abstain from killing, stealing, lying, sexual misconduct, and alcohol. The *eight daylong vows* are the previous five plus to abstain from sitting on high seats, distracting oneself with entertainment, and eating after lunch.

Dependent Arising

This poem was written spontaneously one morning after Tsongkhapa was blessed with a sudden and direct experience of emptiness. The previous night he had dreamed of the great Indian pundits Nagarjuna, Aryadeva, Buddhapalita, Chandrakirti, and others discussing subtle points of Madhyamika philosophy.

Suddenly, Buddhapalita rose with a text he had composed and placed it as a blessing upon Tsongkhapa's head. When he awoke, he plunged into a study of the very same text. While reading he was rewarded with a direct understanding of emptiness.

Chandrakirti was a disciple of Nagarjuna. His *Supplement to the Middle Way* is held by Tsongkhapa as the definitive work on Nagarjuna's Middle Way philosophy.

This translation accords with the commentary of Gen Lamrimpa Ngawang Puntsok, born in 1925, the renowned lama of Drepung monastery, famous for his austere lifestyle and his study and practice of Tsongkhapa's great work, *Lamrim Chenmo*.

Verses of Benediction

A wealthy landowner, Namkha Zangpo, from the region of Neu sponsored the publication of a new edition of twenty-nine sutras that included the *Perfection of Wisdom* as well as other well-known Mahayana sutras, some of which are mentioned. For the success of the publication, he asked Tsongkhapa to write a benediction. The practice of lay people sponsoring religious activity has always been widespread among the Tibetan community.

The *Perfection of Wisdom Sutras* were delivered by the Buddha mainly on Vulture's Peak in Rajgir, near Bodhgaya. They teach, among other topics, the final truth of phenomena according to the highest philosophical view in Buddhist thought, a view that Tsongkhapa is famed for expounding.

Ananda was Buddha's cousin who became his attendant at the age of fifty-five, serving him for twenty-five years. Although he was not an arhat, he was devoted to the Buddha and was known as a kindly soul. He had mastered the ability to memorize word for word every teaching of the Buddha and consequently recited the sutras at the first council.

Those gone to bliss (Skt. *sugata*) is an epithet for buddhas.

Praise of the Protector Dharmaraja

Dharmaraja is the principal protector of the Tibetan Gelug tradition founded by Tsongkhapa. He is extraordinarily ferocious and fearsome to behold. This is because he belongs to class of demons known as *yamas,* who inhabit the underworld and are closely associated with death. Dharmaraja (or Yamaraja) is their king. He was bound over as a protector by Yamantaka or Vajrabhairava, the wrathful form of Manjushri, who made him pledge to serve the Dharma.

Twenty-one Verse Rosary Prayer

This beautiful prayer seems to have been written for recitation almost as a mantra on the rosary. The smallest number of mantras chanted on a rosary is usually twenty-one—an auspicious number. Here Tsongkhapa prays to be reborn in the sacred realm of *Tushita,* where he resides now under the name of Jampal Nyingpo.

To *ripen* living beings means to render them susceptible to the spiritual path.

For As Long As

This is a popular prayer often recited at the end of a meditation session. These kinds of prayers are spiritual investments against an unknown and potentially hostile future. Until one has reached a certain level on the path, the danger of falling back into the suffering of deluded existence is always present.

Vidyadhara means "wisdom holder." The wisdom is that of great bliss held or borne by the profound practices of tantra.

Glossary

Arhat. (Lit. "foe destroyer"). A follower of the Buddhist way who has reached the end of the path of personal salvation. Arhats are free from the cycles of life and death and dwell in nirvana.

Arya. A noble or exalted being. A practitioner of the Buddhist path who has directly experienced the ultimate truth of all phenomena. Once this truth has been experienced, an *arya* will never fall back to the status of an ordinary being.

Bodhi mind, bodhichitta, mind of enlightenment. A mind, moved by intense compassion, directed toward the full enlightenment of a buddha and characterized by the wish to attain such a state for the sake of all living beings.

Bodhisattva. One who has attained the bodhi mind. The path of the bodhisattva is the Mahayana path.

Brahma. A god much associated with purity and cleanliness. He inhabits the realms of form and is said to reside in the Brahma Purohita, the second realm of the first level of meditative concentration (Skt. *dhyana*). He has a beautiful voice, and its sound is said to pervade the universe.

Degenerate times. Buddhist cosmology spans immense periods of time. The teachings of Gautama Buddha were delivered in an era sullied by the *five remains*. These five are the "leftovers" or "dregs" of a golden era enjoyed nearer to the birth of the universe. These times are marked by the proliferation of delusion, the shortening of lifespans of living beings, and the degeneration of views and philosophies.

Dharani. See *Four great powers of retention.*

Form and formless realms. On the higher levels of Mount Meru lie the four realms of form, so called because, although their inhabitants have temporarily freed themselves from the desires that bind others to the desire realm, they are still attracted to form. Access to these realms is by way of high levels of meditative concentration in which the coarser desires are shed. Beings who populate these realms have transparent bodies of light. The god Brahma dwells in the realms of form. The four formless realms do not geographically occupy any position because their worlds are almost totally a creation of mind, in the sense that their inhabitants have abandoned form altogether. Nevertheless, for the sake of inclusion in the world system, they are placed on Mount Meru above the realm of form.

Fourfold logic. This refers to four types of logic that make use of the ways of the world. These are: *the logic of the world*—logic making use of knowledge about worldly processes, such as the fact that water flows downward; *the logic of dependence*—logic making use of knowledge about causality, i.e., that effects arise because of causes, as a sprout arises from a seed; *the logic of functionality*—logic making use of knowledge about the functions of worldly objects, e.g., a rice seed will produce only a shoot of rice and never a shoot of barley; *the logic of valid cognition*—logic making use of knowledge obtained by direct sensory apprehension, sound reasoning, and scripture.

Four great powers of retention. Retention (Skt. *dharani*) refers to the acquired ability to learn and never forget the words and meanings of the teachings. The four powers are: *forbearance*—the ability to meditate on the emptiness of the syllables of the alphabet; *recitation of mantra*—the ability to invoke the power of words of truth; *recollection of words*—the ability not to forget a single word of the teachings; *grasping of meanings*—the ability to easily understand the meanings of the words.

Garuda. A mythical bird of prey, said to be the most powerful of all birds.

Hearers. (Skt. *shravaka*). One of the two classes of followers of the Buddha on the Hinayana path; so named because they listen to the words of Buddha, study them, and teach them to others. They are also known as "those born from the words of the Buddha." Compare *solitary practitioner.*

Hinayana. The Buddhist path of personal salvation or nirvana, as opposed to the Mahayana path of the bodhisattva.

Mara. Mainly used as the personification of obstacles to spiritual development, but the name also refers to a specific being inhabiting the desire realm who, out of jealousy, does his best to cause obstruction to spiritual attainment. There are, therefore, four types of Mara: our own delusions, our physical existence, death, and the specific individual inhabiting the desire realm.

Mount Meru. The great four-sided mountain that, according to Buddhist cosmology, rises up through the center of the universe. Our world lies on its southern face.

Naga. Spirit-like creatures, closely associated with snakes. Sometimes benevolent, but they can often cause harm, especially if offended. They are attracted to water and cleanliness and often inhabit clean pools and lakes. Dirtying or destroying such areas upsets them, and they may retaliate by causing harm to the perpetrator that can manifest as boils and rashes on the body. They are known to guard fabulous riches, and the naga kings possess the wish-fulfilling jewel, ownership of which grants unlimited wealth.

Nagarjuna. The great Buddhist teacher, prophesized by the Buddha, who lived around the second century C.E. Known as one of the "six ornaments of the world," he composed many seminal works, particularly on the Middle Way doctrine of the Buddha.

Perfection of Wisdom. (Skt. *Prajnaparamita*). This refers to both the many sutras on the Perfection of Wisdom and to the wisdom itself, which directly and nonconceptually perceives emptiness.

Rishi. A term literally meaning "straightened" and applied to spiritual practitioners who have straightened out their bodies, speech, and deeds. It is commonly used to describe meditators advanced in Hindu practice.

Samsara. Not a place but a process driven by delusion and karma, throwing us in endless cycles from life to life. We have no control over this process until we destroy ignorance, the root cause of samsara, and thereby attain nirvana.

Shakya. The royal clan or family of northern India of which the Buddha was a prince.

Sixfold clairvoyance. The ability to directly perceive phenomena normally hidden to the senses, of which there are six types: *the eye of the gods*, which sees at great distances and can even see where beings have been reborn after their death; *the ears of the gods*, which understand sounds and languages of other beings; *knowing the minds and dispositions of others*; *knowing the ways of supernatural powers* such as flying and walking on water; *knowing details of previous lives*; and *direct perception of all delusions*, and their degrees of subtlety, to be destroyed on the path to liberation. The sixth ability is possessed only by a buddha.

Solitary practitioner. (Skt. *pratyeka buddha*). One of the two main types of Hinayana practitioner. In the life before attaining freedom from samsara, a solitary practitioner focuses on the twelve links of dependent arising without the assistance of a buddha or a teacher. Compare *Hearers*.

Supernatural sight. Five types are mentioned in the scriptures: the *eye of flesh,* which sees through form; the *celestial eye,* which sees the forms of every world; the *eye of intelligence,* which nonconceptually perceives all conditioned and unconditioned phenomena; the *eye of dharma,* which sees dependent arising; the *eye of wisdom,* which sees all phenomena of the two levels of truth (ultimate and conventional). Only a buddha possesses all five types of supernatural sight.

Ten powers. These are ten powers of nonconceptual wisdom exclusive to buddhas. They are: knowing what is and what is not the basis of happiness and suffering; knowing all aspects of karma and its ripening; knowing the dispositions and tendencies of all beings; knowing the eighteen spheres of phenomena; knowing the differing abilities of all disciples; knowing the paths that lead to enlightenment, nirvana, and to rebirth in the desire realm; knowing the paths, stages, and pitfalls of the meditations of the form and formless realms; knowing all details of past lives; knowing all details of future lives; knowing what constitutes the end of suffering. These ten are detailed in *Praise to Manjushri*.

Three gateways of freedom. Means through which one can approach liberation. Specifically, emptiness, aspirationlessness, and attributelessness.

About the Translator

Gavin Kilty is also author of *Traditions of Tibetan Childbirth* and the translator of *The Sutra of the Wise and Foolish*. For eight years, he studied the monastic curriculum of the Gelug tradition at the Buddhist School of Dialectics in Dharamsala, India, receiving teachings from numerous prominent lamas. Currently he teaches Mahayana Buddhism at the Sharpham College of Buddhism and Contemporary Enquiry and teaches the Tibetan language in Dharamsala for three months a year. Gavin lives in Buckfastleigh, England.

Also from
WISDOM PUBLICATIONS

THE FULFILLMENT OF ALL HOPES
Guru Devotion in Tibetan Buddhism
Je Tsongkhapa
Translated by Gareth Sparham

Devoting oneself to a spiritual teacher is a practice much misunderstood in the West, yet fundamental to the tantric Buddhism of Tibet. *The Fulfillment of All Hopes* is an explanation of this core practice by Tsongkhapa, one of Tibet's most revered scholar-practitioners.

Presented here is a complete translation of Tsongkhapa's commentary on the well-known *Fifty Stanzas on the Guru* accompanied by the original Tibetan text.
160 pp., 0-86171-153-X, $15.95

VAST AS THE HEAVENS
Verses in Praise of Bodhicitta
Khunu Rinpoche
Translated and introduced by Gareth Sparham

Revered by many, the late Khunu Rinpoche devoted his life to the development of the aspiration to achieve enlightenment for the sake of all living beings. *Vast as the Heavens, Deep as the Sea* is a collection of Khunu Rinpoche's inspirational verse—presented here in both English and the original Tibetan.

"To hold in your hands Khunu Rinpoche's own words on bodhicitta is to be given a priceless opportunity—of touching the heart of a master who had made it the guiding light of his entire life."
—Sogyal Rinpoche, author of *The Tibetan Book of Living and Dying*
160 pp., 0-86171-146-7, $16.95

HERMIT OF GO CLIFFS

Timeless Instructions from a Tibetan Mystic

Translated and introduced by Cyrus Stearns

"These tantric songs have a spare elegance and power beautifully rendered into English by Cyrus Stearns... The simplicity and deep contemplative insights of Godrakpa are rendered into evocative English poetry that very much resonates with the style, vigor and power of the original Tibetan songs."

—David Germano, University of Virginia

224 pp., 0-86171-164-5, $19.95

ORDINARY WISDOM

Sakya Pandita's Treasury of Good Advice

Sakya Pandita

Translated by John T. Davenport

"The English translation of Sakya Pandita's *The Treasury of Good Advice* is indeed welcome as it is one of the most popular classics throughout Tibet. In my childhood, I memorized its verses, and they brought me solace during difficult times. John Davenport translated both the verses and the commentary with accuracy and clarity."

—L.P. Lhalungpa, Tibetan scholar and translator of *The Life of Milarepa*

384 pp., 0-86171-161-0, $21.95

THE MEANING OF LIFE

Buddhist Perspectives on Cause and Effect

His Holiness the Dalai Lama

Translated and edited by Jeffrey Hopkins

Each of us struggles with the existential questions of meaning, purpose, and responsibility. In *The Meaning of Life,* the Dalai Lama examines these questions from the Buddhist perspective, skillfully guiding us to a clearer understanding that can liberate us from the prison of selfishness and suffering. The Dalai Lama's incomparable intelligence, wit, and kindness shines through in his explanations on the Buddha's teachings of dependent arising.

164 pp., 0-86171-173-4, $15.95

OPENING THE EYE OF NEW AWARENESS
His Holiness the Dalai Lama
Translated and introduced by Donald S. Lopez, Jr.

"Written for both Tibetan and Western readers, *Opening the Eye of New Awareness* is the Dalai Lama's first religious work. It is not an edited transcript of public lectures, but is His Holiness' own summation of Buddhist doctrine and practice. Completed in 1963, just four years after his escape from Tibet and four years after completing his religious education, it is a work of consummate scholarship by a 27-year-old geshe, wise beyond his years."—Donald Lopez
160 pp., 0-86171-155-6, $14.95

ADVICE FROM A SPIRITUAL FRIEND
Geshe Rabten & Geshe Dhargyey

"Reading this book is akin to taking a personal retreat with two kindly and wise teachers. The instructions for realizing compassion in everyday life are readable and clear, and offer enhanced spiritual skills to readers of any background and orientation."
—*NAPRA ReVIEW*

"Clear, comprehensible, and immensely helpful... unconditionally recommended for all students of mind training."—*Shambhala Sun*
160 pp., 0-86171-193-9, $15.95

PEACOCK IN THE POISON GROVE
Two Buddhist Texts on Training the Mind
Geshe Lhundub Sopa
Edited and cotranslated by Michael J. Sweet and Leonard Zwilling

Geshe Sopa offers insightful commentary on two of the earliest Tibetan texts that focus on mind training. *Peacock in the Poison Grove* presents a powerful technique for dispelling the selfish delusions of the ego, maintaining the purity of our motives. Geshe Sopa's lucid explanations teach how we can realize the truth of emptiness and develop a compassionate, loving attitude toward others.
288 pp., 0-86171-185-8, $19.95

WISDOM ENERGY
Basic Buddhist Teachings
Lama Yeshe and Lama Zopa Rinpoche

"In *Wisdom Energy*, two highly accomplished Tibetan Buddhist teachers demonstrate their remarkable talent for illuminating sometimes complex ideas in a manner that is easily grasped by Westerners. Filled with profound wisdom and useful advice, this lucid introduction to the key principles and practices of Buddhism is directly relevant to modern life. I highly recommend this exceptional book."
—Howard C. Cutler, M.D., co-author of *The Art of Happiness*
160 pp., 0-86171-170-X, $14.95

DOOR OF LIBERATION
Essential Teachings of the Tibetan Buddhist Tradition
Geshe Wangyal

This book contains seven fundamental Buddhist texts—including four texts from Je Tsongkhapa—that the great teacher Geshe Wangyal considered essential to his Western students.

"The scholar-adept Geshe Wangyal was the first to bring Tibetan Buddhism to America. He had extraordinary love and humor as well as ferocity. He taught untiringly.... To live with him was to live with emptiness."—Jeffrey Hopkins, Professor of Religious Studies, University of Virginia
264 pp., 0-86171-032-0, $15.00

THE CLOUDS SHOULD KNOW ME BY NOW
Buddhist Poet Monks of China
Edited by Red Pine and Mike O'Connor

The voices of fourteen eminent Chinese poet monks whose works span twelve centuries (A.D. 700–1900) are presented here in both the original Chinese and in English translation. The poets were chosen by the translators for their insight into the human condition and for the beauty of their poetic expression.

"A thousand years of poetry has been tenderly gathered in from the wind and gently placed upon the page... it is a breath of fresh, crisp, high-altitude air to our hearts."—*NAPRA ReVIEW*
224 pp., 0-86171-143-2, $15.95

Wisdom Publications

Wisdom Publications, a not-for-profit publisher, is dedicated to making authentic Buddhist works available for the benefit of all. We publish translations of the sutras and tantras, commentaries and teachings of past and contemporary Buddhist masters, and original works by the world's leading Buddhist scholars. We publish our titles with the appreciation of Buddhism as a living philosophy and with the special commitment to preserve and transmit important works from all the major Buddhist traditions.

If you would like more information or a copy of our mail-order catalog, please write to us at:

Wisdom Publications
199 Elm Street, Somerville, Massachusetts 02144 USA
Telephone: (617) 776-7416 • Fax: (617) 776-7841
Email: sales@wisdompubs.org
Web Site: http://www.wisdompubs.org

The Wisdom Trust

As a not-for-profit publisher, Wisdom Publications is dedicated to the publication of fine Dharma books for the benefit of all sentient beings and dependent upon the kindness and generosity of sponsors in order to do so. If you would like to make a donation to Wisdom, please contact our Somerville office.

Thank you.

Wisdom Publications is a not-for-profit, charitable 501(c)(3) organization affiliated with the Foundation for the Preservation of the Mahayana Tradition (FPMT).